Weirdest Places in the USA

★★★ ★★★

D1604149

pil

Publications International, Ltd.

Contributing writers: Jeff Bahr, Pete Haugen, Martin Hintz, Linnea Lundgren, Julia Clark Robinson, James Willis

Images from Shutterstock.com

Louis Weber, CEO
Publications International, Ltd.
8140 Lehigh Avenue
Morton Grove, IL 60053

ISBN: 978-1-63938-122-7

Manufactured in China.

8 7 6 5 4 3 2 1

Let's get social!

 @Publications_International

 @PublicationsInternational

www.pilbooks.com

Table of Contents

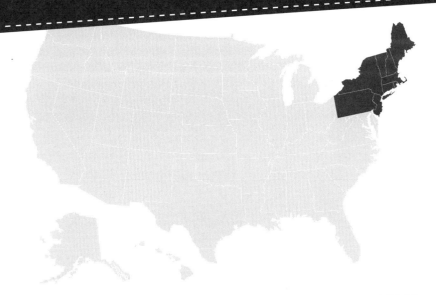

Eartha, the World's Largest Rotating Globe

Yarmouth, Maine

What could put a mapmaking firm on the map? The world's largest globe, of course. DeLorme, a company best known for its road atlases, decided to puff its chest by taking its cartography prowess to the next level. At their national headquarters in Yarmouth, they unearthed "Eartha." According to company spokespeople, the enormous globe features the "largest image of earth ever created."

Housed in a three-story glass atrium, the big blue marble is a sight to behold. Launched into orbit in 1998, the sphere appears to the earthbound eye much as it would to a space traveler. Vivid colors replicate topography, vegetation, major roadways, and cities. Shading suggests ocean depths. In a nod to accuracy, the sphere actually rotates and revolves.

4

At 41.5 feet in diameter, Eartha is recognized by the *Guinness Book of World Records* as the "World's Largest Revolving/Rotating Globe." Says proud parent DeLorme: "Eartha will instill a sense of wonder in people when they first see it and we hope they walk away from it with a better appreciation and knowledge of the world around them." Before Eartha, Italy held the record for largest globe. The Globe of Peace, located in Apeccio, Italy, is 33 feet in diameter.

The Old Lobster Fisherman
Boothbay Harbor, Maine

A fitting mascot for Brown's Wharf Restaurant, Motel & Marina, this stoic, yellow-clad angler consists of wood, steel, and fiberglass and measures 25 feet from boot to cap. Operated by the Brown family since 1944, Brown's Wharf installed the big guy a quarter-century later.

Owls Head Lighthouse
Owls Head, Maine

An older woman dubbed "Little Lady" is frequently seen in the kitchen of this lighthouse. Although most spirits tend to bring cold spots or unease, this one reportedly causes a feeling of calm and warmth. No one is sure who she is, but it is possible that she's keeping the other Owls Head ghost company. Believed to be a previous keeper known for his frugal nature and attention to his post, this ghost makes himself known by turning thermostats down, polishing the brass, leaving footprints in the snow, and occasionally appearing in the tower. He seems to be training his replacement: A resident's young daughter announced one day that fog was coming in and that they should turn on the beacon, something she claimed to have learned from her "imaginary friend."

The Desert of Maine

Freeport, Maine

Despite accusations to the contrary, the owners of the "Desert of Maine" attraction insist, "No, we didn't dump it here!"

Geologists claim that there's really no mystery. A glacier supposedly slid through the area 11,000 years ago and left behind the sand and mineral deposits that today are known as the Desert of Maine.

An alternate explanation holds that bad farming practices were responsible for the desert. In this scenario, sand dunes infiltrated open fields not protected by a layer of grass, much like what occurred during America's "dust bowl" days.

So, who's right? We believe the proper answer is: Who really cares? When you locate a desert in a rainy northern state like Maine, you enjoy it for all it's worth. A couple of bucks are all that separate the masses from this "famous natural phenomenon." What more do we need to know?

Paul Bunyan Statue and Birthplace

Boothbay Harbor, Maine

Since we've crammed this book with all of America's weirdest locations, it's only fitting that we include the Paul Bunyan statue up in Boothbay, Maine. This hardy fellow stands some 31 feet tall and strains scale springs with his 3,700-pound heft.

The giant lumberjack has been standing at Boothbay since 1959. Armed with an equally enormous ax and pick, this figure is reputed to be the largest statue of Paul Bunyan in the world. How do we know this? It says so right at its base.

The Legend of Paul Bunyan

Legend has it that giant lumberjack Paul Bunyan weighed 80 pounds when five storks delivered him as a baby. He grew up so fast that he was wearing his father's clothes within a week. Paul grew up on the coast of Maine but relocated with Babe, his famous blue ox sidekick, to Minnesota. Rumor has it that the young and rambunctious duo created the state's 10,000 lakes with their horseplay. Later, Paul went on to invent the logging industry and chop down vast tracts of forest by himself.

Mud Bowl Championships

North Conway, New Hampshire

Up in New England, touch football has deep roots. The Kennedy boys (yes, those Kennedys) helped popularize the game at their Hyannis port compound. The Mud Bowl Championships run the Kennedys' regal approach right into the dirt. Make that wet dirt, as in mud.

Each September since 1975, teams have gathered in North Conway to get down and dirty. Before the official game begins, a pep rally, bonfire, and "drunkfest" instill the proper mood. As is plain to see, "Here's mud in your eye" has multiple meanings up in these parts.

The "Hogs" out of North Conway have proven their superiority over the years. So much so that they've now constructed the "Hog Coliseum" solely to host the event. If rain dampens their playing field, that's swell. If not, sprinklers get the job done. Let the filthy games begin!

Ruggles Mine

Grafton, New Hampshire

The "World Famous Ruggles Mine" combined good old-fashioned American hucksterism with a captivating environment worthy of a visit. The "Mine in the Sky," as its brochure read, was billed as "the oldest and most spectacular mica, feldspar, beryl, and uranium mine in the USA."

Opened to the public in 1963, the place was so cavernous that human beings looked like fire ants beside its honeycombed tunnels. This lent the mine's "most spectacular" boast much credence and could easily leave visitors spellbound. The mine was closed to visitors in 2016 and then sold to a production company in 2019.

Clark's Bears

Lincoln, New Hampshire

Long before there were theme parks to amuse travelers, one-off places like Clark's Bears ruled the roost. Each operation was as individual and unique as its operators, and you could never be certain what you'd happen upon next.

"Ed Clark's Eskimo Sled Dog Ranch," the original operation begun by Florence and Ed Clark in 1928, featured purebred Eskimo sled dogs. The couple's intent was to bring the far north into New Hampshire's White Mountains—a rough and ready region that attracted outdoor types. In 1931, Ed purchased a live black bear and put it on display. More than any attraction before it, the bear lured so many visitors that more bears were quickly added.

Eventually, sons Murray and Edward began working with the bruins. In 1949, they formed a show that featured bear antics and infused it with wit and educational bits for balance. Clark's bear show was on its way.

Visitors would come from all parts to witness the critters drinking from beer cans, swinging on swings, and shooting "bearskitballs." With an infusion of capital, the operation eventually changed its name to Clark's Trading Post, and later Clark's Bears, and grew to include a steam-powered train ride, a Russian Circus troupe, even a much-beloved, human Wolfman.

Through the years, as perceptions of animal cruelty evolved, Clark's Trading Post came under scrutiny. According to the family, such concerns are completely baseless. They point to the fact that no bear is ever forced to perform. As to concerns about the trainer's well-being, the family patriarch W. Murray Clark explains that every family member has been injured—a fact that causes them to take their jobs very seriously. Nevertheless, they treat the bears with great affection and believe that such goes a long way in keeping the animals content and less likely to attack. This grand throwback to roadside attractions passed its 90th birthday in 2018, and from all indications, it could go another 90 years. People never seem to tire of unique spots such as this. In fact, when it comes to popularity, Clark's Bears (open seasonally) has bearly scratched the surface.

Mount Washington

New Hampshire

If you were asked to name the place on planet Earth responsible for the world's worst weather, we'd guess the state of New Hampshire would not be on your short list. This would be an oversight on your part. Though comparatively small, Mount Washington (aka the "killer mountain") is capable of more harshness than any granite lump has a right to be.

First, a look at the facts: 6,288-foot Mount Washington is located at a spot where three major storm tracks regularly collide. Due to this collision and a funneling-effect attributed to its unique topography (its tree line occurs at a comparatively low 5,000 feet) the mountain produces scary, strong winds. How scary? The mountain's weather is so freakish that a year-round weather observatory has existed at its summit since 1870. In the early days, buildings were actually chained to the mountain to save them from being blown off of it. This sort of thing can occur in an environment where hurricane-force winds occur just about every third day throughout the year.

On April 12, 1934, as if to prove its windy superiority, the mountain let loose with a gust of 231 miles per hour. This was—and still is—the greatest non-tornado blast ever measured on Earth. But wind represents only a portion of Mount Washington's mayhem. Fast-changing weather adds to its knockout blow.

In 1855, 23-year-old Lizzie Bourne and two relatives began a hike to the mountain's summit. The plan was to spend the night at the Tip-Top House. They would walk along the precursor to Mount Washington's famed Auto Road, a steep path that climbs out of the valley and tags the top.

Nearing exhaustion after many hours of exertion, the party finally broke tree line and came within sight of the summit cone. They decided to push on. Almost immediately, windswept rain and plummeting temperatures dogged their attempts. With thick fog shrouding their goal, the party stopped and dug in for a hellish night. Survival was now their chief interest.

It would be Lizzie's last climb. She had underestimated the power of the mountain and died of exposure. But she could hardly be blamed for such foolhardiness. The September 13th day of her death had started off like many other SUMMER days that preceded it, quite warm and sunny. The most heartbreaking part? She and her group had made it to within mere feet of the Tip-Top House. Unfortunately, the mountain's cruel weather had completely masked the object of their salvation.

The Sherman Adams Visitor's Center located at Mount Washington's summit features more than 100 names of other deaths on the mountain. It proves that killers can and do come in all sizes. How about a hike?

Despite a grisly "death statistic" board at the mountain's summit, Mount Washington remains a hiking mecca. Each year, thousands of "peak-baggers" climb up and down the imposing peak and end up none the worse for wear.

The Appalachian Mountain Club (AMC) maintains the Pinkham Notch Visitor's Center at Mount Washington's base. Rangers there will tell you that climbs here are as safe as climbers make them, and that proper gear and an eye on weather is at the crux. Nevertheless, incidents do occur. This fear factor no doubt adds to Mount Washington's allure.

Lake Champlain Monster

Lake Champlain, Vermont

In 1609, French explorer Samuel de Champlain was astonished to see a thick, eight- to ten-foot-tall creature in the waters between present-day Vermont and New York. His subsequent report set in motion the legend of Champ, the "monster" in Lake Champlain.

Even before Champlain's visit, Champ was known to Native Americans as Chaousarou. Over time, Champ has become one of North America's most famous lake monsters. News stories of its existence were frequent enough that in 1873, showman P. T. Barnum offered $50,000 for the creature, dead or alive. That same year, Champ almost sank a steamboat, and in the 1880s, a number of people, including a sheriff, glimpsed it splashing playfully offshore. It is generally described as dark in color (olive green, gray, or brown) with a serpent-like body.

Sightings have continued into modern times, and witnesses have compiled some film evidence that is difficult to ignore. In 1977, a woman named Sandra Mansi photographed a long-necked creature poking its head out of the water near St. Albans, Vermont, close to the Canadian border. She estimated the animal was 10 to 15 feet long and told an investigator that its skin looked "slimy" and similar to that of an eel. Mansi presented her photo and story at a

1981 conference held at Lake Champlain. Although she had misplaced the negative by then, subsequent analyses of the photo have generally failed to find any evidence that it was manipulated.

In September 2002, a researcher named Dennis Hall, who headed a lake monster investigation group known as Champ Quest, videotaped what looked like three creatures undulating through the water near Ferrisburgh, Vermont. Hall claimed that he saw unidentifiable animals in Lake Champlain on 19 separate occasions.

In 2006, two fishermen captured digital video footage of what appeared to be parts of a very large animal swimming in the lake. The images were thoroughly examined under the direction of ABC News technicians, and though the creature on the video could not be proved to be Champ, the team could find nothing to disprove it, either.

As the sixth-largest freshwater lake in the United States (and stretching about six miles into Quebec, Canada), Lake Champlain provides ample habitat and nourishment for a good-size water cryptid, or unknown animal. The lake plunges as deep as 400 feet in spots and covers 490 square miles.

Skeptics offer the usual explanations for Champ sightings: large sturgeons, floating logs or water plants, otters, or an optical illusion caused by sunlight and shadow. Others think Champ could be a remnant of a species of primitive whale called a zeuglodon or an ancient marine reptile known as a plesiosaur, both believed by biologists to be long extinct. But until uncontestable images of the creature's entire body are produced, this argument will undoubtedly continue.

Champ does claim one rare, official nod to the probability of its existence: Legislation by both the states of New York and Vermont proclaim that Champ is a protected—though unknown—species and make it illegal to harm the creature in any way.

Dog Chapel

St. Johnsbury, Vermont

Just after artist Stephen Hunich survived a near-death experience, he claims to have had a vision. According to Hunich, he was instructed to build a dog chapel, "a place where people can go and celebrate the spiritual bond they have with their dogs." Accepting the vision at face value, Hunich constructed his dog chapel in 1999. Since then, St. Johnsbury canines and their owners have grown ever closer, sitting side-by-side in the chapel's pews or moving freely amongst its 400 scenic acres.

Doggy sculptures are spread throughout and include canine heads mounted on pillars, a winged dog affixed to the chapel's steeple, even a businessman taking Fido out for a walk. Hunich also saw fit to include nature trails and swimming ponds in his doggy retreat–all the better to set the mood for enlightenment.

After such embraced spirituality, man (or woman) and best friend can check out Hunich's prints or snap up a copy of his Dog Chapel book. At the dog chapel, it truly is a dog's life.

Knight's Spider Web Farm

Williamstown, Vermont

Peter Parker, AKA Spiderman, has nothing at all on Spiderwebman, AKA Will Knight. While the former was only bitten by an arachnid, the latter lives amongst his eight-legged friends and makes his living off their webs. He even resides on Spider Web Farm Road, lest anyone overlook his life's mission.

Knight first thought of harvesting spider webs in the 1970s. Teaming up with artist wife Terry, the former cabinetmaker set out to capture the artistry of spider webs by mounting them on wood backgrounds.

To obtain his webs, Knight hangs custom-built racks in his backyard. In the morning, after the spiders have done what spiders do, Knight very gingerly positions boards until they come in contact with the sticky webs. Once accomplished, he seals them with lacquer, sends them off to be painted with artistic flowers and the like, and voilà, spider-art is born.

Shelburne Museum

Shelburne, Vermont

The U.S. military possesses an explosive device known as the Mother of All Bombs (MOAB). It is called that simply because it's the largest nonnuclear bomb ever built. The Shelburne Museum, a celebrated Vermont institution where practically everything is featured, might be better served if it were called MOAM, short for mother of all museums. It is that big.

Opened to the public in 1952, the museum was created by Electra Havemeyer Webb (1888–1960), daughter of Henry O. Havemeyer (1847–1907), who founded the Domino Sugar Company. With near limitless funds, Webb acquired an eclectic smorgasbord of items over her lifetime; her collection was some 80,000 objects strong at the time of her death.

These and approximately 70,000 additional items are now housed at the Shelburne Museum in the Lake Champlain Valley. So, just how big is this place? It takes 45 full acres and 39 buildings to display it all, and that's with much if it overflowing onto the grounds.

One of the most revered items found within this hodgepodge is the 1906 steamship *Ticonderoga*. This is no mock-up or reproduction but rather an actual 220-foot-long side-wheel steamer. Webb had it transported from Lake Champlain to the museum, where it's been entertaining visitors since 1955.

Another crowd-pleaser is the Colchester Point Lighthouse. Built in 1871, the Lake Champlain structure originally marked three reefs between Vermont and New York. It was dismantled, reassembled at the museum, and today recalls 19th-century life on the lake.

In addition to these show-stoppers, visitors will find impressionist paintings featuring works by Monet and Degas, historic house interiors from 1790–1950, decorative arts, folk art, decoys, carriages, tools, dolls and dollhouses, toys, quilts, Native American artifacts—the list goes on and on and on. All are contained within eye-pleasing grounds that represent an idyllic slice of Americana. We'd expect no less from the MOAM.

Phineas Gage Memorial

Cavendish, Vermont

On September 13, 1848, an event occurred that was so very freakish, it could turn Robert L. Ripley into a disbeliever. Phineas Gage, a railroad foreman, was setting charges when one of the explosives accidentally detonated. The resulting blast drove an iron rod more than three feet long into his head. The unlikely projectile pierced just above his eye, continued through the top of his skull, and skewered his brain in the process. He should have died. But by some miracle, Gage survived. In fact, he soon regained consciousness and was able to speak on his way to the hospital.

Today, a memorial celebrates Gage's astonishing recovery while also pointing to lessons learned from the incident. Despite living 12 years beyond that fateful day, the plaque tells how Gage's personality was affected, turning him from a hard-working and well-liked man into a shiftless sort who behaved inappropriately and swore incessantly. Finally, medical science had credible evidence that the brain directly affects behavior. The stage for brain mapping had been set.

The monument is located in an empty lot less than one mile from the accident site. Directions to the actual spot are detailed within. Through misfortune came a greater understanding of the human brain. Phineas Gage made it possible.

Williams Hall American Museum of Kitsch Art

Burlington, Vermont

W.H.A.M.K.A. is not really a museum, but a display case in University of Vermont's Williams Hall packed to the gills with some of the tackiest mass-produced objets d'art in manufacturing history, including a velvet "Last Supper," an armada of Pez dispensers, and all sorts of other garish tchotchkes.

Brookfield Floating Bridge

Brookfield, Vermont

Anyone who has crossed Vermont's Brookfield Floating Bridge by car is well aware of its treachery. Anyone who has attempted the same by motorcycle probably took an unplanned swim. This is what happens when a bridge crosses a lake that occasionally crosses it.

The 300-foot-long, all-wooden Brookfield Bridge rests on 380 tarred, oaken barrels that were designed to adjust to the level of Sunset Lake and keep the bridge deck high and dry. But more often than not, they allow the bridge to "sink" several inches below the surface. To a visitor seeing the bridge for the first time, it appears as if an enormous engineering error has been made. Crossing the span does little to convince otherwise.

Why does this bridge float in the first place? Sunset Lake is far too deep to support a traditional, pillared span. Since 1820, impromptu "water ballet" maneuvers have been taking place as vehicles slowly amble across. And every once in a while, a motorcyclist goes Kerplunk!

Haunted Stone's Public House

Since 1834, Stone's Public House has been serving up food and drink to area residents and visitors alike. Should you choose to stop in for a bite, first take a good look at the photo of John Stone hanging over the bar's fireplace, so you'll be sure to recognize his ghost when it appears. Stone's spirit is said to be one of a handful that haunts the inn.

Other spirits include a man that Stone accidentally murdered in an argument during a card game. According to the legend, Stone and several friends buried the man in the basement. The spirits make their presence known by breaking glasses, causing cold breezes, and appearing as shadowy figures.

Home of the Demon

Dover, Massachusetts

For two days in 1977, the town of Dover, Massachusetts, was under attack from a bizarre creature that seemed to be from another world. The first encounter with the beast—nicknamed the Dover Demon—occurred on the evening of April 21. Bill Bartlett was out for a drive with some friends when they saw something strange climbing on a stone wall. The creature appeared to be only about three feet tall but had a giant, oversize head with large, orange eyes. The rest of the body was tan and hairless with long, thin arms and legs.

Several hours later, the same creature was spotted by 15-year-old John Baxter, who watched it scurry up a hillside. The following day, a couple reported seeing the Demon, too. When authorities asked for a description, the couple's matched the ones given by the other witnesses except for one difference: The creature the couple encountered appeared to have glowing green eyes. Despite repeated attempts to locate it, the creature was never seen again.

Hood Milk Bottle
Boston, Massachusetts

Built in 1930 to hawk homemade ice cream, this giant milk bottle was originally some 40 feet tall. In its middle years, it fell into neglect and was acquired by H. P. Hood and Sons, a noted dairy concern. The company refurbished it and donated it to the Boston Children's Museum in 1977. These days, it stands a bit shorter and has been refitted for snack-bar duty. One can only imagine how often "Got Milk?" is "uddered" in its presence.

The Paper House
Rockport, Massachusetts

Beginning in 1922, Elis Stenman layered newspaper, glue, and varnish to create the walls and furnishings of his two-room house. Surprisingly, the place has withstood the test of time. Inside, you can still read the print on the newspapers that make up the desk, tables, chairs, grandfather clock, and bookshelves.

Minots Ledge Lighthouse
Scituate, Massachusetts

Despite the sweet nickname, the ghosts of the "I Love You" lighthouse tell a tragic story. The first Minots Ledge Lighthouse began operating in 1850, and being its keeper was arguably the most frightening assignment around.

Built directly in the rough waters around the Cohasset Reefs, the spidery metal skeleton swayed and buckled in the wind and waves. On April 17, 1851, a sudden nor'easter stranded the keeper on the mainland—he could only watch as the storm slowly destroyed the lighthouse, with his two assistants inside. Their bodies were found after the storm cleared.

A new storm-proof stone tower was built, and the spirits of those who perished in the first lighthouse seem to reside in the new building. Subsequent keepers have heard them working, and sailors see them waving from the external ladder. On stormy nights the light blinks "1–4–3," which locals say is code for "I love you." They believe this is the assistants' message to their loved ones, passing ships, and anyone caught in a storm.

The Mapparium

Boston, Massachusetts

Before Eartha (the World's Largest Globe) came to be, the Mapparium was the preeminent exercise in global largesse. The colorful globe is simply our world when seen from the inside-out. Actually, it's the political world of 1935 as interpreted by its builder, Boston architect Chester Lindsay Churchill.

Viewed from a 30-foot glass bridge that traverses its middle, the three-story, stained glass globe is comprised of 600 concave glass panels and is illuminated by hundreds of lights positioned around it. It's housed inside the Mary Baker Eddy Library, where tour guides explain its reason for being.

"By standing on the crystal bridge, one sees our planet from pole to pole with none of the distortion of area and distance that occur on a flat map," they say rather matter-of-factly. What do we say? Never has a journey to the center of the earth come easier or cheaper.

It may be a bit dated, but what's not to like?

Jordan's Furniture Store and Trapeze School

Reading, Massachusetts

At some point, Americans apparently grew bored with single-purpose stores, and establishments now seem bent on offering wildly unrelated things under one roof.

Jordan's Furniture chain heads up this charge with a theme park experience at its Massachusetts stores. Its outlet in Reading happens to feature a trapeze school. Makes perfect sense to us.

Like any good furniture "circus," Jordan's also features a sideshow. "Beantown" offers a wall covered with jelly beans, while the "Green Monster" features a giant rendition of Boston's Fenway Park mascot squeezing the life out of a New York Yankee. Encircling such fun bits are the expected furniture shopping opportunities and—of course—the trapeze school itself.

If not put off by its array of 30-foot towers and safety nets, anyone can sign up to take a swing. There's even an area where well-wishers (or those who wish for the swinger's early demise) can cheer their heroes on.

Now, about that futon...

Museum of Bad Art

Boston, Massachusetts

If one longs to visit an art museum that self-appointed sophisticates will avoid like the plague, a trip to Boston's Museum of Bad Art (MOBA) is the ticket. The museum, which celebrates the very worst in self-expression, began with a terrible painting that founder Scott Wilson retrieved from the trash in 1993. Whimsically titled "Lucy in the Field with Flowers," it depicts an elderly woman in a frumpy housedress performing an off-kilter dance amongst a field of flowers.

Somehow, Wilson was able to see beyond the painting's bile-inducing veneer and into its very soul. "The motion, the chair, the sway of her breast, the subtle hues of the sky, the expression on her face; every detail combines to create this transcendent and compelling portrait, every detail cries out 'masterpiece,' " declares Wilson. Ahem, we'll take his word for it.

With entire collections found under divisions of portraiture, landscapes, and "unseen forces" (a conglomeration of truly horrendous styles), a museum visitor is never far from a belly laugh or stomach upset. "Art too bad to be ignored" is the museum's slogan, and believe us, these fine folks are not exaggerating.

Dr. Seuss National Memorial Sculpture Garden

Springfield, Massachusetts

Who could ever forget such books as *Green Eggs and Ham* or *The Cat in the Hat?* Dr. Seuss, AKA Theodor Seuss Geisel (1904–1991) produced zany books that children actually wanted to read. As a result, the offbeat writer from Springfield, Massachusetts, has become a beloved legend. Recognizing this, his hometown raised more than $6 million to create a national memorial in his honor.

Geisel's step-daughter, Lark Grey Dimond-Cates, sculpted bronze figures of Seuss's most beloved characters. These include the Lorax, Thidwick the Big-Hearted Moose, the Grinch and his dog Max, Horton the Elephant, and of course, the Cat in the Hat. There's even a sculpture of Geisel at his drawing board engrossed in the process of liberating his youthful followers.

Dr. Seuss wasn't actually a doctor at all. Although Oxford-educated, the budding writer failed to snare a sheepskin. The "Dr." in his pen name is a nod to his father's unfulfilled hopes in this area.

Jack Kerouac Park

Lowell, Massachusetts

Before he wrote *On the Road*, Jack Kerouac spent his formative years in Lowell. The nomadic scribe is honored in his hometown by a monument in an eponymous park that includes excerpts from his novels as well as Roman Catholic and Buddhist symbols that reflect the late writer's diverse beliefs.

Great American Road-Trip Books

- *On the Road*, Jack Kerouac
- *Blue Highways: A Journey into America*, William Least Heat-Moon
- *Travels with Charley: In Search of America*, John Steinbeck
- *The Electric Kool-Aid Acid Test*, Tom Wolfe
- *Roads: Driving America's Great Highways*, Larry McMurtry
- *Zen and the Art of Motorcycle Maintenance*, Robert Pirsig
- *The Lost Continent: Travels in Small-Town America*, Bill Bryson

Witch History Museum

Salem, Massachusetts

If a visitor wishes to get up-close-and-personal with the witch hysteria of the late 1600s, this is the place. With first-person narrations and an unsettling basement diorama featuring devil-possessed girls dancing with wild abandon, the Witch History Museum centers on little-known stories from the witching era.

The "Graveyard" and "Witch in the Night" dioramas are particularly creepy. As are the voice tracks that seem to come from nowhere. While a visit to this bewitching spot is advised, perhaps it's best done in pairs. Yikes!

House of Seven Gables

Salem, Massachusetts

In the 1851 novel *The House of the Seven Gables*, American author Nathaniel Hawthorne (1804–1864) alludes to a "rusty wooden house, with seven acutely peaked gables." While it certainly sounds as if the fictional place were patterned after Salem's "House of the Seven Gables," AKA the Turner-Ingersoll Mansion, it was not. In fact, Hawthorne went out of his way to note that his book was based on no house in particular.

Nevertheless, this 1668 dwelling in Salem's witch country has become famous for its longevity (it's thought to be the oldest surviving 17th-century wooden mansion in New England) as well as its interesting features. It's listed on the National Register of Historic Places, and tours of its many rooms are available. These days, Nathaniel Hawthorne's birth house has been relocated to the grounds, and a museum featuring more than 2,000 artifacts completes the lure.

The Great Molasses Flood

Boston, Massachusetts

On an unusually warm January day in 1919, a molasses tank burst near downtown Boston, sending more than two million gallons of the sticky sweetener flowing through the city's North End at an estimated 35 miles per hour. The force of the molasses wave was so intense that it lifted a train off its tracks and crushed several buildings in its path.

When the flood finally came to a halt, molasses was two to three feet deep in the streets, 21 people and several horses had died, and more than 150 people were injured. Nearly 90 years later, people in Boston can still smell molasses during sultry summer days. You can still visit the site today.

Where It Rains Frogs

Leicester, Massachusetts

On September 7, 1953, clouds formed over Leicester, Massachusetts—a peaceful little town near the middle of the state. Within a few hours, a downpour began, but it wasn't rain falling from the sky—thousands of frogs and toads dropped out of the air. Children collected them in buckets as if it was a game. Town officials insisted that the creatures had simply escaped from a nearby pond, but many of them landed on roofs and in gutters, which seemed to dispute this theory. It is still unclear why the frogs appeared in Leicester or why the same thing happened almost 20 years later in Brignoles, France.

Harvard's Poisoned Puddings and Puritanism

Cambridge, Massachusetts

Today, Harvard is famed for a vast endowment, but its early days were marked by a struggle to get by with quarter-bushels of wheat donated by local farmers.

The School's Scandalous First Leader

In 1640, the tiny college of Harvard was in crisis. Founded four years before by the Massachusetts Bay Colony, Harvard had a student body of nine; a "yard" liberated from cows; and a single, hated instructor.

Harvard's 30-year-old schoolmaster, Nathaniel Eaton, was known to beat wayward students. Other students charged

Eaton's wife, Elizabeth, of putting goat dung into their cornmeal porridge, or "hasty pudding." (Harvard's theatrical society is named for the dish.) Finally, Master Eaton went too far and was hauled into court after clubbing a scholar with a walnut-tree cudgel. He was also accused of embezzling 100 pounds (then an ample sum).

In 1639, Eaton and his wife were sent packing. Master Eaton returned to England, was made a vicar, then died in debtor's prison. Following the Eaton affair, Harvard's reputation lay in tatters; its operations were suspended, and its students were scattered.

The Roots of Learning

The money and work Massachusetts had put into the school seemed for naught. The colony's General Court had allotted 400 pounds for a college in what became known as Cambridge, Massachusetts—across the Charles River from Boston. The school was named for John Harvard, a clergyman from England's Cambridge University, which at the time was known to be a hotbed of Puritanism, the severe, idealistic faith opposed to the dominant Church of England.

John Harvard was a scholar whose family had known William Shakespeare. When the plague felled his brothers and his father, John inherited a considerable estate, including the Queen's Head Tavern. After immigrating to the Boston region, he became a preacher in Charleston, but his career was short. In 1638, at the age of 31, he died of consumption, having bequeathed money and his personal library to the planned college.

Comeback Under the First President

In 1640, the colony's founders were desperate for educational cachet. They offered the post of Harvard president to Henry Dunster, a new arrival from England and another graduate of Cambridge University.

The energetic Dunster tapped into the colony's inherent educational edge. Many of the new Puritan arrivals had studied at the Oxford and Cambridge academies: Some

130 alumni of the two schools were in New England by 1646. Dunster himself was a leading scholar in "Oriental" languages, that is, biblical tongues such as Hebrew.

Led primarily by a Protestant culture that stressed reading the Bible, Boston set up the first free grammar school in 1635; within 12 years, every town in Massachusetts was required by law to have one. Harvard's new president mandated a four-year graduation requirement and rode out angry students who protested over a commencement fee. Dunster obtained Harvard's charter and authored the school's "Rules and Precepts." He bankrolled the facilities through donations of livestock and, over the course of 13 years, some 250 pounds of wheat. He took a modest salary, being underpaid through 14 years of service, and piled up personal debts. Fortunately, his wife, Elizabeth Glover, kept a printing press in their home. It was the American colonies' first press, and its profits underwrote her husband's work. Dunster managed to turn the school around. Harvard's reputation soared, and students from throughout the colonies, the Caribbean, and the mother country flocked to newly built dorms.

Religious Schisms and a President's Heresies

Yet Dunster tripped up on one of the many religious disputes roiling the Puritan colony. In 1648, it was a criminal offense to engage in "Blasphemy, Heresie, open contempt of the Word preached, Profanation of the Lord's Day"; separation of church and state was unknown.

A source of controversy was infant baptism, which the Puritan fathers required by law. Drawing on his biblical knowledge, Dunster noted that John the Baptist had baptized the adult Jesus, but he could find no biblical examples of children being baptized.

In 1653, he refused to have his son Jonathan baptized. At Cambridge's Congregational Church, Dunster preached against "corruptions stealing into the Church, which every faithful Christian ought to [bear] witness against."

This put the Puritans of Boston and Cambridge in a quandary. Dunster's views made him a heretic, yet he was much liked for his work at the college. Early the next year, the colony's officers wrote that Dunster "hath by his practice and opinions rendered himself offensive to this government." They assembled a conference of 11 ministers and elders to interrogate him. Egged on by this assembly, in May 1654 the General Court forbade schools to employ those "that have manifested themselves unsound in the faith, or scandalous in their lives." Dunster resigned from Harvard.

The ex-president then petitioned the court to let him to stay in the colony until he could repay the many debts he'd accumulated from his work. Court authorities coldly responded that "they did not know of [such] extraordinary labor or sacrifices. For the space of 14 years we know of none." Dunster, with Elizabeth and their youngest child ill, then beseeched the court to at least let his family stay the winter. The magistrates agreed grudgingly, but the following spring they banished the Dunster family to the backwater town of Scituate. Harvard's first president died there four years later, at the age of 47.

Lizzie Borden Bed & Breakfast Museum

Fall River, Massachusetts

> Lizzie Borden took an axe,
> And gave her mother forty whacks.
> And when she saw what she had done,
> She gave her father forty-one.

August 4, 1892, began quite uncomfortably for the Borden family. Rather mysteriously, family members had been stricken with food poisoning and were in more than a little distress. Andrew Borden, one of Fall River's wealthiest men, and his second wife Abby were resting on the first and second floors of the house respectively. As it worked out, their recovery would be short-lived. An ax-wielding murderer was in their midst.

Daughter Lizzie was the first person to discover her father's lifeless body. She screamed to a maid, "Come down quick—father's dead. Somebody came in and killed him!" Soon,

Lizzie and a neighbor would discover the mangled body of Abby Borden who, like her husband Andrew, had been bludgeoned to death. After an investigation, Lizzie Borden would be charged with the crimes.

History shows that despite a preponderance of evidence, Borden was acquitted on all charges. Such knowledge is standard fare more than a century later. What is not standard is the fact that the Borden house still exists. It currently operates as a bed and breakfast, of all bizarre things, and actually encourages people to sleep and move about the infamous "death" rooms.

The Greek-Revival home features six bedrooms (one of them the room where Abby Borden went all to pieces), and visitors are invited to "learn the true facts about Lizzie Borden and the murders of 1892." The parlor where Andrew Borden met the business end of an ax is also open to guests. What first appears to be the actual couch upon which he was bludgeoned is actually a reproduction. There was "way too much blood" on the original piece, we soon learn.

The tour is given by guides extremely well-versed in the murders. When one of them is asked if she believes Lizzie to be guilty or innocent, her words leave her lips with a measured cadence, with much thought and knowledge clearly applied to her answer. "In my opinion, Lizzie Borden was undoubtedly..." Be sure to swing by for the answer. Chop, chop.

Big Blue Bug

Providence, Rhode Island

How do you make a giant bug sculpture lovable? Design him as a termite and give him the name "Nibbles Woodaway." At 58 feet long, we don't suppose many would contest Nibbles's grandiose claim of world superiority, particularly if they live in wood-framed houses.

But Nibbles is even tougher than his nibbling suggests. When built in 1980 at a cost of $20,000, the enormous winged creature was designed to withstand the force of a hurricane. The giant bug's deep-blue hue easily catches the eye, and he's outfitted in different garb for major holidays. Somehow the thought of a 58-foot termite wearing an Uncle Sam hat appeals to us. You?

Waterfire

Providence, Rhode Island

Waterfire, an environmental art installation, is made up of more than 100 bonfires that rage just above the three rivers (Woonasquatucket, Moshassuck, and Providence) of Waterplace Park. It's staged after dusk for maximum effect.

Created by artist Barnaby Evans in 1994, Waterfire blazes before an ever-changing background of classical and world music and offers visitors a uniquely artsy experience. The show sometimes draws as many as 65,000 people, a statistic that brings great joy to its creator.

It was Evans's deep fascination with liquid and flame that led to Waterfire. Says the artist: "Water will quench a fire, but fire can boil water away to invisibility." When combined, they can also entertain. A visit to Waterfire serves as scorching proof.

Frog Bridge

Willimantic, Connecticut

This whimsical bridge pays tribute to two disparate phenomena. The spools are monuments to the thread industry that was the backbone of the local economy in the 19th century. The frogs perched atop the spools are reminders of the infamous "Battle of the Frogs" of 1754, when the cries from dying, drought-ravaged bullfrogs seriously alarmed locals during the thick of the French and Indian War.

Museum of Natural and Other Curiosities

Hartford, Connecticut

Built in 1796, Hartford's Old State House was also home to a museum that displayed the unusual collection of deacon and painter Joseph Steward from 1797 to 1808. The style and substance has been re-created for today's visitor with a collection that includes two-headed livestock, mummified body parts, and plenty of catch-all "other curiosities."

Barnum Museum

Bridgeport, Connecticut

At first glance, it's hard to believe a museum so downright classy could spring from a man considered to be something just a bit less. In his defense, Phineas T. Barnum, for all his hucksterism, exaggeration, and deceit, was in fact the consummate showman. And as they say in the business, the man "went over big." Real big. So, perhaps it's not so surprising that a fabulous Bridgeport display has been featuring snippets from the showman's colorful life since 1893.

Divided amongst three levels, the former Barnum Institute of Science and History features a wealth of Barnum memorabilia, as well as bits that tie in with Bridgeport's industrial and social heritage. P.T. Barnum: Bethel to Broadway to Bridgeport traces the showman's life and career and displays such artifacts as a reproduction of his bizarre Feejee Mermaid (half mammal, half fish) and a piece of wedding cake preserved from the 1863 union of General

Tom Thumb—Barnum's diminutive mega-star. It concludes with P. T. Barnum's Greatest Show on Earth, precursor to the Ringling Brothers Barnum and Bailey Circus.

Another gallery houses a 1,000-square-foot model of a five-ring circus. Completely hand-carved, the replica contains some 3,000 miniature sculptures and is considered one of the finest carved circus models in America. A 4,000-year-old mummy occupies the third-floor gallery. As the oldest artifact in the museum, it captures some of the wonderment of a 19th-century Barnum sideshow but fails to capture the playful huckster that epitomized the man.

Dinosaur State Park
Rocky Hill, Connecticut

In 1966, some 2,000 dinosaur tracks were unearthed during excavation for a new state building. Realizing the importance of the find, the Connecticut Department of Environmental Protection took action. The result is Dinosaur State Park, a dino-centric spot where 500 of these impressions exist under a geodesic dome.

While no one can say with certainty just what species left the tracks (called *Eubrontes* by geologist Edward Hitchcock), scientists currently lean toward the carnivore *Dilophosaurus*. But the point is nearly moot. After some 200 million years, whatever left them is worthy of preservation–a fact underscored by the park's Registered National Landmark status.

Gillette Castle State Park
East Haddam, Connecticut

If the name sounds familiar, you're probably off track. This particular Gillette had nothing to do with shaving and everything to do with the stage.

Theater buffs may recall William Hooker Gillette (1853–1937), an American actor who delivered the very first stage performance of Sherlock Holmes. If equally versed in castles, they'll also know that Gillette built himself a humdinger of a fortress high up on a bluff overlooking the Connecticut River.

Upon Gillette's death, his will stipulated that his circa-1919 castle not fall into the hands of any "blithering sap-head who has no conception of where he is or with what surrounded." In 1943, the actor got his wish when the State of Connecticut took possession of the unique property and christened it Gillette Castle State Park.

Since then, millions of visitors have gawked at the castle's stone exterior and admired its interior woodwork of southern white oak. With 14 dissimilar doors leading inside, visitors get a glimpse of a man who treasured uniqueness and creativity above all else. The castle includes a system of hidden mirrors, which makes it possible to monitor the public areas from the master bedroom.

New England Carousel Museum

Bristol, Connecticut

What comes around goes around, and what comes around at the New England Carousel Museum (NECM) keeps going, and going, and going. It appears the display's guardians would have it no other way.

If its title isn't descriptive enough, allow us to fill in the blanks. The NECM is a place that harkens back to a time before Blackberries, Palm Pilots, and theme parks. It speaks to the childish wonder in all of us through the magic of old-time carousels.

The museum's mission statement reads in part: "The New England Carousel Museum is dedicated to the acquisition, restoration and preservation of operating carousels and carousel memorabilia..." Nicely put and fairly inclusive, but we think it can be simplified beyond this. Here goes: Did you ever get your chance to grab for the brass ring; to give your all in a free-spirited attempt at circle-clenching glory? As one of America's largest collections of antique carousels, this is one place that fully understands this primal desire. Perhaps you should give it a spin?

Moodus Noises Cave

East Haddam, Connecticut

The Moodus Noises are thunderlike sounds that emanate from caves near East Haddam, Connecticut, where the Salmon and Moodus Rivers meet. The name itself is derived from the Native American word *machemoodus*, which means "place of noises." When European settlers filtered into the area in the late 1600s, the Wangunk tribe warned them about the odd, supernatural sounds. Whether or not anything otherworldly exists there is open to debate.

In 1979, seismologists showed that the noises were always accompanied by small earthquakes (some measuring as low as magnitude 2 on the Richter scale) spread over a small area some 5,000 feet deep by 800 feet wide. But this doesn't explain the fact that no known faultline exists at Moodus. Nor does it describe how small tremors—producing 100 times less ground motion than is detectable by human beings—can generate big, bellowing booms. The mystery and the booms continue.

Ringing Rocks County Park

Bucks County, Pennsylvania

Visitors looking to entertain themselves at Pennsylvania's Ringing Rocks Park often show up toting hammers. Seems odd, but they're necessary for the proper tone. Ringing Rocks is a seven-acre boulder field that runs about ten feet deep. For reasons that are still unexplained, some of these rocks ring like bells when struck lightly by a hammer or other object. Because igneous diabase rocks don't usually do this, the boulder field has caused quite a stir through the years. In 1890, Dr. J. J. Ott held what may have been the world's first "rock concert" at the park. He assembled rocks of different pitches, enlisted the aid of a brass band for accompaniment, and went to town.

Carbon County Jail

Carbon County, Pennsylvania

In 1877, Carbon County Prison inmate Alexander Campbell spent long, agonizing days awaiting sentencing. Campbell, a coal miner from northeastern Pennsylvania, had been charged with the murder of mine superintendent John P. Jones. Authorities believed that Campbell was part of the Molly Maguires labor group, a secret organization looking to even the score with mine owners. Although evidence shows that he was indeed part of the Mollies, and he admitted that he'd been present at the murder scene, Campbell professed his innocence and swore repeatedly that he was not the shooter.

The Sentence

Convicted largely on evidence collected by James McParlan, a Pinkerton detective hired by mine owners to infiltrate the underground labor union, Campbell was sentenced to hang. The decree would be carried out at specially prepared gallows at the Carbon County Jail. When the prisoner's day of reckoning arrived, he rubbed his hand on his sooty cell floor then slapped it on the wall proclaiming, "I am innocent, and let this be my testimony!" With that, Alexander Campbell was unceremoniously dragged from cell number 17 and committed, whether rightly or wrongly, to eternity.

The Hand of Fate

The Carbon County Jail of present-day is not too different from the torture chamber that it was back in Campbell's day. Although it is now a museum, the jail still imparts the horrors of man's inhumanity to man. Visitors move through its claustrophobically small cells and dank dungeon rooms with mouths agape. When they reach cell number 17, many visitors feel a cold chill rise up their spine, as they notice that Alexander Campbell's handprint is still there!

"There's no logical explanation for it," says James Starrs, a forensic scientist from George Washington University who investigated the mark. Starrs is not the first to scratch his head in disbelief. In 1930, a local sheriff aimed to rid the jail of its ominous mark. He had the wall torn down and replaced with a new one. But when he awoke the following morning and stepped into the cell, the handprint had reappeared on the newly constructed wall!

Many years later Sheriff Charles Neast took his best shot at the wall, this time with green latex paint. The mark inexplicably returned. Was Campbell truly innocent as his ghostly handprint seems to suggest? No one can say with certainty. Is the handprint inside cell number 17 the sort of thing that legends are made of? You can bet your life on it.

The Haunted Gettysburg National Military Park

Gettysburg, Pennsylvania

The Battle of Gettysburg holds a unique and tragic place in the annals of American history. It was the turning point of the Civil War and its bloodiest battle. From July 1 through July 3, 1863, both the Union and Confederate armies amassed a total of more than 50,000 casualties (including dead, wounded, and missing) at the Battle of Gettysburg. All that bloodshed and suffering is said to have permanently stained Gettysburg and left the entire area brimming with ghosts. It is often cited as one of the most haunted places in America.

First Ghostly Sighting

Few people realize that the first sighting of a ghost at Gettysburg allegedly took place before the battle was over. As the story goes, Union reinforcements from the 20th Maine

Infantry were nearing Gettysburg but became lost as they traveled in the dark. As the regiment reached a fork in the road, they were greeted by a man wearing a three-cornered hat, who was sitting atop a horse. Both the man and his horse appeared to be glowing.

The man, who bore a striking resemblance to George Washington, motioned for the regiment to follow. Believing the man to be a Union general, Colonel Joshua Chamberlain ordered his regiment to follow the man. Just about the time Chamberlain starting thinking there was something odd about the helpful stranger, the man simply vanished.

As the regiment searched for him, they suddenly realized they had been led to Little Round Top—the very spot where, the following day, the 20th Maine Infantry would repel a Confederate advance in one of the turning points of the Battle of Gettysburg. To his dying day, Chamberlain, as well as the roughly 100 men who saw the spectral figure that night, believed that they had been led to Little Round Top by the ghost of George Washington himself.

Devil's Den

At the base of Little Round Top and across a barren field lies an outcropping of rocks known as Devil's Den. It was from this location that Confederate sharpshooters took up positions and fired at the Union soldiers stationed along Little Round Top. Eventually, Union soldiers followed the telltale sign of gun smoke and picked off the sharpshooters one by one.

After Devil's Den was secured by Union forces, famous Civil War photographer Alexander Gardner was allowed to come in and take photos of the area. One of his most famous pictures, "A Sharpshooter's Last Sleep," was taken at Devil's Den and shows a Confederate sharpshooter lying dead near the rocks. There was only one problem: The photograph was staged. Gardner apparently dragged a dead Confederate soldier over from another location and positioned the body himself. Legend has it that the ghost of the Confederate soldier was unhappy with how his body was treated, so his ghost often causes cameras in Devil's Den to malfunction.

Pickett's Charge

On July 3, the final day of the battle, Confederate General Robert E. Lee felt the battle slipping away from him, and in what many saw as an act of desperation, ordered 12,000 Confederate soldiers to attack the Union forces who were firmly entrenched on Cemetery Ridge. During the attack, known as Pickett's Charge, the Confederates slowly and methodically marched across open fields toward the heavily fortified Union lines. The attack failed miserably, with more than 6,000 Confederate soldiers killed or wounded before they retreated. The defeat essentially signaled the beginning of the end of the Civil War.

Today, it is said that if you stand on top of Cemetery Ridge and look out across the field, you might catch a glimpse of row after ghostly row of Confederate soldiers slowly marching toward their doom at the hands of Union soldiers.

Jennie Wade

While the battle was raging near Cemetery Ridge, 20-year-old Mary Virginia "Ginnie" Wade (also known as Jennie Wade) was at her sister's house baking bread for the Union troops stationed nearby. Without warning, a stray bullet flew through the house, struck the young woman, and killed her instantly, making her the only civilian known to die during the Battle of Gettysburg.

Visitors to the historical landmark known as the Jennie Wade house often report catching a whiff of freshly baked bread. Jennie's spirit is also felt throughout the house, especially in the basement, where her body was placed until relatives could bury her when there was a break in the fighting.

Farnsworth House

Though it was next to impossible to determine who fired the shot that killed Jennie Wade, it is believed that it came from the attic of the Farnsworth house. Now operating as a bed-and-breakfast, during the Battle of Gettysburg the building was taken over by Confederate sharpshooters. One in particular, the one who may have fired the shot that killed Jennie Wade, is said to have holed himself up in the attic.

No one knows for sure because the sharpshooter didn't survive the battle, but judging by the dozens of bullet holes and scars along the sides of the Farnsworth house, he didn't go down without a fight. Perhaps that's why his ghost is still lingering—to let us know what really happened in the Farnsworth attic. Passersby often report looking up at the attic window facing the Jennie Wade house and seeing a ghostly figure looking down at them.

Spangler's Spring

As soon as the Battle of Gettysburg was over, soldiers began relating their personal experiences to local newspapers. One story that spread quickly centered on the cooling waters of Spangler's Spring. It was said that at various times during the fierce fighting, both sides agreed to periodic ceasefires so that Union and Confederate soldiers could stand side-by-side and drink from the spring. It's a touching story, but in all likelihood, it never actually happened.

Even if it did, it doesn't explain the ghostly woman in a white dress who is seen at the spring. Some claim that the "Woman in White" is the spirit of a woman who lost her lover during the Battle of Gettysburg. Another theory is that she was a young woman who took her own life after breaking up with her lover years after the war ended.

Pennsylvania Hall at Gettysburg College

One of the most frightening ghost stories associated with the Battle of Gettysburg was originally told to author Mark Nesbitt. The story centers around Gettysburg College's Pennsylvania Hall, which was taken over during the battle by Confederate forces, who turned the basement into a makeshift hospital. Late one night in the early 1980s, two men who were working on an upper floor got on the elevator and pushed the button for the first floor. But as the elevator descended, it passed the first floor and continued to the basement.

Upon reaching the basement, the elevator doors opened. One look was all the workers needed to realize that they had somehow managed to travel back in time. The familiar surroundings of the basement had been replaced by bloody, screaming Confederate soldiers on stretchers. Doctors stood over the soldiers, feverishly trying to save their lives. Blood and gore were everywhere.

As the two men started frantically pushing the elevator buttons, some of the doctors began walking toward them. Without a second to spare, the elevator doors closed just as the ghostly figures reached them. This time the elevator rose to the first floor and opened, revealing modern-day furnishings. Despite repeated return visits to the basement, nothing out of the ordinary has ever been reported again.

The Roxborough Antenna Farm

Philadelphia, Pennsylvania

As drivers creep along I-76 just west of Philadelphia, they witness a stand of super-tall broadcasting masts towering over a suburban neighborhood. The Roxborough Antenna Farm is to broadcasting towers what New York City is to skyscrapers. In the land of broadcasting, height equals might, so the higher the tower, the better the signal strength.

With eight TV/FM masts jutting above the 1,000-foot mark (the tallest stretches to 1,276 feet), the array easily outclasses most skyscrapers in height. The reason these big sticks exist in such a concentrated area? Location, location, location.

The Roxborough site is a unique setting that features geographical height, proper zoning clearances, and favorable proximity to the city—a trifecta by industry standards.

Pratt Rocks

Prattsville, New York

South Dakota has Mount Rushmore, but nestled in the Catskill Mountains is the town of Prattsville, New York, which features Pratt Rocks—a set of relief carvings begun 84 years before its famous western counterpart. Zadock Pratt, who founded the world's largest tannery in the 1830s, commissioned a local sculptor to immortalize his visage high up on a mountainside.

The numerous stone carvings include a coat of arms, Pratt's own bust, his business milestones, and even his personal accomplishments, such as his two terms in the U.S. House of Representatives. Carvings also include a shrine to Pratt's son George, who was killed during the Civil War. But the strangest bit found at this site is a recessed tomb that was intended to house Pratt's decaying corpse for eternity. It leaked, Pratt balked, and the chamber remains empty.

Boldt Castle

Heart Island, New York

It's rather poetic that Boldt castle should be located on Heart Island, for it was built by a heart filled with love. George C. Boldt (1851–1916), manager of the New York's Waldorf Astoria Hotel, loved his wife Louise so much that he decided to memorialize his devotion by presenting her with a dream castle.

For four splendid years, the Boldts and their children summered on Heart Island as the castle's construction advanced. The family marveled at the 6-story, 120-room bulk of the structure. Its mass was offset by ornate trim and flourishing Italian gardens. Unfortunately, in 1904, just as the castle was nearing completion, Louise died suddenly.

With his beloved wife taken from him, a heartbroken Boldt saw no reason to continue building an empty shrine. He ordered the castle's construction halted and never again set foot on the island.

The castle stood vacant for decades. Then, in 1977, the Thousand Islands Bridge Authority acquired the property and devised a funding mechanism to ensure that it would be preserved for future generations. Today, the castle's sad story is powerful enough to bring tears to the eyes of some visiting tourists.

Perhaps this is the greatest testament to the power of one man's love.

Cardiff Giant

Cooperstown, New York

It seems people will believe anything if they want to badly enough. Take for instance the Cardiff Giant, a ten-foot-tall petrified stone man "discovered" in 1869 on a farm in Cardiff, New York. Could the giant be the missing link? Perhaps a visitor from another planet? Might he even have biblical implications? People wanted to know.

The answer, as it turns out, was none of the above. In reality, the Cardiff Giant was a divine hoax perpetrated by the farm's owner William C. "Stub" Newell and his pal George Hull. Concocted partly as a joke but also to turn a profit, the pair charged visitors fifty cents apiece to see the huge stone man up close. There were thousands of takers.

Eventually, the pranksters grew bored of the ruse and sold the giant to a group of businessmen for $37,500. Once the petrified man was placed on display at Syracuse, New York, a closer examination revealed the truth. Oddly, it didn't seem to matter. People were still fascinated by the giant and came out in droves to see "Old Hoaxey" in person. These days, the giant remains a major draw at the Farmers Museum in Cooperstown (home of the Baseball Hall of Fame), New York. Good show, big guy.

The Kaatskill Kaleidoscope

Mt. Tremper, New York

You have to admire American ingenuity and the spirit that drives it. Only in this land of milk and honey could the thought of constructing the world's largest kaleidoscope seem so terribly vital. Lucky for us!

The Kaatskill Kaleidoscope at Emerson Place Spa screams "fun" from the get-go. Housed in a converted grain silo, the 60-foot-tall world champ was originally jacketed in a sky-blue façade on which a strange set of eyes had been painted. Now it's shrouded in stealthy flat black. And the interior? Try to imagine what it would be like to magnify a hand-held kaleidoscope. Once inside the tube you'd feast your eyes on an ever-changing psychedelic world so vivid it would impress Peter Max. This is a lot like that.

Designed by Isaac Abrams, the giant kaleidoscope has stood in this Catskill Mountain Valley since 1996. The artist has ambitiously deemed his creation the "first cathedral of the third millennium." We can't speak to that, but the terms "groovy" and "far out" do spring to mind.

Lucy the Elephant

Margate City, New Jersey

There are elephants and there are elephants. Jumbo, the famous pachyderm that P. T. Barnum featured in the 1880s, was one enormous fellow. If we're to believe the famously deceptive showman, Jumbo was some 13-feet-tall at the shoulder. In reality, he probably came closer to 11 feet. But even Jumbo in all of his magnificence paled in comparison with Lucy, the elephant from Margate.

Now, some may argue that Jumbo was a real living elephant, whereas Lucy is just a reproduction made from wood and tin. A mere technicality, we say. Besides, if one attempted to climb up into Jumbo's nether regions, that person would likely be trampled. Lucy not only allows such antics, she encourages them.

Built in 1881 by developer James V. Lafferty, Lucy was created as an attention-grabbing centerpiece that would put the former "South Atlantic City" and his business on the map. At 65-feet-tall by 60-feet-long and weighing some 90 tons, she was hard to miss.

Lucy is the only example of "zoomorphic architecture" left in the United States. Staircases in her legs lead to rooms inside. Over the years, Lucy has served as a summer home, tavern, and tourist attraction. Preservationists completed a loving restoration in 2000.

These days, tours of Lucy's cavernous "guts" are conducted daily, and most patrons emerge slack-jawed in appreciation. Lucy is considered the largest elephant on planet Earth. But there may be something about her that's even better. No one has to follow this elephant around with a shovel.

Lucy was named a National Historic Landmark in 1976. In the spring of 2006, Lucy was struck by lightning. Evidence of this brush with mother nature can be seen on the tips of her tusks, which were blackened by the episode.

S.S. Atlantus

Cape May, New Jersey

When a joke fails, it's said to have gone over like a "lead balloon." The implication is obvious since a lead balloon can't float. With this in mind, one must wonder why President Wilson saw fit to commission a fleet of concrete ships during World War I. Had the prospect of drowned seamen suddenly become funny to the statesman?

Despite beliefs to the contrary, concrete ships really did float. The president approved the construction of 24 such vessels simply because the war effort had made steel scarce.

Launched on December 5, 1918, the S.S. *Atlantus* would carry troops and transport coal until 1920, when she'd be deemed too heavy and retired to a salvage yard.

In March 1926, a plan was hatched. The 250-foot-long *Atlantus* would become a half-submerged ferry dock at Cape May, New Jersey. The ship was towed to its new site. Before a channel could be dug to firmly anchor it, a storm hit. The ship drifted and beached 150 feet off the coast where she rests to this very day. To some, the ship's a slowly decaying conversation piece; to others, she's a renowned New Jersey landmark. To all, she's the SS *Atlantus*, the ship that went over like a "lead balloon."

Martian Landing Site
Grover's Mill, New Jersey

To say that American people were more gullible in 1938 is to totally miss the point. While it's true that Orson Welles scared the tar out of them with his infamous "War of the Worlds" radio broadcast—a transmission so realistic that many thought America was actually being invaded by little green men from Mars—it's also true that this was an era that predated television, instant news, satellites, and cell phones.

In those days, when a broadcaster issued a bulletin, people listened. Then too, Welles had craftily mixed genuine details into his attack scenario. There really was a Grover's Mill, New Jersey. When people heard that it had suddenly become a Martian ground-zero, they understandably panicked.

To memorialize the unique event, the town of Grover's Mill has erected a monument at Van Nest Park, the very spot where the fictional spaceships were said to have landed. It depicts Welles behind his microphone and a petrified family huddled around the family radio, hanging onto his every word. Rather curiously, nearby Grover's Mill Pond is colored an ethereal green. This likely stems from algae and other such organisms. Then again, if a Martian made a water-landing one would expect such a verdant hue. You don't suppose...?

World Trade Center Memorial Replica

Tinton Falls, New Jersey

Some sculptures are abstract, some more literal. When 9/11 memorials popped up around New Jersey, most included the names of those lost that terrible day and a sketch or photograph of the Twin Towers as they once appeared. The town of Tinton Falls did things a bit differently. They erected a dead-ringer monument to the towers that's so very lifelike, it sends shivers down the spines of those who witnessed the tragedy firsthand.

The towers stand majestically on the front lawn of Tinton's firehouse. At eight feet high, the towers can't be mistaken for the real thing, yet compared with other monuments they are huge. While their size is intriguing, it's their attention to detail that really sets them apart.

The silver-hue of their façade is historically correct, as is the antenna mast on the north tower. Some 40,000 drilled holes faithfully represent windows. There's even an "X" at the point where the airliners impacted each building.

But it's at night that the memorial turns downright eerie. This is when interior lights are flicked on and reality suddenly becomes fuzzy—particularly to those New Jerseyans who once viewed the twin towers from across the Hudson. If his goal was to keep people from forgetting, designer Jared Stevens has clearly done his job.

Admiral Fell Inn

Baltimore, Maryland

The Admiral Fell Inn, located just steps away from the harbor on historic Fell's Point in Baltimore, was named for a shipping family who immigrated from England in the 18th century. With parts of the inn dating back to the 1700s, it's a charming place with stately rooms, an intimate pub, and wonderful service. It is also reportedly home to a number of spirits.

The ghosts at the Admiral Fell Inn include a young boy who died from cholera, a woman in white who haunts Room 218, and a man who died in Room 413. Staff members claim this room is always chilly and has strange, moving cold spots.

In 2003, during Hurricane Isabel, the hotel's guests were evacuated to safety, but several of the hotel managers stayed behind. At one point in the night, they reported the sounds of music, laughter, and dancing from the floor above the lobby. When they checked to see what was going on, they discovered no one else in the building.

Chesapeake Bay Monster?

Chesapeake Bay, Maryland

Chesapeake Bay, a 200-mile intrusion of the Atlantic Ocean into Virginia and Maryland, is 12 miles wide at its mouth, allowing plenty of room for strange saltwater creatures to slither on in. Encounters with giant, serpentine beasts up and down the Eastern seaboard were reported during the 1800s, but sightings of Chessie, a huge, snakelike creature with a football-shape head and flippers began to escalate in the 1960s. Former CIA employee Donald Kyker and some neighbors saw not one, but four unidentified water creatures swimming near shore in 1978.

Then in 1980, the creature was spotted just off Love Point, sparking a media frenzy. Two years later, Maryland resident Robert Frew was entertaining dinner guests with his wife, Karen, when the whole party noticed a giant water creature about 200 yards from shore swimming toward a group of people frolicking nearby in the surf. They watched the creature, which they estimated to be about 30 feet in length, as it dove underneath the unsuspecting humans, emerged on the other side, and swam away.

Frew recorded several minutes of the creature's antics, and the Smithsonian Museum of Natural History reviewed his film. Although they could not identify the animal, they did concede that it was "animate," or living.

The Chessie Challenge

Some believe Chessie is a manatee, but they usually swim in much warmer waters and are only about ten feet long.

Also, the fact that Chessie is often seen with several "humps" breaking the water behind its head leads other investigators to conclude that it could be either a giant sea snake or a large seal.

One Maryland resident has compiled a list of 78 different sightings over the years. And a tour boat operator offers sea-monster tours in hopes of repeating the events of 1980 when 25 passengers on several charter boats all spotted Chessie cavorting in the waves.

God's Ark of Safety
Frostburg, Maryland

Faith is said to move mountains. It can also build arks. We could be referring to a famous ship commanded by a fellow named Noah. We are not. God's Ark of Safety is a modern incarnation of that biblical boat that totally skips the middle man. And it's made from steel!

In May 1974, Pastor Richard Green had a series of visions featuring a large ark on a hillside. Through these revelations, Green believes God asked him to build his new church as a replica of Noah's Ark. According to Green it would be a "sign to the world of God's love and the soon return of Jesus." The pastor complied. On Easter day in 1976, the first spade of dirt was turned, and God's Ark of Safety was underway.

More than five decades later the ark stands as a rusting hulk less than half-finished. Faith may move mountains, but construction requires labor and money, each of which arrives in drips and drabs. When/if finished, the ark will measure an astounding 450 feet long by 75 feet wide.

Undaunted, the congregation meets each Sunday at a temporary church located beside the ark. Church members are certain that Pastor Green's vision will one day be realized. It has to be. God himself commanded it.

Grotto of Lourdes Replica

Emmitsburg, Maryland

If cash-strapped pilgrims can only dream of a journey to the Grotto of Lourdes in France, they're in for a treat. The National Shrine Grotto of Our Lady of Lourdes in Emmitsburg, Maryland, has brought the miracle to them.

When young Bernadette Soubiroux saw the Blessed Virgin Mary at a grotto in southern France in 1858, she caused quite a stir. Since then, people have flocked from all parts of the globe to experience the purported healing powers of the Grotto's spring at Lourdes.

The replica in Emmitsburg dates to 1875. It emerged from the combined efforts of Father John Dubois (founder of the adjacent Mount Saint Mary's College in 1808) and Saint Elizabeth Ann Seton (founder of the Sisters of Charity).

A meandering path encounters altars and chapels on its way to the "Grotto Cave," a close replica of the site where Soubiroux was said to receive her revelations. The grounds are of such uncommon beauty, secularists and people of other faiths should appreciate them at a level similar to their Christian counterparts. Such can be the beauty of faith.

The Awakening Sculpture

Oxen Hill, Maryland

In a classic bit of American weirdness, "The Awakening," a 70-foot-long by 17-foot-high "screaming" sculpture by J. Seward Johnson, Jr., was moved from its Hains Point, Washington D.C., home to Oxen Hill, Maryland, in 2008.

The aluminum behemoth whose wildly contorted facial expressions suggest a perpetually bad day, had struggled at Hains Point in his half-buried state since the 1970s. For reasons that escape lovers of the offbeat, the National Park

Service suddenly turned on the tin man and issued him his walking papers. This, of course, was an oversight on their part since this giant has never stood on his own two feet.

Luckily, billionaire developer Milton Peterson stepped in and rescued the grumpy giant. Peterson even saw fit to provide him with new "digs" on a faux beach at National Harbor, Maryland—the playground for the upwardly mobile. Now, "power walkers" and chic restaurant patrons can catch a daily glimpse of the man who's clearly having a worse day than they. Progress!

Haunted Point Lookout Lighthouse

St. Mary's County, Maryland

Built in 1830, the historic Point Lookout Lighthouse is located in St. Mary's County, Maryland, where the Potomac River meets Chesapeake Bay. It is a beautiful setting for hiking, boating, fishing, camping, and ghost-hunting.

Point Lookout Lighthouse has been called America's most haunted lighthouse, perhaps because it was built on what later became the largest camp for Confederate prisoners of war.

Marshy surroundings, tent housing, and close quarters were a dangerous combination, and smallpox, scurvy, and dysentery ran rampant. The camp held more than 50,000 soldiers, and between 3,000 and 8,000 died there.

Park rangers and visitors to the lighthouse report hearing snoring and footsteps, having a sense of being watched, and feeling the floors shake and the air move as crowds of invisible beings pass by. A photograph of a former caretaker shows the misty figure of a young soldier leaning against the wall behind her, although no one noticed him when the photo was taken during a séance at the lighthouse. And a bedroom reportedly smelled like rotting flesh at night until the odor was publicly attributed to the spirits of the war prisoners.

The Lost Ghost

In December 1977, Ranger Gerald Sword was sitting in the lighthouse's kitchen on a stormy night when a man's face appeared at the back door. The man was young, with a floppy cap and a long coat, and peered into the bright room. Given the awful weather, Sword opened the door to let him in, but the young man floated backward until he vanished entirely. Later, after a bit of research, Sword realized he had been face-to-face with Joseph Haney, a young officer whose body had washed ashore after the steamboat he was on sank during a similar storm in 1878.

The Host Ghost

One of Point Lookout's most frequent visitors is the apparition of a woman dressed in a long blue skirt and a white blouse who appears at the top of the stairs. She is believed to be Ann Davis, the wife of the first lighthouse keeper. Although her husband died shortly after he took the post, Ann remained as the keeper for the next 30 years, and, according to inspection reports, was known for clean and well-kept grounds. Caretakers claim to hear her sighing heavily.

Who Said That?

Point Lookout's reputation drew Hans Holzer, Ph.D., a renowned parapsychologist, who tried to capture evidence of ghostly activity. Holzer and his team claimed to have recorded 24 different voices in all, both male and female, talking, laughing, and singing. Among their recordings, the group heard male voices saying "fire if they get too close," "going home," and more than a few obscenities.

Take Care, Caretaker

One former caretaker reported waking in the middle of the night to see a ring of lights dancing above her head. She smelled smoke and raced downstairs to find a space heater on fire. She believes that the lights were trying to protect her and the lighthouse from being consumed by flames.

The lighthouse was decommissioned in 1966, after 135 years of service. In 2002, the state of Maryland purchased it, and it is now open for tours and paranormal investigations. The Point Lookout Lighthouse continues to have a steady stream of visitors—even those who are no longer among the living.

World Championship Punkin Chunkin
Millsboro, Delaware

An annual tradition since 1986, this competition strives to answer the question: Exactly how far can a pumpkin fly? While the first chunkin resulted in a 126-foot chunk for the gold medal, the record is now over 4,000 feet. There are a number of classes, ranging from air cannons to catapults to human power; explosives are not permitted.

An ideal road-trip destination, Punkin Chunkin usually draws 20,000 spectators to its playing field every November, but as of 2023, the Punkin Chunkin organizers are looking for a new home to host the world championship. If you know someone who owns 200 acres in the greater Delaware area, visit www.punkinchunkin.com.

Woodburn—The Governor's Mansion
Dover, Delaware

Located in Dover, Delaware, Woodburn was constructed in the late 1700s and is a classic example of Colonial-style architecture. Before it became the official governor's mansion in 1965, it had several owners, as well as several ghosts—including one with a fondness for alcohol spirits.

According to legend, early owners of the house frequently left wine-filled decanters out for the thirsty entity, only to find them completely empty the next morning. One staff member claimed to have actually seen the ghost enjoying its beverage; he described the specter as an older man who was wearing Colonial-era attire, including a powdered wig. Former owner Dr. Frank Hall told friends that he occasionally found mysteriously empty wine bottles in the pantry.

The spirit-loving spirit may be the most active ghost in the house, but it isn't the only one that resides there. In 1805, an apparition nicknamed "the Colonel" made an appearance before evangelist Lorenzo Dow, who was in town for a series of revival meetings. Dow mentioned to his hosts that he had passed a gentleman in the upstairs hall; the hosts were surprised because Dow was their only guest at the time.

Other ghosts that have been witnessed at Woodburn include a young girl wearing a checkered gingham dress and a man who, in life, was rumored to have been involved in slave kidnapping and is known for rattling chains on the grounds of the estate.

The slave kidnapper was part of a pro-slavery mob that attacked the mansion, which was a stop on the Underground Railroad at the time; however, the mob was rebuked by a group of Quakers. According to legend, the kidnapper hid in an old tree, where he hanged himself. Whether his death was an accident or a suicide remains a mystery; either way, the incident seems to have kept his spirit earthbound.

Fort Delaware Prison

Delaware City, Delaware

Pea Patch Island. Sounds quaint, doesn't it? Hardly the name of a place that you'd imagine would host a military prison...or the ghosts of former inmates who still can't seem to escape, even in death. But then, the hardships and horrors that were experienced there might just trump the loveliness that the name suggests.

Shaped like a pentagon, Fort Delaware Prison was completed in 1859, just prior to the Civil War. With a moat surrounding its 32-foot-high walls, it was a very secure place to hold Confederate POWs.

With no extra blankets or clothing, Fort Delaware's inmates struggled to keep warm and suffered through the cold, harsh winters that are typical in the Mid-Atlantic region. Malaria, smallpox, and yellow fever were commonplace, and they traveled quickly through the facility; estimates suggest that between 2,500 and 3,000 people may have died there—and many tormented souls seem to remain.

Now Appearing...

One ghost that has been seen by many workers at the Fort Delaware Prison—which is now a living-history museum—is not the spirit of a prisoner at all: It's that of a former cook who now spends her time hiding ingredients from the current staff. Visitors have reported hearing a harmonica in the laundry area, where a ghost has been spotted threading buttons in a long string.

In the officer's quarters, a spectral child is known to tug on people's clothes and a ghostly woman taps visitors on the shoulder. Books fall from shelves, and chandelier crystals swing back and forth by themselves.

And then there are the darker, more sinister spirits—the ones that suffered in life and found no relief in death. Moans, muffled voices, and rattling chains fill the basement with spooky sounds of prisoners past. The halls echo with noises that resemble the sounds of someone trying to break free from chains. Apparitions of Confederate soldiers have been seen running through the prison, and sailors have witnessed lights on shore where there were none. Screams and desperate voices plead for help, but so far, no one has been able to calm these restless souls.

Ghost Hunter Endorsed

If you're searching for proof that these ghosts are the real deal, check out a 2008 episode of *Ghost Hunters* that was shot at Fort Delaware. Jason Hawes, Grant Wilson, and their team of investigators found quite a bit of paranormal activity when they visited the old prison. In the basement's tunnels, they heard unexplained footsteps and voices, as well as something crashing to the ground. A thermal-imaging camera picked up the apparition of a man who appeared to be running away from the group. And in the kitchen, the investigators heard a very loud banging sound that seemingly came from nowhere.

In the Spirit of Things

It's not all terror at the old prison. Today, Fort Delaware is part of a state park that's open to tourists and offers many special programs. One event that appeals to athletes and history buffs alike is the "Escape from Fort Delaware" triathlon: Each year when the starting musket blasts, participants reenact the escape route of 52 inmates who broke out of Fort Delaware Prison during the Civil War.

During the Civil War, so much misery was experienced at Camp Sumter—a prison for captured Union soldiers near Andersonville, Georgia—that the absence of a haunting there would be remarkable. It only served as a POW camp for a little more than a year, but during that time, 13,000 Union soldiers died there. Captain Henry Wirz, who was in charge of the prison, was hanged after the war for conspiracy and murder. His angry spirit still wanders the compound, and many visitors have smelled a vile odor that they attribute to his ghost.

World's Oldest Edible Ham

Smithfield, Virginia

P. D. Gwaltney, Jr., the originator of the famous Smithfield Ham, found his bosom buddy completely by accident. Sifting through his warehouse in 1922, he came across a 20-year-old ham that had miraculously escaped shipping. As a testament to his company's curing process, the ham appeared remarkably appetizing—even if it had lost some 65 percent of its original weight.

Recognizing the meatiness of the situation, the pork huckster quickly bolted into action. With the instincts of a showman and an eye on publicity, Gwaltney took out a $1,000 insurance policy on his newfound "friend." How long might his pet ham last, he wondered? He aimed to find out.

By most accounts the unlikely duo were inseparable. Like a proud papa, Gwaltney would drag his prized ham to exhibitions, food fairs, get-togethers—anywhere ham-loving (buying?) people might gather. But even with this burden, Gwaltney never felt hamstrung. In fact, the two were only getting started.

In 1932, Ripley's Believe It or Not would feature Gwaltney's pal as the world's oldest ham, an honor that would bring with it national recognition and separate it from scores of other "ham and eggers."

Eventually, Gwaltney had a brass collar fitted to his slowly decaying pal. This served two purposes. First, it cleared up any doubt to ownership by proclaiming the petrified porker, "Mr. Gwaltney's Pet Ham." Second, it provided a way to chain his feted treasure to the ground.

For 14 long years the two pals moved happily about in gastronomic circles, until one awful day in 1936 when P. D. Gwaltney, Jr., headed off to that big curing center in the sky. Would this tragic event signal the end of his beloved porker as well? "Not a HAM CHANCE!" fans seemed to say.

Happily rescued by the residents of Smithfield, Gwaltney's pride and joy would carry on. In 2002, the ham celebrated its 100th anniversary. In 2003, Ripley's Believe It or Not again honored Gwaltney's friend as the world's oldest ham.

Today, the porker seems as gamy as ever as it begs for notice at Smithfield's quaint Isle of Wight Museum. There, stored safely beneath protective glass, the storied ham rests beside a life-size cardboard cutout of its beloved master.

Occasionally, visitors observe wistful glances between Gwaltney and the ham as they ride out eternity, side-by-shank. For the sake of all that's strange, we can only hope these folks aren't lying. A man and his meat, such as it were, should never be trifled with.

From World's Oldest Ham to World's Largest Ham Biscuit

Smithfield commemorated its 250-year anniversary by hamming it up. Literally. On September 28, 2006, the town prepared the world's largest ham biscuit. The creation was eight feet in diameter and was piled with 500 pounds of ham. Let's give the "ham" let of Smithfield a hand!

American Celebration on Parade

Shenandoah Caverns, Virginia

Earl Hargrove, Jr., had a dream. As the head honcho of a company that staged conventions and trade shows, the fanatical collector needed a space to house his beloved floats, props, and parade materials. His dream materialized when he purchased the Shenandoah Caverns attraction and erected a 40,000-square-foot building strictly for that purpose.

American Celebration on Parade's floats trace to past Thanksgiving parades, Miss America processions, even President Bill Clinton's 1996 inaugural parade. But parade floats represent only a portion of the collector's bounty. Visitors will also find truly wacky items such as a 30-foot-tall genie, a humongous puppy in a wagon, and an enormous American flag made from 5,000 square yards of crushed silk.

"People enjoy seeing the floats—how big they are, how complicated they are, and how well dressed out they are," Hargrove, Jr., explains. "Our visitors get a sense that they are seeing a little bit of history here."

In addition to the floats, the museum, open seasonally, contains an eclectic potpourri of items fairly begging for discovery. There's a parrot overlooking an arctic scene that features a ferocious polar bear. Beside the bruin, a giant rabbit seeks out his next conquest. Pelicans, elephants, and a stuffed bison add to the mix. When asked to name a favorite item at his vast repository, the patriotic man cuts right to the chase. "I guess it would be the American flag because we've had so many great experiences with it." No doubt.

Flying Circus Air Show

Bealeton, Virginia

It's up, up, and away each Sunday (May through October) at Bealeton as old-time flyers relive the golden age of aviation. A weekly tradition that got off the ground in 1971, the Flying Circus Air Show features aerobatic maneuvers, wing walkers, skydivers, formation flyers, and a multitude of other winged pursuits.

Vintage aircraft recalls barnstorming days and features 1930s and 1940s Stearman and Waco biplanes, as well as other open cockpit craft. If attendees wish to take to the wide, blue yonder, a cash fee will put them in the passenger seat. Not a bad deal for the rising Red Barons among us.

Commodore Theater

Portsmouth, Virginia

Dinner theaters that combine food and a live stage show are fairly common, and it's easy to understand why. After all, what could be more fun than pairing entertainment with food? Portsmouth's Commodore Theater may have hit upon the answer to that particular question: coupling a fine-dining restaurant with a movie auditorium.

The restored 1945 Art Deco movie palace now features a modern 41X 21-foot screen and full digital sound. But it wasn't always so. When rescued by present owner Fred Schoenfeld in 1987, the building had been vacant for nearly 12 years.

Originally designed to hold more than 1,000 moviegoers, the Commodore now seats 188 patrons in its dining area and 318 in its balcony. The dinner theater's menu features hearty American fare, soft drinks, and beer, as well as popcorn by the bucketful. One can only imagine the visceral thrill of slicing into a rare steak while watching a "slasher" movie.

Blennerhassett Hotel

Parkersburg, West Virginia

The Blennerhassett Hotel was designed and built in 1889 by William Chancellor, a prominent businessman. The hotel was a grand showplace and has been restored to its original condition in recent years. These renovations have reportedly stirred the ghosts who reside there into action.

There are several ghosts associated with the hotel, including a man in gray who has been seen walking around on the second floor and the infamous "Four O'Clock Knocker," who likes to pound on guest room doors at 4:00 a.m. There is also a ghost who likes to ride the elevators, often stopping on floors where the button has not been pushed. But the most famous resident spirit is that of hotel builder William Chancellor. Guests and employees have reported seeing clouds of cigar smoke in the hallways, wafting through doorways, and circling a portrait of Chancellor that hangs in the library.

1952 Close Encounter

Flatwoods, West Virginia

While playing football on the afternoon of September 12, 1952, a group of boys in Flatwoods, West Virginia, saw a large fireball fly over their heads. The object seemed to stop near the hillside property of Bailey Fisher. Some thought the object was a UFO, but others said it was just a meteor. They decided to investigate.

Darkness was falling as the boys made their way toward the hill, so they stopped at the home of Kathleen May to borrow a flashlight. Seeing how excited the boys were, May, her two sons, and their friend, Eugene Lemon, decided to join them. The group set off to find out exactly what had landed on the hill.

Walking Through the Darkness

As they neared the top of the hill, the group smelled a strange odor that reminded them of burning metal. Continuing on, some members of the group thought they saw an object that resembled a spaceship. Shining their flashlights in front of them, the group was startled when something not of this world moved out from behind a nearby tree.

The Encounter

The description of what is now known as the Flatwoods Monster is almost beyond belief. It stood around 12 feet tall and had a round, reddish face from which two large holes were visible. Looming up from behind the creature's head was a large pointed hood. The creature, which appeared to be made of a dark metal, had no arms or legs and seemed to float through the air. Looking back, the witnesses believe what they saw was a protective suit or perhaps a robot rather than a monster.

When a flashlight beam hit the creature, its "eyes" lit up and it began floating toward the group while making a strange hissing noise. The horrible stench was now overpowering and some in the group immediately felt nauseous. Because she was at the head of the group, Kathleen May had the best view of the monster. She later stated that as the creature was moving toward her, it squirted or dripped a strange fluid on her that resembled oil but had an unusual odor to it.

Terrified beyond belief, the group fled down the hillside and back to the May house, where they telephoned Sheriff Robert Carr, who responded with his deputy, Burnell Long. After talking with the group, they gathered some men and went to the Fisher property to investigate. But they only found a gummy residue and what appeared to be skid marks on the ground. There was no monster and no spaceship. However, the group did report that the heavy stench of what smelled like burning metal was still in the air.

The Aftermath

A. Lee Stewart, a member of the of the search party and co-publisher of the *Braxton Democrat*, knew a good story when he saw one, so he sent the tale over the news wire, and almost immediately, people were asking Kathleen May for interviews. On September 19, 1952, May and Stewart discussed the Flatwoods Monster on the TV show *We the People*. For the show, an artist sketched the creature based on May's description, but he took some liberties, and the resulting sketch was so outrageous that people started saying the whole thing was a hoax.

Slowly, though, others came forward to admit that they too had seen a strange craft flying through the sky near Flatwoods on September 12. One witness described it as roughly the size of a single-car garage. He said that he lost sight of the craft when it appeared to land on a nearby hill.

Since that night in 1952, the Flatwoods Monster has never been seen again, leaving many people to wonder what exactly those people encountered. A monster? An alien from another world? Or perhaps nothing more than a giant owl? One thing is for sure: There were far too many witnesses to deny that they stumbled upon something strange that night.

Prabhupada's Palace of Gold

Moundsville, West Virginia

Opulence is a word that's tossed about with abandon, but when it's truly deserved, there will be no doubt. Such is the case with Prabhupada's Palace of Gold. As its name implies, the palace, built as a "gift of love" by Hare Krishna devotees of Swami Srila Prabhupada, is lavishly laden in 22-karat gold.

Called "America's Taj Mahal" by the *New York Times*, the citadel has looked upon the West Virginia countryside since 1979. Constructed by monastic volunteers, its turrets, minarets, and marble-bedecked rooms personify beauty and show what can be accomplished when ordinary people gather for a shining cause.

You might have to see this one to actually believe it. The Palace grounds feature a dazzling array of flowers and more than 100 fountains—not to mention the swan boat that graces its artificial lake. Inside, you'll find ten elaborate marble rooms, including a 30-ton main dome with a 4,200-piece crystal ceiling. If that doesn't amaze you, maybe the 31 stained glass windows will catch your eye?

Haunted Harper's Ferry

Harper's Ferry, West Virginia

Harpers Ferry, West Virginia, is a picturesque town that has been at the center of a great deal of American history, most notably during the mid-19th century, when abolitionist John Brown staged a raid that proved to be a catalyst for the American Civil War. However, Harpers Ferry is also known for its ghosts. Here are a few of the many spirits that haunt this historic town:

Rachael Harper

In the mid-18th century, Robert Harper founded the town of Harpers Ferry. After he and his wife Rachael lost their first house in a flood, Harper began construction of a much grander home. But this was during the American Revolution, when laborers were hard to find, so the aging Harper did much of the work himself. He was quite concerned about lawlessness during this uncertain time, so legend has it that he instructed Rachael to bury their gold in a secret location and tell no one about it. Harper passed away in 1782, and after Rachael died unexpectedly following a fall from a ladder, the secret location of their gold was buried with her.

For many years, the Harper House has been considered haunted. People who pass it swear that they see a woman in old-fashioned clothes staring out from an upstairs window. Perhaps it's Rachael, remaining watchful and vigilant over the family's gold.

18th Century Soldiers

In the waning years of the 18th century, an army was sent to Harpers Ferry in preparation for a possible war between the United States and France. The army wound up waiting for a conflict that never happened, so to relieve their boredom, the soldiers paraded to fife and drum music. Unfortunately, a cholera epidemic struck the army while it sat idle, and many men died. Today, the spirits of the men seem to remain. Almost everyone in town has heard the faint sounds of feet marching, drums beating, and fifes playing as an invisible phantom army sweeps through town, doomed to repeat its nightly musical ritual for eternity.

John Brown

John Brown is probably the most noteworthy figure associated with the town of Harpers Ferry. Many people are familiar with his gaunt, white-bearded image, so perhaps it's not surprising that many have seen someone looking exactly like him around town. The resemblance to Brown is so uncanny that tourists have taken photos with the spirit; however, when the pictures are developed, "Brown" is not in them.

John Brown's ghost has also been spotted several miles outside of town at the Kennedy Farmhouse. It was there that Brown and his men stayed for several months while planning the raid. Even today, phantom footsteps, disembodied male voices, and snoring can be heard coming from the empty attic where the conspirators once stayed. It's no wonder that particular area of the house is largely shunned.

Dangerfield Newby

Another ghost seen at Harpers Ferry is that of Dangerfield Newby, a former slave who joined Brown's raid out of desperation after a cruel slave owner stymied his attempts to free his wife and child. Newby was the first of Brown's band to die in the raid; he was struck in the throat by a jagged spike. Vengeful townspeople mutilated his body and left it in an alley for wild hogs to devour.

Dressed in old clothes and a slouch hat, Newby's specter continues to roam the streets of Harpers Ferry, perhaps still trying to save his family or take revenge on those who treated his corpse so badly. Across his neck is a horrific scar from the spike that killed him.

The Hundred Days' Men

Like many other ghosts, the spirits of the Hundred Days' Men were born out of the violence of war. In 1864, at the height of the Civil War, the governor of Ohio proposed a plan that called for several northern states to enlist large numbers of men for a short period of 100 days.

One such group was sent to Harpers Ferry, where they camped at Maryland Heights. One wet day, the inexperienced troops sought dry ground on which to build a fire and cook their dinner. Unfortunately, someone decided to stack some artillery shells to make a dry surface on which to place wood and vegetation. Soon a roaring fire was under way—atop the artillery shells! Inevitably, the shells exploded and many of the Hundred Days' Men were killed.

Mysterious fires are sometimes reported at Maryland Heights, but locals believe that it's just the Hundred Days' Men, trying to eat a meal that they began more than a century ago.

St. Peter's Catholic Church

During the Civil War, St. Peter's Catholic Church was used as a hospital for wounded soldiers. One day, a wounded young soldier was brought into the churchyard and left lying on the ground as others with more severe injuries were tended to. Hours passed, and the young man's condition worsened as he slowly bled to death. By the time doctors got to him, it was too late. As he was carried into the church, he whispered weakly, "Thank God I'm saved." Then he died.

Over the years, many people have seen a bright light on the church's threshold and heard faint whispers say, "Thank God I'm saved." Some have also watched as an elderly priest emerges from the church's rectory; he turns and walks into the church—right through the wall where the front facade once stood.

Jenny the Vagrant

Another ghost of Harpers Ferry is that of a poor girl named Jenny, who lived in an old storage shed that had been abandoned after the railroad came to Harpers Ferry in the early 1830s. One night, Jenny's dress was set ablaze when she ventured too close to the fire she was using to heat the shed. Jenny bolted out of the shed screaming in a blind panic. Unfortunately, she ran straight onto the railroad tracks and was hit by a train.

Since then, engineers have reported hearing unearthly screams for help and seeing a ball of light careening wildly down the train tracks. Frantically, they blow their whistles, but it's too late: Each engineer feels a bump as if his train has struck something, but when he goes to investigate, he finds nothing.

West Virginia State Penitentiary Tour
Moundsville, West Virginia

This fortress-like facility, which was built in 1866 and closed in 1995, is a throwback to "retribution" prisons. Here, under deplorable conditions in claustrophobic five-by-seven cells, emphasis was placed on punishment, not rehabilitation.

Today, tours lead "prisoners" past such areas as the Wagon Gate, a portion of the prison that features a trap door responsible for 85 hangings, and the North Hall, where the prison's most unruly spent 22 hours of each day in seclusion.

In addition to its harsh history, the prison is said to be haunted. A midnight tour provides visitors with a 90-minute overview of the place, then allows them to roam unaided until 6:00 a.m. The spookfest is the penitentiary's most popular tour. The West Virginia State Penitentiary was the second public building established in the new state after the Civil War. We wonder what the first public building was. Grocery store, maybe?

George Washington's Bathtub

Berkeley Springs, West Virginia

George Washington often visited Berkeley Springs to avail himself of the "healing" mineral baths fed by the area's natural warm springs. Each spring the town honors this heritage with George Washington's Bathtub Celebration. Washington-themed events include a period dinner, readings from his diary entries, and of course, visits to "the only outdoor monument to presidential bathing."

Philippi Mummies

Philippi, West Virginia

If you were entrusted with the preservation of 120-year-old mummies, would you: A. Store them in a museum? B. A train depot? C. A restroom? D. All of the above? If you answered "D" you may already know about the Philippi Mummies. If not, read on.

In 1888, self-appointed scientist Graham Hamrick purchased two female cadavers from the West Virginia Hospital for the Insane. His plan? To re-create embalming techniques used by the ancient pharaohs. Whatever method Hamrick employed, it apparently worked. Today, 120 years later, the ladies appear fairly healthy—if a bit stone-faced.

The mummies traveled a convoluted path after expiring. They reportedly did the European circus act with P. T. Barnum, were misplaced for a few decades, spent time in a barn, and eventually ended up in the home of a local citizen. A severe flood sent them off to the front lawn of Philippi's post office, where they were dried out and tended to.

Today, the rigid ladies are housed in the Barbour County Historical Museum at the former B & O Railroad Station in what used to be a bathroom. Does it get any weirder than this? You'll have to read on to see!

Home of the Mothman

Point Pleasant, West Virginia

Legend has it that from 1966 to 1967, the town of Point Pleasant was terrorized by a mysterious, shrieking winged creature. The figure most closely resembled a moth with humanlike features and stood between six and seven feet tall, with featherless wings and red eyes. Local lore indicated that dozens of townspeople had encounters with the mothlike creature before a 1967 bridge collapse that resulted in the death of 46 people, which the Mothman was said to have predicted.

Today, the town pays homage to this tall, dark stranger from its past with a 12-foot-fall stainless-steel sculpture and the world's only Mothman Museum. A yearly Mothman festival takes place every September. *The Mothman Prophecies*, a book by journalist John Keel, documents the story of this fearsome creature with firsthand accounts from people who reportedly saw it. The book was later turned into a 2002 film by the same name starring Richard Gere.

Coal House

Williamson, West Virginia

This soot-black structure appears so for a very good reason—it's constructed entirely of coal. Built in 1933 by architect H. T. Hicks, the coal house weighs in at some 65 tons and features two-foot-thick walls.

Why was it built? Since Williamson is first and foremost a coal town, it seems only right and proper that it should have its own coal building. A plaque proclaiming, "This Building Constructed of Winefrede Seam Coal," proudly tells of the structure's carbonized origins. The unique structure is listed on the National Register of Historic Places. It currently serves as an office for the Tug Valley Chamber of Commerce.

Shell-Shape Filling Station

Winston-Salem, North Carolina

Built in 1930 by the Quality Oil Company (a local Shell Oil marketer), gas-thirsty visitors immediately knew what brand of dino-juice this shell-shape station pumped. Originally one of eight such "scallops" in the Winston-Salem area, it stands as the sole survivor.

After its gas-pumping days had passed, the station served a second life as a lawn-mower repair shop. Falling into disrepair by the late 1990s, it was rescued by Preservation North Carolina.

Today, the bright orange building is spiffier than new, and two old-time pumps (donated by Shell Oil) appear ready to "fill 'er up." But alas, it's just a pretty facade. In reality, this primo example of novelty architecture serves as a satellite office for Preservation North Carolina.

Devil's Tramping Ground

Siler City, North Carolina

What would you call a 40-foot barren circle, situated in the middle of a productive forest, that hasn't grown so much as a weed for hundreds of years? North Carolinians call it the Devil's Tramping Ground.

Since the Department of Agriculture can't explain the phenomenon, dark theories abound. These include extra-terrestrial visits and appearances by the devil himself.

A more down-to-earth explanation involves a particularly high salt level in the soil. Still, this doesn't account for the tramping ground's near perfect circular shape.

Another nod to the occult comes by way of firsthand reports. Amongst other things, these state that objects placed in the circle overnight will vanish by morning, never to be found again.

In 1949, journalist John William Harden added to the legend when he wrote: "The Devils Tramping Ground, the Chatham natives say...There, sometimes during the dark of night the Majesty of the Underworld of Evil silently tramps around that bare circle –thinking, plotting, and planning against the god, and in behalf of wrong. So far as is known no person has ever spent the night there to disprove this is what happens." Any volunteers?

Phantom Lights at Brown Mountain
Morgantown, North Carolina

Although scoffed at as nothing more than reflected train lights, the multicolored light show in the foothills of North Carolina's Blue Ridge Mountains has fascinated humans since an early explorer reported it in 1771, and even earlier according to Native American legend. Several centuries ago, many people were killed during a battle between the Cherokee and the Catawba tribes. Legend has it that the Brown Mountain Lights are the spirits of those lost warriors.

Another tale states that a plantation owner got lost hunting on Brown Mountain and that one of his slaves came looking for him, swinging a lantern to light his way. The slave never found his owner but still walks the mountainside with his eternal lantern. Still another legend claims the lights come from the spirit of a woman murdered on the mountain by her husband in 1850.

Whatever the source of the colorful lights, they come in many shapes, from glowing orbs to trailing bursts to still, white areas. Crowds flock to at least three locations to view the lights, but one of the most popular is the Brown Mountain overlook on Highway 181, 20 miles north of Morganton.

The Lost Colony

Roanoke Island, North Carolina

Twenty years before England established its first successful colony in the New World, an entire village of English colonists disappeared in what would later be known as North Carolina. Did these pioneers all perish? Did Native Americans capture them? Did they join a friendly tribe? Could they have left descendants who live among us today?

Timing Is Everything

Talk about bad timing. As far as John White was concerned, England couldn't have picked a worse time to go to war. It was November 1587, and White had just arrived in England from the New World. He intended to gather relief supplies and immediately sail back to Roanoke Island, where he had left more than 100 colonists who were running short of food. Unfortunately, the English were gearing up to fight Spain. Every seaworthy ship, including White's, was pressed into naval service. Not a one could be spared for his return voyage to America.

Nobody Home

When John White finally returned to North America three years later, he was dismayed to discover that the colonists he had left behind were nowhere to be found. Instead, he stumbled upon a mystery—one that has never been solved.

The village that White and company had founded in 1587 on Roanoke Island lay completely deserted. Houses had been dismantled (as if someone planned to move them), but the pieces lay in the long grass along with iron tools and farming equipment. A stout stockade made of logs stood empty.

White found no sign of his daughter Eleanor, her husband Ananias, or their daughter Virginia Dare—the first English child born in America. None of the 87 men, 17 women, and 11 children remained. No bodies or obvious gravesites offered clues to their fate. The only clues—if they were clues—that

White could find were the letters CRO carved into a tree trunk and the word CROATOAN carved into a log of the abandoned fort.

No Forwarding Address

All White could do was hope that the colonists had been taken in by friendly natives.

Croatoan—also spelled "Croatan"—was the name of a barrier island to the south and also the name of a tribe of Native Americans that lived on that island. Unlike other area tribes, the Croatoans had been friendly to English newcomers, and one of them, Manteo, had traveled to England with earlier explorers and returned to act as interpreter for the Roanoke colony. Had the colonists, with Manteo's help, moved to Croatoan? Were they safe among friends?

White tried to find out, but his timing was rotten once again. He had arrived on the Carolina coast as a hurricane bore down on the region. The storm hit before he could mount a search. His ship was blown past Croatoan Island and out to sea. Although the ship and crew survived the storm and made it back to England, White was stuck again. He tried repeatedly but failed to raise money for another search party.

No one has ever learned the fate of the Roanoke Island colonists, but there are no shortage of theories as to what happened to them. A small sailing vessel and other boats that White had left with them were gone when he returned. It's possible that the colonists used the vessels to travel to another island or to the mainland. White had talked with others before he left about possibly moving the settlement to a more secure location inland. It's even possible that the colonists tired of waiting for White's return and tried to sail back to England. If so, they would have perished at sea. Yet there are at least a few shreds of hearsay evidence that the colonists survived in America.

Rumors of Survivors

In 1607, Captain John Smith and company established the first successful English settlement in North America at Jamestown, Virginia. The colony's secretary,

William Strachey, wrote four years later about hearing a report of four English men, two boys, and one young woman who had been sighted south of Jamestown at a settlement of the Eno tribe, where they were being used as slaves. If the report was true, who else could these English have been but Roanoke survivors?

For more than a century after the colonists' disappearance, stories emerged of gray-eyed Native Americans and English-speaking villages in North Carolina and Virginia. In 1709, an English surveyor said members of the Hatteras tribe living on North Carolina's Outer Banks—some of them with light-colored eyes—claimed to be descendants of white people. It's possible that the Hatteras were the same people that the 1587 colonists called Croatoan.

In the intervening centuries, many of the individual tribes of the region have disappeared. Some died out. Others were absorbed into larger groups such as the Tuscarora. One surviving group, the Lumbee, has also been called Croatoan.

The Lumbee, who still live in North Carolina, often have Caucasian features. Could they be descendants of Roanoke colonists? Many among the Lumbee dismiss the notion as fanciful, but the tribe has long been thought to be of mixed heritage and has been speaking English so long that none among them know what language preceded it.

Blackbeard's Ghostly Stomping Grounds

Ocracoke Island, North Carolina

Perhaps the most famous buccaneer of all was Edward Teach, better known as Blackbeard. His career was built on fear and intimidation, and apparently he hasn't changed— even in death.

Blackbeard's reign of terror on the high seas lasted for more than two years. During that time, he commanded a fleet of captured vessels and ambushed any ship he pleased. He pillaged and murdered up and down the East Coast until he turned himself in and was pardoned in July 1718.

After receiving his pardon, it didn't take long for Blackbeard to return to a life of piracy. In November 1718, Virginia Governor Alexander Spotswood ordered Lieutenant Robert Maynard to capture Blackbeard. On November 22, Maynard and his men finally caught up with the famed pirate and his crew just off Ocracoke Island. A battle ensued, during which Blackbeard and Maynard exchanged gunfire. The men then drew their swords, and Blackbeard managed to break Maynard's blade, but before he could kill the officer, a member of Maynard's party slit Blackbeard's throat. It took a total of 5 gunshot wounds and 20 sword strokes to bring down the notorious pirate, and to ensure that he was dead, he was decapitated; his head was suspended from the bowsprit of Maynard's vessel.

Home Is Where the Head Is

Since that fateful day, Blackbeard's bloody specter has been seen on Ocracoke Island carrying a lantern, apparently searching for his missing head. The island is known locally as "Teach's Hole," and visitors and residents alike have reported seeing his phantom swimming along the shore at night; some have even watched him rise up from his watery grave and continue his search along the shore. Fishermen in Pamlico Sound have dubbed any strange lights viewed on North Carolina's Outer Banks "Teach's Lights." The few souls brave enough to follow the unearthly glow of Blackbeard's lantern ashore never find footprints or other signs of life when they investigate. Try as he might to find his missing head, some local legends suggest that Blackbeard is looking for his noggin in the wrong place.

Death to Spotswood!

In the 1930s, North Carolina judge Charles Whedbee claimed to have seen Blackbeard's skull. According to the judge, when he was in law school at the University of North Carolina, he was invited to join a secret society. His induction into the group involved a large silver chalice and the chanting of the mysterious phrase, "Death to Spotswood." Whedbee was told that a silversmith had made the cup from Blackbeard's skull after stealing it from atop a pole at the mouth of the Hampton River more than two centuries prior. The macabre chalice seems to have been lost to time, but it isn't the only treasure that Blackbeard is said to have left behind.

Annual Salley Chitlin' Strut Festival

Salley, South Carolina

To raise funds for their Christmas decorations, the town of Salley held its first Chitlin' Strut Festival in November 1966. For those not up on southern cuisine, chitlins are really chitterlings, a cutesy name for fried hog intestines.

Although the delicacy sounds off-putting to some, nothing proves their popularity better than the continuing success of the festival. As the locals say, it's a real humdinger of an event that draws as many as 50,000 during peak years.

So what can be found here other than pig innards? Parades, arts and crafts, carnival rides and midways, country music, even a Chitlin' Strut dance contest. When these "little piggies" go to market, a good time is had by all. Although the festival was cancelled for a few years due to COVID-19 concerns, it resumed triumphantly in November, 2022.

South of the Border

Dillon, South Carolina

It seems some of the greatest places have billboards that sing their praises from hundreds of mile away. Think Wall Drug or Rock City, or in this case, South of the Border. Despite its Mexican pretensions, this classic tourist attraction is not positioned south of the border, unless, of course, one is referring to the borderline of North and South Carolina.

South of the Border is located directly on I-95, just below the North Carolina line in Dillon, South Carolina. This location, not coincidentally, is the approximate halfway point to Florida for drivers making the trek out of New York. The crafty Pedro realized that drivers might be a bit road-weary at this point and set out to right this eminent wrong. Boy, did he succeed!

The first clues arrive some 200 miles out when the first of Pedro's many billboards are encountered. With clever cracks like, "Pedro's Weather Forecast: Chili today, hot tamale" and "You never Sausage a Place! You're always a Weiner at Pedro's!" travelers begin to wonder what all the hoopla is about and wait with baited breath for the next sign to appear. If they're making the ride at night, a virtual explosion of light will let them know when they've finally arrived.

Sticking out like a gaudy piñata, a 165-foot-tall neon-lighted sombrero welcomes visitors. This stands beside a 97-foot-tall neon Pedro figure so enormous his legs can be driven through. Within this "Mexican" city, visitors will find over-the-top restaurants, motels, fireworks stores, souvenir stands, an RV park, even a chapel that performs real weddings.

Visitors who ascend the sombrero tower quickly realize that this is a funky-fun oasis of activity existing in a region of near nothingness. All thanks to Pedro.

Pawley's Island

South Carolina

One of the oldest summer resorts on the East Coast, Pawleys Island is a small barrier island located along the coast of South Carolina. Only a handful of people live there year-round, and one of the perennial residents is the Gray Man. Many say that this restless spirit has no face. However, that seems to be a minor inconvenience; after all, when it comes to warning the living of impending doom, a pretty face—or any face at all—is hardly necessary.

Apparition Identity Crisis

According to legend, before every major hurricane that has hit Pawleys Island since the early 1820s—including Hurricane Hugo in 1989—the Gray Man has appeared to certain folks on the island to warn them to leave before the approaching storm strikes. When they return after the storm, the people who encountered the Gray Man find their homes undamaged, while other buildings nearby have been destroyed.

The identity of the Gray Man is unknown, but there are several candidates. One theory suggests that it's Percival Pawley, the island's first owner and its namesake; others believe that the helpful spirit is Plowden Charles Jennett Weston, a man whose former home is now the island's Pelican Inn.

But the more romantic legends say that the Gray Man is the ghost of a young man who died for love. Stories about how he perished vary: One tale says that on his way to see his beloved, he fell into a bed of quicksand and died. Soon after, while the object of this deceased man's affection was walking along the beach, a figure in gray approached her and told her to leave the island. She did, and that night a hurricane slammed into the area, destroying just about every home—except hers.

Another story concerns a woman who married a man after she thought that her beloved had died at sea. Later, when she met a man who had survived a shipwreck off Pawleys Island, she realized that he was her lost love, waterlogged but still very much alive. However, he didn't take the news of her marriage too well; he slinked away and died shortly thereafter. But according to legend, ever since then, he's been warning folks to flee when they're in danger from an upcoming storm.

The Ghostly Lifesaver

No matter who this ghost was in life, he has supposedly appeared before hurricanes in 1822, 1893, 1916, 1954, 1955, and 1989. And for decades, local fishermen have told stories of the Gray Man appearing to them hours before a sudden storm roiled up that would have put their lives in jeopardy.

The Gray Man is credited with saving many lives before the advent of contemporary forecasting techniques. In 1954, a couple was spending their honeymoon on the island when they heard a knock on their door at around 5 a.m. When the husband opened the door, he saw a figure in gray whose clothes reeked of salty brine and whose features were obscured by a gray hat. The man in gray said that the Red Cross had sent him to warn people to evacuate because a huge storm was heading for the island. Before the honeymooning husband could question him further, the man in gray vanished. Realizing that this was no ordinary Red Cross worker, the man and his new bride left the island.

Later that evening, ferocious Hurricane Hazel struck the island with the deadly force of a Category 4 storm, with winds gusting as high as 150 miles per hour. In her wake, Hazel left thousands of homes destroyed and 95 people dead. The newlywed couple, however, had been spared by the ghostly grace of the Gray Man.

A Ghost Who Keeps on Giving

The Gray Man apparently doesn't care much for modern technology—he was still on the job as recently as 1989. That year, just before Hurricane Hugo hit, a couple walking along the beach spotted the Gray Man. Although the phantom vanished before the couple could speak to him, his reputation preceded him, and the couple fled the island. When they returned, their home was the only one in the area that had not been devastated by the storm. This incident got the Gray Man a moment in the national spotlight: He was featured on an episode of Unsolved Mysteries in 1990.

Jimmy Carter Peanut

Plains, Georgia

To honor our peanut-producing past president (try saying that three times fast) a mighty peanut stands proud at Jimmy Carter's Plains, Georgia, hometown. Built by Indiana residents James Kiely, Doyle Kifer, and Loretta Townsend, the 13-foot-tall peanut originally oversaw a 1976 campaign visit to Evanston, Indiana. After the ceremonies, the big nut was shipped off to Plains.

The peanut, flaunting a toothy smile that could only come from Carter's happy kisser, suffered great indignities over time. While berthed at the Plains train depot, souvenir-hunters nearly gouged it to pieces, and yearly wear and tear took its toll.

Thankfully, the local Davis E-Z Shop stepped in, filled the peanut's bottom with concrete, and anchored it down in front of their store. Successive repairs have rendered it good enough to eat.

St. Simon's Island Lighthouse

St. Simon's Island, Georgia

This lighthouse may have been cursed from the start. Originally constructed in 1811, the first building was destroyed by Confederate soldiers. While the lighthouse was being rebuilt, the architect fell ill and died of yellow fever. Then, on a stormy night in 1880, a dispute between the lighthouse keeper and his assistant resulted in gunshots. The keeper died after days of suffering from his wounds, but the assistant was never charged with the crime. The new keeper maintained he could hear strange footsteps on the spiral staircase to the tower. To this day, subsequent lighthouse keepers, their families, and visitors have also heard the same slow tread on the tower's 129 steps.

Trash Statue of Liberty

McRae, Georgia

In 1986, the local Lions club undertook the building of a second Lady Liberty. This was done to commemorate the green lady's 100th anniversary and to remind people of America's true meaning. With nothing more than pieces of old Styrofoam, a tree stump, and other discarded materials, they erected a one-twelfth scale "trash" Statue of Liberty that closely approximates the original.

The "artists" used old photos for cues as they went along, but perhaps their picture of the base was somewhat lacking. For whatever reason, the replica tapers toward the top (like the original) then grows wide again just before the statue is reached (decidedly unlike the original). Can you say "artistic license"?

BabyLand General Hospital
Cleveland, Georgia

Who could forget the Cabbage Patch Doll craze of the early 1980s? For parents of young daughters, obtaining one of these beady-eyed moppets became a mission second only to guarding their child's life. While the fad has died down, the dolls still continue to sell.

Like all offspring, the Cabbage Patch Kids hail from somewhere. Legend has it that they arrive not by stork but via the BabyLand General "Hospital," located in the mountains of northern Georgia.

Creator Xavier Roberts began producing the dolls in his homeland of Cleveland, Georgia, in 1978. Originally marketed as "Little People," the dolls were said to have emerged from a cabbage patch. Eventually, a name change to Cabbage Patch would attest to their lineage and earn them a place in toy-making history.

Today, the hospital/factory continues to attract tourists. Visitors can watch dolls being "born" in the cabbage patch and observe the cutie-pies as they attend school. All staff members wear crisp white doctor's and nurse's uniforms.

Lunchbox Museum

Columbus, Georgia

Children from a not-too-distant era happily carried lunch boxes to school. These lightweight metal containers emblazoned with the names and pictures of popular television shows, heartthrobs, cowboy heroes, and the like, kept kid's lunches safe and secure. They were as individual as each child and favored by most.

Then, from out of the blue, an entity known as "progress" came marching along. This "concerned" force systematically snatched these lunch pails from the hands of children. A colorful era in American pop culture had come to a grinding halt.

Alan Woodall has tapped into this past craze with a vast collection of these colorful lunch houses. Billed as the "World's Largest Lunchbox Museum," Woodall's collection at the Rivermarket Antique Mall numbers in the thousands and shows no sign of letting up.

Visitors to the museum can feast their eyes upon such lunch box favorites as Hopalong Cassidy, David Cassidy, Daniel Boone, Bonanza, Flipper, Charlie's Angels, Bobby Sherman, Superman, the Dukes of Hazzard, Mickey Mouse, and literally thousands of others. If the subject matter held some form of popularity during the 1950s through 1960s, chances are good that a lunch box paid it homage.

Thermoses and coolers round out the collection and bring back happy memories to more than a few. For those wondering why lunch boxes finally rode off into the sunset, the owner points directly at the Florida legislature. In 1986, they ruled that each metal lunch box should be viewed as a "lethal weapon." Funny, we thought that was a movie. In fact, we think a Mel Gibson/Danny Glover lunch box would be the cat's pajamas!

U.S. National Tick Collection

Statesboro, Georgia

Just when you think you've seen it all, the U.S. National Tick Collection (USNTC) repository comes along. The Statesboro facility houses 850 different species and more than one million specimens of ticks. Researchers study the parasites hoping to gather the good and bad from each, but the US-NTC isn't all about business. One day each week, the facility conducts tours and educates the public on the profound differences between each species. Microscopes get visitors up close and personal with each tick.

Owned by the Smithsonian Institution, the enterprise features ticks that tick us off, such as those responsible for Lyme disease and Rocky Mountain Spotted Fever, as well as agreeable ones that show promise within the medical realm. Think of it as a zoo for bloodsuckers.

Providence Canyon State Park

Stewart County, Georgia

Providence Canyon has been dubbed Georgia's "Little Grand Canyon"—and for good reason. Peering up at its walls from the valley floor, visitors are treated to a striking array of orange, red, pink, and purple hues, similar to those found at the famous Arizona canyon. In reality, soft canyon soil provides this tapestry of colors, not element-weathered rock.

The 150-foot-deep canyon encompasses more than 1,100 acres. It was formed through erosion after settlers clear-cut the land in the 1800s. In the 1930s, the Civilian Conservation Corp planted trees and plants in an effort to slow the process. In 1971, the unique area became a state park.

Despite its unlikely roots, the park provides breathtaking vistas, numerous hiking trails, fossilized areas, and a chance to commune with nature.

Pasaquan
Buena Vista, Georgia

Pasaquan is the creation of folk artist St. EOM, also known as Eddie Owens Martin. After returning home in 1957 after a long stint in New York City, St. EOM spent the last 30 years of life turning Pasaquan into a multihued fantasyland of artistic fusion, in between telling fortunes for those who sought out "The Wizard of Pasaquan."

The Big Chicken
Marietta, Georgia

Originally the home of a greasy spoon called Johnny Reb's, this eatery, adorned with a 56-foot-tall sheet-metal chicken, has been a Kentucky Fried Chicken location since 1974. KFC considered demolishing the place after high winds damaged the bird in 1993, but public outcry led to a complete restoration.

The Haunted Riddle House
West Palm Beach, Florida

Built in 1905 as a gatekeeper's cottage, this pretty "Painted Lady" seemed incongruent with the cemetery it was constructed to oversee. Cloaked in grand Victorian finery, the house radiated the brightness of life. Perhaps that's what was intended: A cemetery caretaker's duties can be gloomy, so any bit of spirit lifting would likely be welcomed. Or so its builders thought. In the case of this particular house, however, "spirit lifting" took on a whole new meaning.

The first ghost sighted in the area was that of a former cemetery worker named Buck, who was killed during an argument with a townsperson. Shortly thereafter, Buck's ghost was seen doing chores around the cemetery and inside the cottage. Luckily, he seemed more interested in performing his duties than exacting revenge.

In the 1920s, the house received its current name when city manager Karl Riddle purchased it and took on the duty of overseeing the cemetery. During his tenure, a despondent employee named Joseph hung himself in the attic. This sparked a frenzy of paranormal phenomena inside the house, including the unexplained sounds of rattling chains and disembodied voices.

After Riddle moved out, the reports of paranormal activity slowed down—but such dormancy wouldn't last.

By 1980, the Riddle House had fallen into disrepair and was abandoned. The city planned to demolish the building but instead decided to give it to John Riddle (Karl's nephew). He, in turn, donated it for preservation. The entire structure was moved—lock, stock, and barrel—to Yesteryear Village, a museum devoted to Florida's early years. There, it was placed on permanent display as an attractive token of days long past. There, too, its dark side would return—with a vengeance.

When workers began to reassemble the Riddle House, freshly awakened spirits kicked their antics into high gear. Ladders were tipped over, windows were smashed, and tools were thrown to the ground from the building's third floor. Workers were shocked when an unseen force threw a wooden board across a room, striking a carpenter in the head. The attacks were blamed on the spirit of Joseph, and the situation became so dangerous that work on the structure was halted for six months. After that, however, the Riddle House was restored to its previous glory.

During the dedication of the Riddle House in the early 1980s, two unexpected guests showed up for the ceremony. Resplendent in Victorian garb, the couple added authenticity to the time period being celebrated. Many assumed that they were actors who were hired for the occasion; they were not. In fact, no one knew who they were. A few weeks later, century-old photos from the Riddle House were put on display. There, in sepia tones, stood the very same couple that guests had encountered during the dedication! Ethereal stirrings at the Riddle House continue to this day. Unexplained sightings of a torso hanging in the attic window represent only part of the horror. And if history is any indicator, more supernatural sightings and activity are certainly to come.

Christ of the Abyss

Key Largo, Florida

Should spiritual beliefs be neglected in the underwater realm? Italian Sculptor Guido Galletti answers with a resounding "no." His *Christ of the Abyss* statue in Key Largo's Pennekamp Park (aka Key Largo Coral Reef Preserve) has attracted scuba divers and snorkelers from around the world since 1966.

The nine-foot bronze statue is anchored to a 4,000-pound base and is situated some 25 feet below the ocean's surface. To reach it, visitors must take a three-mile boat ride from Key Largo. The statue is actually a cast of a 1954 forerunner placed underwater in the Mediterranean Sea near Genoa, Italy. The original piece *Il Cristo Degli Abissi* translates (in English) to *Christ of the Abyss*.

Coral Castle

Homestead, Florida

Homestead is known for its Coral Castle—a miraculous construction brought to life by a mysterious man named Edward Leedskalnin (1887–1951).

The chief difference between Edward Leedskalnin's castle and other single-builder fortresses lies in its building materials. Coral Castle is comprised of huge coral blocks, some weighing as much as 30 tons. How Leedskalnin moved these into place, completely by himself and using early 1900s technology, has been equated with the mystery of the Great Pyramids. For the record, Leedskalnin was about five feet tall and tipped the scales at an underwhelming 100 pounds.

Mind-boggling features can be found everywhere at the castle. A raised obelisk weighs a whopping 28 tons. A wall surrounding the palace stands eight feet tall and also pushes the scale into the multiple tons.

To show further engineering savvy, a nine-ton swinging gate is balanced so precisely, the touch of a finger sets it into motion. Some stones at Coral Castle weigh twice as much as the ones used at the Pyramids of Giza. How could one man possibly move these into place?

Leedskalnin, a Latvian immigrant, began his project in 1920 and continued through 1940. Almost inexplicably, no one is reported to have witnessed the one-man building dynamo as he quarried, fashioned, and ultimately moved his huge coral stones into place. The belief that Leedskalnin worked at night gives a hint to his secretiveness.

With no hard facts upon which to draw, theories concerning the construction abound. Some say Leedskalnin levitated the blocks using ethereal powers. Others say the diminutive man unlocked the secrets of antigravity. For his part, Leedskalnin was an outspoken believer in the power of magnetic current and suggested that this was responsible for his Coral Castle.

Could this scientific phenomenon be responsible for Coral Castle? Only Edward Leedskalnin knows for sure, and that information was buried with him in 1951.

During the dedication of the Riddle House in the early 1980s, two unexpected guests showed up for the ceremony. Resplendent in Victorian garb, the couple added authenticity to the time period being celebrated. Many assumed that they were actors who were hired for the occasion; they were not. In fact, no one knew who they were. A few weeks later, century-old photos from the Riddle House were put on display.

There, in sepia tones, stood the very same couple that guests had encountered during the dedication!

Fountain of Youth

St. Augustine, Florida

The site of a natural spring that Spanish explorer Juan Ponce de Leon mistook for the legendary Fountain of Youth in 1513 is now a kitschy attraction with touristy diversions of all kinds. The spring's water is free for the taking—but you have to buy the souvenir bottle in which to take it home.

Solomon's Castle

Ona, Florida

Howard Solomon was a sculptor whose primary medium was found and recycled objects. His biggest undertaking—at 10,000 square feet—was his personal residence, which he started building more than 30 years ago. With a shimmering facade of recycled printing-press plates, a tower with a bed-and-breakfast suite, and numerous galleries to showcase his unusual art, the castle is an incredible destination now run by his children.

Xanadu

Kissimmee, Florida

Once a prototype home of the future (with sister structures in Wisconsin Dells, Wisconsin, and Gatlinburg, Tennessee), Xanadu looked more like a home of the past. Built from plastic bubbles sheathed in spray-on white foam, the house showcased such futuristic oddities as a video fireplace and wireless communicators.

But in the 21st century, Xanadu met its fate of demolition, the fate that its Tennessee and Wisconsin counterparts had already undergone.

Jules Undersea Lodge

Key Largo, Florida

Like its descriptive name implies, Jules Undersea lodge is located undersea. If this sounds just a trifle deadly, don't worry. Jules (named for science-fiction writer Jules Verne) is accessible to folks who use scuba gear. This includes seasoned sport divers as well as beginners.

The dive drill is simple. Descend 21 feet to the lodge and enter by swimming up into the "wet" room. Remove your gear and kick back. Like any modern lodge, air-conditioning, hot showers, music, and television await. When the hunger gong is sounded, a fully stocked galley provides caloric comfort. These lures, coupled with this unique environment, have snared some famous guests. Canadian Prime Minister Pierre Trudeau has taken the plunge, as have rockers Steven Tyler from Aerosmith and quite fittingly, Jon Fishman from Phish.

The brainchild of ocean researchers Neil Monney and Ian Koblick, the underwater motel might not be situated "20,000 Leagues Under the Sea" as Verne envisioned it, but it is under the sea. That's got to count for something!

Skunk Ape Research Headquarters

Ochopee, Florida

Glomming onto the Bigfoot craze, the elusive Skunk Ape makes an appearance. Rarely, that is. For better than a half-century, the seven-foot-tall, frightfully hairy creature is said to have roamed and terrorized the hinterlands of South Florida.

Men of science doubt the creature's validity, as men of science usually do when it comes to such fantastic things—but that hasn't stopped Dave Shealy, a self-appointed expert in everything Skunk Ape. As founder of the Skunk Ape Research Headquarters, Shealy attempts to enlighten nonbelievers. Photos, newspaper clippings, grainy videos, even a plaster cast of a Skunk Ape's footprint do their best to convince these "doubting Thomases." Says Shealy, "I don't have a choice to believe, because I've seen [the Skunk Ape] three times." We'll take his word for it.

International Hamburger Hall of Fame

Daytona Beach, Florida

To fully appreciate this fun museum it's best to arrive hungry. While "Hamburger Harry" doesn't actually serve the beloved sandwich, at tour's end we're certain most will fancy one. German immigrant and collector Harry Sperl has amassed more than 1,000 burger-related items in his shrine to red meat, and the patties just keep on coming.

Visitors will find a hamburger-shape waterbed and operational motorcycle, burger banks and clocks, salt and pepper shakers, music boxes, biscuit jars, badges, magnets—virtually everything that can be plastered with a hamburger on its side or shaped along its contours. If there's a hot dog heaven, certainly one must exist for the venerable hamburger. From the look of things, this may just be it.

Weeki Wachee Springs

Weeki Wachee, Florida

Since 1947, Florida's Weeki Wachee Springs has enthralled people with its natural beauty, glass-bottomed boat tours, and world-famous "mermaids." In 1946, when former U.S. Navy frogman Newton Perry perfected hose breathing (the ability to breathe underwater via a compressor-fed air hose) at Weeki Wachee Springs, a door opened. Now it was suddenly possible to stage underwater shows in the 72-degree, crystal-clear spring. Newton Perry set out to do just that.

By 1947, the first underwater theater was completed. This enabled tourists to view underwater proceedings from below-ground rooms. It also ushered in the Weeki Wachee Mermaids. There's something fabulously unreal about fish-tipped ladies performing an underwater ballet. From a campy act that includes more than a little humor, to captivating choreographed moves that sometimes find the mermaids hanging motionless as if in space, the show has become a staple of Weeki Wachee. But it isn't the only thing out of the ordinary at the spring.

Glass-bottomed boat tours pick up where the underwater show leaves off. As the small boats make their way about the 45-foot-deep spring (the spring links to a cave system that's been explored to 403 feet, making it the deepest naturally formed spring in the United States), manatees, fish, turtles—even the occasional alligator—come into view. Every so often, the mermaids are spotted doing their act, captivating the crowd as they hold their breath for up to two-and-one-half minutes.

St. Augustine Lighthouse
St. Augustine, Florida

St. Augustine is often called America's most haunted city, and the lighthouse there might claim its own "most haunted" title. So many different spirits are rumored to haunt this light that it's probably a bit crowded. Visitors report seeing a young girl with a bow in her hair. She is thought to be the ghost of a girl who died during the tower's construction. A tall man is often seen in the basement of the keeper's house, and doors unlock mysteriously, footsteps follow visitors, and cold spots move around the buildings. The spirits seem harmless, but construction workers have complained of foreboding feelings and freak accidents.

★★★ South Central ★★★

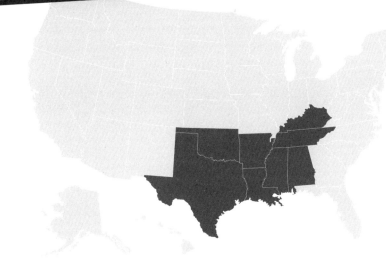

The Marfa Lights

Marfa, Texas

The famed Marfa Lights of Marfa, Texas, have become almost synonymous with the term ghost lights. Since 1883, they have been spotted in an area southwest of the Chisos Mountains, some 200 miles south of El Paso. The lights appear almost playful in their gyrations, skimming over the fields, bobbing like a yo-yo, or chasing visitors. One woman reportedly witnessed a white ball of light three feet in diameter that bounced in slow motion alongside her car as she drove through the Chisos one night. Some of the lights have been attributed to auto headlights miles away across the desert, but the Marfa Lights were witnessed long before automobiles came to the area.

The Driskill Hotel

Southern hospitality abounds at the Driskill Hotel in downtown Austin, Texas. Built in 1886 by local cattle baron Colonel Jesse Lincoln Driskill, this lodging is hardly short on amenities. As a member of Historic Hotels of America and Associated Luxury Hotels International, the Driskill offers every comfort imaginable: From fancy linens and plasma-screen TVs to fine dining and complimentary shoeshines, this Austin institution has it all—including a few resident ghosts.

Since it opened, the Driskill has been a magnet for the rich and famous: Lyndon and Lady Bird Johnson had their first date at the hotel's restaurant, and Amelia Earhart, Louis Armstrong, and Richard Nixon have all sought respite there. At the Driskill, the upscale clientele mixes with the invisible guests that reside there full-time—the true spirits of the hotel.

Meet the Ghosts

Considered one of the most haunted hotels in the United States, the Driskill is the eternal home of many spirits. First and foremost would have to be the ghost of Colonel Driskill himself. He makes his presence known by entering random guest rooms and smoking the cigars that he once loved so dearly. Driskill is also said to play with the lights in bathrooms, turning them on and off for fun.

Hotel guests and employees have seen water faucets turn on and off by themselves; some have even reported hearing the sound of noisy guests coming from an empty elevator. Others have felt as if they were being pushed out of bed, and some wake in the morning to find that their room's furniture has been rearranged during the night.

A Ghost With Fashion Sense

When singer Annie Lennox stayed at the Driskill Hotel in the 1980s while performing in Austin, she laid out two dresses to consider after she got out of the shower. When she emerged from the bathroom, only one dress was still on the bed; the other was once again hanging in the closet.

A ghost dressed in Victorian-era clothing has been seen at night where the front desk used to stand, and guests have detected the scent of roses in the area. This is believed to be the spirit of Mrs. Bridges, who worked at the Driskill as a front-desk clerk in the early 1900s.

The spirit of a young girl haunts the lobby on the first floor; she is believed to have been the daughter of a senator. In 1887, she was chasing a ball on the grand staircase when she tripped and fell to her death. Today, her ghost is often heard laughing and bouncing a ball up and down those same stairs.

The spirit of Peter J. Lawless might still be residing in Room 419, where he lived from 1886 until 1916 or 1917. Although the housekeeping crew cleans and vacuums that room like all the others, they often report finding rumpled bedclothes, open dresser drawers, and footprints in the bathroom—after they've already cleaned the room. Lawless is typically blamed for this mischievous behavior, and his specter is also often spotted near the elevators on the fifth floor. He pauses to check his watch when the doors open—then he promptly disappears.

In the Spirit of Things

A more modern ghost that hangs around the Driskill is the "Houston Bride." When her fiancé called off their wedding plans in the 1990s, the young woman did what many other jilted brides would be tempted to do: She stole his credit cards and went shopping! She was last seen on the hotel elevator, loaded down with her packages. Retail therapy was apparently not the cure, however: She was found dead a few days later, the victim of a gunshot wound to the abdomen. Some guests have seen her apparition with her arms full of packages; others have spotted her in her wedding gown.

Oddly, it seems to be those guests who are at the hotel for weddings or bachelorette parties that are most likely to see her. And even stranger, some brides consider it good luck to catch a glimpse of the tragic "Houston Bride" before their own weddings. Maybe she counts as "something blue."

Cockroach Hall of Fame
Plano, Texas

Before you depart this big blue marble called Earth, you owe yourself a few chuckles. That's where pest control specialist Michael Bohdan comes in. He dressed up a number of creepy crawly cockroaches, placed them in themed dioramas, and started a museum.

Famous types of every crawl make an appearance at the offbeat attraction (which also doubles as the business address for Bohdan's retail store). Have a laugh with comic David Letterroach or enjoy a piano concerto by Liberoachi? How about a visit to Roach Liberty, where the famous statue lifts her roach beside the golden door?

Perhaps the strangest bug is the one that welcomes unwary visitors to the Combates Motel. As a takeoff on the movie *Psycho*, the white-wigged roach wields a knife and slides along a track between the motel and a spooky house. In this creepy scenario, it's the humans who check in but don't check out. Ah, sweet revenge!

Hutto Hippos

Driving through Hutto, Texas, one thing quickly becomes apparent: Hutto is hippopotamus country. In fact, Hutto reveres the enormous beast like none other. How do they show their affection for the ungainly mammal? By distributing hippo statues virtually everywhere.

An exhibit called "Hippo Lure" explains how an old circus trail once passed through town. When a hippo broke loose and wandered to Cottonwood Creek, the town had a new mascot.

Various sights have included a Lone Star Hippo, a Stars and Stripes Hippo, a Texas Longhorn Hippo, and a Hippo Crossing amongst other hippopotami. There's even a stationary 725-pound concrete hippo that's designed to be "ridden." Just the thing for a safari on the cheap.

Toilet Seat Art Museum

The Colony, Texas

Self-proclaimed "toilet seat artist" Barney Smith has created more than 700 unique toilet seat works and placed them in his garage-turned-museum for viewing. As a retired master plumber, Smith knows commode lids better than just about anyone.

More than 30 years ago, Smith modified his first toilet seat when he used one to mount a set of deer antlers. From that point forward, Smith has been "sitting down on the job," so to speak.

His creations include license plate seats; tribute seats; Elks, Lions Club, and Rotary seats; seats that feature cutlery, pens, and fragrances; and a whole slew of other crazy toilet-art pieces.

Cadillac Ranch

Amarillo, Texas

The man behind Cadillac Ranch, helium baron Stanley Marsh 3 (he favors the Arabic numeral over the "pretentious" Roman III) is both beloved and despised in his hometown. Some see him as a genius of modern public art, and others believe he's dragging Amarillo's property values into the gutter. In 1974, Marsh commissioned a San Francisco art collective named The Ant Farm to create this unusual work of roadside art. The Ant Farm buried 10 vintage Cadillacs up to their midsections at the angle of the Great Pyramid. Cadillac Ranch, since moved two miles west to escape the city's growth, is open to the public, who are free to photograph or spray paint as they like.

Balmorhea Pool

Balmorhea State Park, Texas

There's no antidote for a hot summer day like a dip in the pool, especially if it's the world's largest spring-fed swimming pool. Supplied with over 20 million gallons a day from San Solomon Springs, the 1930s-era pool has a surface area around 1.75 acres and a depth of about 25 feet.

Old Rip

Eastland, Texas

Built in 1897, the Eastland County Courthouse in northern Texas had a legend living in its cornerstone until the wrecking ball came calling in 1928. Defying all biological explanation, a horned toad somehow lived to see daylight after dwelling in the cornerstone for 31 years. Hoax or not, locals dubbed the reptile "Old Rip" (after Rip Van Winkle) and took him on tour. The famous toad even met President Calvin Coolidge. He passed away soon thereafter and has called the new Eastland County Courthouse home ever since: His embalmed body is on display under glass.

Big Texan Steak Ranch

Amarillo, Texas

You see the billboards long before the motels lining the Amarillo stretch of I-40 come into sight: "Home of the FREE 72-ounce Steak!!!!" The catch: You've got to finish the whole thing in an hour—or else pay a steep price. Regardless of your appetite, the Big Texan is a bastion of cowboy kitsch, inside and out.

AIA Sandcastle Competition

Galveston, Texas

Since the mid-1980s, thousands of architects and designers have headed to Galveston Island for the annual American Institute of Architects Sandcastle Competition. Using nothing but sand, water, tools, and hands, contestants have eight hours to craft the sandcastle of their dreams— or just about anything else. The results are impressive and include dragons, mermaids, and happy walruses alongside sandcastles inspired by the Mayans, Romans, Alfred E. Neuman, and J.R.R. Tolkien.

Petrified Wood Gas Station

Decatur, Texas

Proprietor E. F. Boydston put a veneer of locally quarried petrified wood on his gas station to attract customers to his

Texas Tourist Camp, which also included a restaurant and rental cabins. It's alleged that long before the gas station closed in 1989, infamous bank robbers Bonnie and Clyde once spent the night in one of the cabins. The place remains a local attraction.

National Museum of Funeral History
Houston, Texas

We all have to go sometime. If founder Robert L. Waltrip has his way, our destination will be the National Museum of Funeral History in Houston, Texas.

This vast, 20,000-square-foot museum is packed to the rafters with caskets, coffins, hearses, and other items that relate in some way to the death process.

Opened in 1992 as a way to honor "one of our most important cultural rituals," the scope of the operation is impressive, as are some of its more unusual exhibits.

A real "crowd" pleaser comes in the form of a 1916 Packard Funeral Bus. This bizarre vehicle seems to ask, "Why deal with long funeral processions when this all-in-one baby can do it all?" Designed to carry a coffin, pallbearers, and up to 20 mourners, the bus was retired after it tipped over during a San Francisco funeral in 1952, ejecting mourners and the mourned into the street.

Rather playfully, a sign in the museum reads, "Any day above ground is a good one." In general, we agree. But after checking out the museum's ultra-cool eternity collection, "six feet under" doesn't seem all that bad.

The museum features a collection of 12 "fantasy coffins." These hand-painted Ghanaian "art" coffins are designed to capture the spirit of the departed and are carved into such shapes as a car, an airplane, and a lobster. The grouping is believed to be the largest such collection outside of Africa.

Orange Show Monument

Built by folk artist and postal worker Jefferson Davis McKissack, the Orange Show Monument pays homage to one of America's most beloved fruits.

The craftsman erected his 3,000-square-foot shrine to citrus between 1956 and 1979. For building materials, McKissack used such things as concrete, steel, and brick. For adornments, the junk man came to the rescue with discarded tiles, wagon wheels, tractor seats, old mannequins, and statuettes.

Sporting an orange-and-white color scheme, the monument features educational boards that tout the orange's many plusses. An oasis, wishing well, pond, stage, museum, and gift shop provides a nifty backdrop for McKissack's favorite fruit.

When McKissack died in 1980, a nonprofit organization calling itself the Orange Show Foundation stepped in to preserve his monument.

In 1988, the group commissioned a display of mobile art they called the Fruitmobile. And this is how the celebration known as the Art Car Parade was born. At the Houston Art Car parade, artists get to show off their idiosyncrasies in a mobile medium. The parade features wacky cars that make vehicles from *Mad Max* appear almost ordinary.

Take, for example, the Hen-A-Tron II, a hen/car hybrid that represents the type of auto lunacy that prevails at the parade. From here, the asphalt is the limit.

Past parade entries have included a Volkswagen Beetle with another upside-down Beetle welded to its roof, a Sunflower car where driver and friends sit high in an elevated sun pod, and a giant Gold Star car that looks to be uncontrollable. Each year the entries get more artistic, intricate, and dare we say, weirder. Bravo!

The Haunted Fort Worth Stockyards

Fort Worth, Texas

The Stockyards used to have quite a few head of beef, but now they mostly have tourists. Today the Fort Worth Stockyards are a historic district (or a tourist trap, depending on perspective) like Vancouver's Gastown or Wichita's Cowtown. Fort Worthians revel in the ghosty spice that seasons the Stockyards' history. For a slight fee, some will take you on a tour. Here are some of the highlights.

Good Golly...

One of the Stockyards' most famous haunted spots is Miss Molly's Hotel, formerly a boardinghouse, speakeasy and bordello. Seven themed and named rooms are lush with all the all the attendant décor you'd expect. The Cattleman's and Cowboy's rooms are notorious for ghost sightings. Most commonly, the apparitions look like young women, perhaps the spirits of past 'soiled doves' who too often came to grief in the old West. One modern housekeeper quit after extra coins kept appearing after she'd already collected her tips!

Cantina Cadillac

This hopping night spot is so haunted that at night, it always has at least two staffers. Tills are often short or over, with the shortage or overage made up the next day. This could just be human error, except that it happens here suspiciously more often than in most establishments. One day, while closing out downstairs, the Cantina crew heard noise topside. They went up to find all the furniture shoved into the middle of the dance floor. Clever prank or ghost? We don't know.

Cattlemen's Steakhouse

Would you like some spirits with your enormous medium rare rib eye? Can do, if you can get staff to take you downstairs at the Cattlemen's—they go in pairs. Disembodied voices call their names, doors open and close unattended, and stuff gets moved around at random. Ghost hunters have bagged some nice orb photos here, and an actual ghost photo adorns the upstairs wall—an odd face behind a bolo-hat-wearing mortal.

Maverick Building

It has seen many uses, including its current incarnation as a western apparel store. Of old, the Maverick was a saloon, and reputedly Bonnie Parker's (as in Bonnie and Clyde) favorite gambling joint. The ghost upstairs is believed to be female, probably hailing from the brothel days of the early 20th century.

Even when the Stockyards mostly smelled of cattle, and what goes into and comes out of them, one could smell roses upstairs. Years back, someone experimented by leaving a bouquet of roses upstairs. She came back later to find them tastefully distributed throughout the rooms.

White Elephant Saloon

In the old days, this was one of the rougher and sleazier drunkeries, and was in a different location. When that old structure crumbled, owners moved all the memorabilia here with the name. It seems that the unseen inhabitants came along, or were perhaps already in residence.

Three violent deaths have occurred in the basement of the current building, leaving it with a creepy sensation. As with many hauntings, the staff describe glasses and implements mysteriously moving to new locations.

Knife Alley...

...is an alley no more, since people roofed and walled it. Today you can buy some of the finest blades in Texas in this shop. You can also watch the power go out, which the local utility finds very suspicious, considering that they have replaced the transformer three times.

Ghost hunters reckon that paranormal activity might be to blame, since all mundane explanations have been ruled out.

Cumberland Falls

Cumberland Falls State Resort Park, Kentucky

Some waterfalls boast of being the highest; others brag about spilling more water than the rest; but as far as we know, only one lays claim to producing a genuine "moonbow."

If you're unfamiliar with the word, suffice to say that a moonbow is the nighttime equivalent of a rainbow. The major difference is the latter uses lunar, not solar, rays to produce the colorful phenomenon.

At 68 feet tall by 125 feet wide, Cumberland Falls has been dubbed "Little Niagara" by waterfall buffs. On nights featuring a full moon, the elusive moonbow sometimes appears. The event relies on a number of variables including proper water temperature, agreeable mist cloud, and clear skies, but when the moonbow does come it's pure magic. The phenomenon is so popular, Web sites regularly track "optimal moonbow dates" so aficionados won't miss out. Take that, Niagara!

Cave City

Barren County, Kentucky

If you are enticed by terms like "world's biggest" and "world's hokiest," you'll definitely want to plan a visit to Cave City, Kentucky. This offering in south-central Kentucky's cave country is locked in a glorious time warp of 1950s era roadside fun and adventure.

First and foremost, the town owes its lifeblood to a giant hole in the ground.

In a world of braggadocio, Mammoth Cave should win an award for truth in advertising. With more than 350 miles of mapped passages discovered thus far, the 379-foot-deep cave system is considered the world's longest by a healthy margin. Each day, tourists arrive in throngs to explore its famed passageways and eat in its underground "Snowball Dining Room." But Mammoth Cave is merely the main lure to Cave City. There are many strange and unusual bits lurking about its periphery.

Take Dinosaur World, for example. With 150 full-size dinosaur statues arranged in a jungle setting, the attraction offers visitors a chance to meet these prehistoric giants up close and personal. If that doesn't suit your fancy, the site also offers kids the opportunity to search for their very own fossils—which they can then keep!

Guntown Mountain, another exercise in kitsch, features the time-honored "Old West" theme. This offering adds a touch of questionable authenticity to the genre since Jesse James was thought to have hidden out in area caves. Gunfights and high-living abound.

By the way, Cave City is not called Cave City solely for Mammoth Cave. The geology that produced the giant has populated the area with a number of underground chambers. Examples run the gamut from the kitschy to the more kitschy. When it's time to batten down the hatches and retire from spelunking, archeology, and gunfights, the Wigwam Village Motel is the perfect place to put one's 1950s roadside trip to bed. Literally.

Vent Haven Ventriloquist Museum

Fort Mitchell, Kentucky

"Hard work never killed anybody, but why take a chance?" So quipped famous ventriloquist dummy Charlie McCarthy during an act with his partner (and true voice) Edgar Bergen. For the sake of McCarthy's legacy, it's a good thing ventriloquist William S. Berger didn't follow the dummy's lead.

Berger, a collector of all things ventriloquist, was the hard-working president of the International Brotherhood of Ventriloquists from the late 1940s up until 1960. Having no heirs and fearing his collection would be lost, he helped pave the way for Vent Haven, a museum devoted to the art of ventriloquism.

The facility, open seasonally, includes more than 700 ventriloquist's dummies, a library of ventriloquist books, photographs, playbills, and other trade bits.

Lost River Cave
Bowling Green, Kentucky

Why trudge through a cave when you can glide across it in a boat? Bowling Green's Lost River Cave bills itself as offering the only underground boat tour in the state—and it's easy to see the attraction.

As one of a handful of watered cave systems in America, Lost River Cave features an agreeable river walk leading to one of the largest cave entrances east of the Mississippi River. From there, visitors can embark upon a 25-minute underground boat ride.

Ripley's Believe It or Not categorizes the Lost River as the shortest and deepest in the world, and the inimitable Jesse James and his gang are said to have visited the cave. Who could blame them? With all their tiresome running, the desperados probably fancied a cruise.

Harland Sanders Café and Museum
Corbin, Kentucky

Long before Colonel Sanders sold "finger-lickin' good" chicken from a chain of Kentucky Fried Chicken franchises, he stirred the pot here at his first store. Actually, "store" is an overstatement. In 1930, white-bearded Sanders operated a service station with a small six-seat lunchroom attached. In short order (pun intended), word spread about his uncommonly tasty fried chicken.

In 1937, Sanders enlarged his enterprise and built Sanders Café, a restaurant with accommodations for 142 customers. Kentucky Fried Chicken was on its way to fast-food superstardom. Today, the restored Harland Sanders Café stands at the "Birthplace of Kentucky Fried Chicken." Next door, a modern KFC restaurant wows hungry patrons with their super-secret "11 herbs and spices." Yum!

World Chicken Festival

Kentucky pays homage to Colonel Sanders through its annual World Chicken Festival, which takes place in London, Kentucky. The festival features the world's largest stainless-steel skillet—10 feet, 6 inches in diameter and 8 inches deep with an 8-foot handle. The skillet weighs a whopping 700 pounds! Visitors to the festival can purchase chicken fried in this sizeable skillet, which can cook 600 quarters of chicken at once. Anyone want seconds? How about thirds?

The Blue People of Kentucky

Hazard, Kentucky

There exists a rare blood disorder called methemoglobinemia that affects a very small percentage of the population. The disorder happens when a Caucasian person's blood carries a higher than normal level of methemoglobin, a form of hemoglobin that does not bind oxygen. Too much methemoglobin can make the blood dark brown and give the skin a distinctly bluish tint. A person can get this disorder via exposure to certain drugs in the antibiotic and bromate family, but the most famous occurrences of methemoglobinemia were caused by genetics.

The Blue Fugates

In the early 1800s, a man named Martin Fugate lived in the Appalachian Mountains with his wife, who was said to have carried the recessive gene that causes methemoglobinemia, or metHB for short. One carrier of metHB won't make a blue person, but two will: The Fugates married into the Smith family, who also carried the gene. In 1832, a blue baby was born. Now, a blue baby or two might not make news, but because of serious inbreeding among the clans, eventually there was a concentration of these "Blue Fugates" near Troublesome Creek, an area in the hills near Hazard, Kentucky.

In the 1960s, a hematologist named Madison Cawein diagnosed them with metHB and treated them with an injection of the chemical methylene blue, effectively replacing the missing enzyme in their blood. The results were amazing, though temporary: The Fugates who were treated were restored to a pinkish hue that lasted as long as they took regular doses of the chemical.

A Shade of the Past

Now that people get around more easily and inbreeding is more of a social taboo, the gene that carries metHB is becoming even rarer than before. The "blue people of Kentucky" are increasingly harder to find, though with nature's infinite combinations, it's still possible to encounter a blue man or woman at Troublesome Creek.

World's Largest Baseball Bat

Louisville, Kentucky

Here's where they turn out bats for everyone from Little Leaguers to the game's greatest stars. And they've been doing it since 1884. Honus Wagner signed on to have them exclusively make his bats in 1905. (He was the first player to have his autograph on the bat.) You can get a bat with your own name on it at the gift shop.

Leaning against the Slugger Bat Factory and Museum is a bat that has no equal, measuring 120 feet from tip to tip and weighing in at 34 tons. The steel bat is a scale replica of Babe Ruth's 34-inch Slugger. Close at hand are the World's Largest Baseball and the World's Largest Baseball Glove.

The Peabody Ducks

Memphis, Tennessee

If it walks like a duck and quacks like a duck, it must be a duck, right? Not if it's a Peabody duck from the esteemed troupe of marching ducks at the Peabody Hotel. To call one of these thoroughbreds by such a pedestrian name is akin to confusing opera with pop music.

The grand tradition began in 1933 when prankster and General Manager Frank Schutt put three live ducks in the hotel's fountain. His stunt backfired. Guests actually loved the sight so much the hotel replaced the three with five Mallard ducks.

In 1940, bellman and former circus animal trainer Edward Pembroke offered to assist in duck duties and eventually taught the ducks to march. He became the official Peabody "Duckmaster" and remained in that capacity until 1991. Eight decades later, the "quackers" are still moving in lockstep. Here's the drill:

Every day at 11:00 a.m., the ducks are led by their duckmaster to the Peabody Grand Lobby. A red carpet is unfurled and the ducks commence marching to the tune of John Philip Sousa's "King Cotton March." At 5:00 p.m., the ceremony is reversed, and the cultured ducks retreat to their penthouse lair for the evening.

Surprisingly, the regal birds don't live the uppity life for very long. Every three months, a new team is trained, and the veterans are returned to farms to live out their lives. This must be pretty hard on the quackers. Would you want to dine on farm muck after you'd sampled beef wellington?

Rock City: Lookout Mountain

Lookout Mountain, Georgia, near Chattanooga, Tennessee

Rock City is one of those roadside attractions that seems to have it all. Especially if the "See Rock City" ads are to be believed. This classic tourist draw, which is essentially an expanded mountaintop overlook, got its start in 1932 when Garnet Carter (the inventor of miniature golf) opened it under the name "Freida's Rock City Gardens."

"See Seven States," reads a slate map at Rock City's lookout point. While the claim has never been substantiated, the view up top is truly inspirational. Surprisingly, Rock City's owners didn't originate the boast. It emerged from the Civil War diaries of a Union officer and a Confederate nurse who were here during the Battle of Lookout Mountain. Chalk one up for authenticity.

While it's true that Rock City's most famous feature is its lookout, there are other lures. Chief amongst these is a 140-foot waterfall that takes its majestic plunge mere feet from the precipice. Clearly, Rock City has its scenic bases covered.

On the "Enchanted Flagstone Trail," visitors are led past the very best Lookout Mountain has to offer. Who wouldn't want to follow the trail to see the "1,000-ton Balanced Rock" or to attempt to pass through "Fat Man's Squeeze," a hopelessly narrow passageway? The precarious "Swing-Along Bridge" seems as if it were designed to induce vertigo and seasickness simultaneously. It's high times in Rock City!

On the artificial side of things, gloriously whimsical objects arrive in the form of Fairyland Caverns and Mother Goose Village. Both are as tacky as all get-out, but that's precisely the point. "See Rock City," reads the ad copy. We're certainly glad we did.

Mimicking South Dakota's Wall Drug and South Carolina's South of the Border, the mass of "See Rock City" signs that lead visitors to the Chattanooga, Tennessee, attraction have taken on a life of their own.

Shortly after Rock City opened in 1932, employee Clark Avery Byers negotiated a deal with American farmers, offering them $3 a year for the right to paint a message on their barns. Nine hundred enterprising men gave Byers the go-ahead, and the result was an army of "See Rock City" barns that added to the attraction's coffers as it weaved its way into the American psyche.

Today, only a fraction of the barns remain, but the ones that do usually catch the eye. Clark Avery Byers would be right proud of that.

Graceland
Memphis, Tennessee

The home of Elvis Presley is now a prime road-trip destination, attracting visitors as both a rock landmark and the Taj Mahal of American kitsch. The King of Rock 'n' Roll bought the place in 1957 and lived there until his 1977 death. Elvis stamped each room of the mansion with his unusual taste. The jungle room houses Polynesian-inspired furnishings and has a waterfall coursing down the wall. The pool room isn't dominated by the pool table, but by the walls and ceiling, which are swathed in the loudest fabric money can buy.

Gatlinburg Space Needle
Gatlinburg, Tennessee

The Great Smoky Mountains' answer to the Seattle landmark went up less than a decade after the original but never garnered the same level of fame. Featuring a 3,600-square-foot observation deck 342 feet above town, the tower is now the centerpiece of an amusement park.

Salt and Pepper Shaker Museum

Gatlinburg, Tennessee

Proving that no object is too ordinary to build a museum around, this shrine to salt and pepper shakers is one woman's spicy dream come true.

Owner Andrea Ludden is a trained archeologist. Originally from Belgium, she has managed to collect more than 20,000 salt and pepper shakers. She houses them in fastidious order in her multiroom museum in Gatlinburg but already the venue is packed to overflowing. It's not the first time Ludden has run out of space.

Building her collection for well over two decades, Ludden first opened a museum in Cosby, Tennessee. That building proved too small for her ever-burgeoning inventory, and she was forced to relocate. She moved to her present space in 2004, but history may repeat itself since Ludden's collecting bug shows no sign of abating.

Ludden's salt and pepper shakers come from everywhere and anywhere, and are made from glass, plastic, wood, metal, crystal, walnut shells, sea shells, nuts, eggs—the list goes on.

There are shakers shaped like ears of corn, tractors, apples, gumball machines, log cabins, people, places, animals; if it can be imagined, it was probably manufactured.

In addition, there are shakers that celebrate pop culture, with the Beatles heading up the British invasion; and shakers that question good "taste", such as the human foot and toilet offerings.

Will Andrea Ludden's enterprise outgrow its present home and force her to relocate once again? If things "shake" out the way we think they will, it's almost a certainty. We don't suppose Ludden would want it any other way.

Eiffel Tower Replica

Paris, Tennessee

If a town is named Paris and its inhabitants swim in civic pride, what's the next logical step? They build a replica of the Eiffel Tower to cement their association with the European land of brie and chardonnay.

In this case, the replica is vastly shorter than the original (70 feet versus 986 feet), but who's counting? It features most every metal bit that the original does and is even painted a similar hue.

The tower was originally created at Christian Brothers University in Memphis, Tennessee, and was some ten feet shorter. When Paris, Tennessee, learned that Paris, Texas, had built a 65-foot replica, they pushed their pinnacle to 70 feet. Viva la difference!

The Paris, Tennessee, replica consists of 500 pieces of Douglas fir, 6,000 steel rods, and 10,000 hours of volunteer labor.

Parthenon

Nashville, Tennessee

Anyone who claims to see the Greek goddess Athena while standing beside Nashville's Parthenon should be excused. They are not dreaming. In keeping with their "Athens of the South" nickname, the city of Nashville chose to build this full-scale replica for the Tennessee Centennial Exposition in 1897.

Originally constructed of wood, plaster, and brick, Nashville's Parthenon was rebuilt out of concrete in the 1920s. If placed side by side with its Greek counterpart, it's actually more faithful to the original design since the ravages of time have not yet taken their toll.

Today, the Parthenon operates as an art gallery and well-known landmark in Centennial Park. In 1990, a 41-foot, 10-inch statue of Athena Parthenos was added. Artist Alan LeQuire's work faithfully replicates Athens' long-lost sculpture. The Athena Parthenos statue holds a unique honor—it's the tallest indoor statue in the Western world.

Oklahoma's Spook Light

Quapaw, Oklahoma

The Tri-State Spook Light (aka the Hornet Spook Light) is an orb that appears almost nightly near Quapaw, Oklahoma. While many claim that it's merely the headlights from cars on Route 66, the phenomenon was witnessed in the area long before cars were even invented; in fact, local Native American tribes knew of it centuries ago. The orb maintains a careful distance from those who gather to see it; it pulses and varies in intensity and then disappears when cars on the road approach it.

Many theories speculate as to what (or who) the orb is: Some believe that it's the ghost of a miner carrying a lantern; others believe that it is two Native American lovers who killed themselves because their romance was forbidden; and still others speculate that it is a solitary Native American, or even a portal to another world.

Blue Whale

Catoosa, Oklahoma

A surviving icon along historic U.S. Route 66, the smiling blue whale tells quite a tale. Hoping to show wife Zelta (a whale figurine collector) a whale of a good time for their wedding anniversary, Hugh Davis constructed the blue giant out of pipe and concrete in the early 1970s.

Built over a spring-fed pond, the whale features a sliding board and a mouth so large it could swallow people whole. Eventually, word of the great beast spread, and Davis commercialized the operation. A sandy beach, picnic tables, and lifeguards now welcomed would-be "Captain Ahabs" interested in a refreshing dip.

Everything went swimmingly at the "Fun and Swim Blue Whale" until 1988 when the attraction went belly up. In short order, nature began to reclaim the site. In 2000, concerned Catoosa citizens stepped in and restored the whale. While no longer operated as a swimming concession, the blue whale continues to trigger double takes from nostalgic Route 66 travelers. And that's no fish story.

World's Largest Concrete Totem Pole
Foyil, Oklahoma

If the thought of beholding the World's Largest Concrete Totem Pole gets your engine running, beat a hasty retreat to Foyil, Oklahoma, home of Ed Galloway's Totem Pole Park. Eleven years in the making, the giant pole was completed in 1948 by retired Galloway, who was looking for "something to do." Adorned with owls, spirit lizards, and Indian chiefs, the artistic post pays homage to Native American culture.

Okie Catfish Noodling Tournament
Paul's Valley, Oklahoma

Noodling involves catching a catfish with one's hands. Really. The annual Okie Catfish Noodling Tournament pits crafty humans against equally cagey fish. Usually performed with the aid of a "spotter," a noodler dives underwater to depths approaching 20 feet to retrieve his quarry, which are usually hiding out under rocks. With winning specimens weighing as much as 50 to 60 pounds, this is no small feat.

The 24-hour tournament started in 2000. Anglers (noodlers) are permitted to catch their prey in any body of water statewide but must bring their catch to a central point for weighing. Afterward, cheers and jeers are exchanged, and noodlers set their sights on the next contest, often lamenting "the one that got away."

Mobile Carnival Museum

Mobile, Alabama

This museum, which traces the history of Carnival in Mobile, acts as a Mardi Gras primer. Who knew that Mardi Gras (French for "Fat Tuesday", the final and most spectacular day of Carnival) was first celebrated more than 300 years ago? And how many realize that Mobile beat New Orleans to the punch as the birthplace of Mardi Gras in America?

Through displays, exhibits, artifacts, and art, the Mobile Carnival Museum educates as it entertains. Visitors will find elaborate gowns and trains worn by past Carnival queens alongside flamboyant outfits worn by Mardi Gras's many jesters. Posters, ball invitations, and interactive exhibits round out the celebratory repertoire.

Amelia Gayle Gorgas Library

Tuscaloosa, Alabama

From 1883 to 1907, Amelia Gayle Gorgas served as the first female librarian at the University of Alabama. She is believed to haunt this facility, which was built in 1939 and named in her honor. She makes her presence known by stopping the elevator on the floor that holds the special collections—even when the elevator bank is locked down. When the doors open, the errant elevator is always empty.

Africatown

Plateau, Alabama

Beginning in 1808, it was technically illegal to bring slaves from Africa into the United States; this law was often violated, however. The last recorded case of a slave ship entering the United States was in 1859, when the *Clotilde* docked in Mobile Bay, Alabama, with more than 100 slaves from an area of western Africa near present-day Benin. More than 30 of the slaves escaped and established the settlement Africatown in southern Alabama, where they practiced the customs of their homeland. One of Africatown's leaders, Cudjo Lewis, was the last survivor of the Clotilde slaves. He died in 1935 at age 114, impoverished and embittered toward the Americans who had bought him and the Africans who had sold him.

Ghosts of Huntingdon College

Montgomery, Alabama

If you visit Pratt Hall at Huntingdon College in Montgomery, Alabama, you might just encounter the ghost of a young lady named Martha. Better known today as the "Red Lady," Martha left her native New York and enrolled at Huntingdon in the early 1900s because it was her grandmother's alma mater. She was known on campus for her love of red: She decorated her room with red drapes and a red rug, and she often wore red dresses. Lonely and taunted by her peers, Martha killed herself in despair.

She now haunts Pratt Hall (which once housed her dorm), where residents occasionally catch a glimpse of a young lady dressed in red. In recent years, she seems to have gotten bolder, as students have reported cold blasts of air surrounding those who are caught picking on their classmates.

The Dexter Avenue Baptist Church

Montgomery, Alabama

Dr. Martin Luther King, Jr., became pastor of the Dexter Avenue Baptist Church in Montgomery, Alabama, in 1954. By then, he had become deeply involved in the cause of civil rights for African Americans, and in 1955 he led the Montgomery Bus Boycott,which lasted 382 days. During that time, King was arrested, his home was bombed, and he was subjected to tremendous personal abuse. But as a result of that protest, the United States Supreme Court declared unconstitutional all laws requiring segregation on buses. For the first time in history, blacks and whites could ride municipal buses as equals.

The Montgomery Bus Boycott placed King in the national spotlight and established him as a leading spokesman in the fight for civil rights. In 1957, he was elected president of the Southern Christian Leadership Conference, which was organized to provide leadership for the burgeoning movement. King traveled the nation and the world on behalf of injustice, advocating nonviolent protest to enact social change.

In the years that followed, King worked tirelessly to ensure equal rights for all. He promoted voter registration drives for African Americans in Alabama and directed a peace march on Washington, D.C., that drew a quarter of a million people. It was during that event, on the steps of the Lincoln Memorial, that King delivered his famous "I Have a Dream" speech, in which he passionately advocated for racial equality and the end of discrimination.

Ave Maria Grotto

Cullman, Alabama

This "Jerusalem in Miniature" is the lifework of Benedictine Monk Joseph Zoettl (1878–1961). Using stone, concrete, and whatever building materials he could scrounge together, Brother Zoettl reproduced 125 of the world's most famous buildings and shrines in miniature and deposited them in a steep hillside.

Spread over a four-acre site, Zoettl's creations include the Vatican's St. Peter's Basilica, the Monte Casino Abbey, the Alamo, the Leaning Tower of Pisa, and the Hiroshima Peace Church.

Zoettl spent some 50 years building his miniature city—no small feat given the fact that the holy man was afflicted with a hunched back. Still, the talented monk persevered and was able to move mountains. Little ones, in this case, but mountains nonetheless.

Tom's Rock Wall

Florence, Alabama

If love can move a mountain it can certainly build a wall. Such was the mindset of Tom Hendrix, who built a stone partition in honor of his Native American ancestor—a woman who suffered great heartbreak along the Trail of Tears.

The story holds that Te-lah-nay (Hendrix' great-great grandmother) so missed her native Oklahoma, she endured a four-year odyssey to once again embrace its soil. During her walk from Alabama, she carried a small rock originally taken from her homeland. From this stone, Hendrix drew his inspiration.

Hendrix's rock wall, a work in perpetual progress featuring free-laying stones and numerous impromptu builders, is one of the largest monuments to a woman in America.

Unevenly contoured, the wall bends here and there and is higher in certain places than others. According to Hendrix, this symbolizes the "difficult journey his ancestors took in life ... A journey through life is never straight." Indeed.

Unclaimed Baggage Center

Scottsboro, Alabama

At the Unclaimed Baggage Center (UBC), shoppers will find a wealth of bargains. Unfortunately, their gain is directly linked to someone else's loss. Horror stories concerning lost luggage are as common as flight delays these days. Many frequent flyers actually expect to lose a bag over the course of a year. When this unfortunate occurrence takes place, a portion of the bounty can end up here.

After a 90-day waiting period (just to make things right and proper) the free-for-all begins. UBC carries virtually everything that people drag onto airplanes, so its departments read much like Macy's. Looking for ladies and men's clothing? They're here. Digital cameras and electronics float your boat? Dig in. From fine jewelry to Persian rugs, artwork to luggage (surprise!), this place has you covered. Greatest find thus far? A 41-karat natural emerald.

Since the inventory is constantly revolving, treasure-hunting types consider the place more of a happening than a mere store. "Unclaimed Baggage Center gets nearly one million visitors annually, making it one of Alabama's top attractions," says Rand McNally. Sounds about right and wrong when you get right down to it.

Over the years, the Unclaimed Baggage Center has had some unusual finds. Like the rattlesnake employees found packed away in an unclaimed suitcase. Or the doll with $500 hidden inside. Sounds like every day is an adventure at this place!

World's Largest Office Chair

Anniston, Alabama

An apt advertisement for Miller Furniture in downtown Anniston, this 33-foot chair trumps numerous big chairs scattered across the planet. This is one chair you don't want to lean too far back—it might flatten a brick building.

Spear Hunting Museum

Summerdale, Alabama

Eugene C. Morris desperately wants the world to know that he's a spear hunter. Plastered on the side of his museum is this boastful proclamation: "The Greatest Living Spear Hunter in the World." Since Morris claims to have taken 408 big-game animals with his trusty lance, we'll have to take his word for it.

Within his 7,600-square-foot display, Morris's fleshy spoils are displayed beside a vast assortment of spears. Realizing that many peaceful people take exception to his chosen sport, the hunter offers no apologies. "They are just plain, flat-out not rational or even sane," says the spear-chucker when he describes the "don't kill anything" crowd.

In the souvenir area, a four-bladed steel "killer" spear is offered for sale beside a host of other deadly implements. While we'll "spear" clear of the great hunting debate, we will say that the Spear Hunting Museum comes right to the point. Take that as you will.

Lee County Library

Tupelo, Mississippi

The Lee County Library was constructed in 1971, on the site of the former home of Congressman John Mills Allen. Although the house was torn down, some of its original features were used in the library, including the glass panels and doors in the Mississippi Room. Apparently, Allen's spirit remains as well. Whenever staff members find books removed from shelves and spread across the floor, the congressman is deemed responsible. His ghost is also blamed for removing items from the book drop.

The Haunted McRaven House

Vicksburg, Mississippi

Located near Vicksburg, Mississippi, the McRaven House was haunted even before it became a Civil War hospital.

The oldest parts of the estate known as McRaven House were built in 1797. Over the next 40 years, its owners gradually added to the property until it became a classic southern mansion, standing proudly among the magnolia blossoms and dogwood trees of the Old South.

And like nearly all such mansions, it has its share of resident ghosts. Today, McRaven House is often referred to as "the most haunted house in Mississippi." Some researchers believe that environmental conditions on the property make it particularly susceptible to hauntings: Ghosts that may not be noticeable in drier, less humid climates seem to be more perceptible in the dews of the delta. Of course, it helps that the McRaven House has seen more than its share of tragedy and death during its 200-year history.

The Ghost of Poor Mary

In the early 1860s, the house's supernatural activity seemed to center on an upstairs bedroom in which Mary Elizabeth Howard had died during childbirth in 1836 at age 15. Mary's brown-haired apparition is still seen descending the mansion's grand staircase. Her ghost is blamed for the poltergeist activity—such as pictures falling from the wall— that is often reported in the bedroom where she died. And her wedding shawl, which is occasionally put on display for tourists, is said to emit heat.

Ghosts of the Civil War

Mary Elizabeth's ghost alone would qualify McRaven House as a notably haunted reminder of Mississippi's antebellum past, but she is far from the only spirit residing there, thanks in part to the bloody atrocities of the Civil War.

The Siege of Vicksburg, which took place in 1863, was one of the longest, bloodiest battles of the entire conflict. When General Ulysses S. Grant and his Union forces crossed the Tennessee River into Mississippi, Confederate forces retreated into Vicksburg, which was so well guarded that it was known as a "fortress city." But as more and more Union forces gathered in the forests and swamps around Vicksburg, Confederate General John C. Pemberton was advised to evacuate. Fearing the wrath of the local population if he abandoned them, Pemberton refused.

By the time the siege began in earnest, the Confederate troops were greatly outnumbered. Rebel forces surrendered the city of Vicksburg on July 4, 1863, after more than a month of fighting. Nearly all of the Confederate soldiers involved in the battle—around 33,000 in all—were captured, wounded, or killed. The Union victory put the entire Mississippi River in northern hands, and combined with the victory at Gettysburg that same week, it marked the beginning of the end for the Confederacy.

Captain McPherson's Last Report

In the middle of the action stood McRaven House. In the early days of the siege, it served as a Confederate hospital, and, at that time, it was full of the screams of anguished and dying men. Cannons from both armies shot at the mansion, destroying large portions of it.

Later, after Union forces captured the house, it served as the headquarters for General Grant and the Union army. One of the officers put in charge of the house was Captain McPherson, a Vicksburg native who had fled to the North to fight for the Union. Sometime during the siege, he disappeared. Soon after, according to legend, McPherson's commanding officer awoke to find the captain in his room.

He was furious at the intrusion until he noticed McPherson's mangled, bloody face and torn uniform. The commanding officer then realized that this was not McPherson himself—it was his ghost, which had returned to deliver the message that Rebels, who couldn't forgive him for abandoning the

South, had murdered him. McPherson's ghost reputedly still wanders the grounds dressed in Union blue with blood oozing from a bullet wound in his forehead.

Other Civil War Ghosts

Nearly a year after the siege ended, John Bobb—the owner of McRaven House at the time—spotted six Union soldiers picking flowers in his garden. Outraged by the trespassers, Bobb threw a brick at them and hit one of the Yankees in the head. After going to the local field commander to report the intruders, Bobb returned home to find 25 Union soldiers waiting for him; they marched him into the nearby bayou and shot him to death. His ghost has been seen roaming the property ever since.

The Haunted King's Tavern

Natzchez, Mississippi

Did a love triangle and murder produce a spirit that resides at King's Tavern in Natchez, Mississippi? It seems likely. But the ghost of Madeline isn't the only disembodied soul flitting about at this historic pub (closed as of this printing).

From Fort to Tavern

The Old Natchez Trace—a 500-mile trail stretching from Natchez, Mississippi, to about 17 miles southwest of Nashville, Tennessee—was cut by Native Americans centuries before Europeans arrived and was used as a crude highway to transport goods and people. It also attracted miscreants in the form of highwaymen, and during Colonial times, robberies and murders were common on the trail. Nevertheless, the path remained popular, and businesses catering to travelers sprouted up along it out of necessity. One such enterprise was King's Tavern. Originally built as a blockhouse for a fort, the building was acquired in 1799 by wealthy New Yorker Richard King, who turned it into a bar and inn. It was a great success, but it would also bring drama into King's life.

Cheating Ways

Despite having a loving wife, King succumbed to the oldest of temptations when he hired a young woman named Madeline as a server and subsequently seduced her. Attractive and industrious, Madeline was only too happy to become the rich man's mistress. Their tryst didn't last long, however: When King's irate wife learned of the affair, she took steps to end it. What occurred next is open to debate: Some believe that Mrs. King hired highwaymen to murder Madeline, while others say that she performed the deed herself. Either way, Madeline vanished without a trace. But without a body, there was officially no murder, so nothing further came of King's wife's permanent solution to her husband's tawdry affair.

Mystery Solved

In 1932, King's Tavern underwent significant renovations. While workers were repairing the fireplace in the pub's main room, they were horrified to find three human skeletons—two male and one female—hidden behind the bricks.

The identities of the men were anyone's guess, but many believed that the female was Madeline, the young temptress who'd been done in by the jealous Mrs. King more than a century prior. When a Spanish dagger—a weapon that was quite popular during Colonial times—was discovered nearby, the theory became even more plausible. The bodies were buried in a local cemetery and the remodeling job was completed. A mysterious chapter in the tavern's history had been put to rest...or had it?

Manifestations

After the renovation, apparitions and other unexplained phenomena arrived like waves on a beach. Shadowy figures were often spotted walking up the staircases or passing directly through them. A spectral man wearing a top hat moved freely about the tavern; sporting a black jacket and tie string, his garb was consistent with that of the era in which the murders occurred. Members of the waitstaff who witnessed the apparition felt that he embodied evil, and many believed that he was involved in the murders somehow—either as a perpetrator or a victim.

But ghosts of grown men aren't the only spirits lingering at the tavern: The unsettling sound of a crying baby has also been reported, and small footprints—presumably left by a woman—appear from out of nowhere on freshly mopped floors. Many believe that Madeline is responsible for the footprints, which usually move across the room directly toward startled employees. Madeline's ghost has also been blamed for spilling pitchers onto the floor, knocking jars from shelves, turning faucets and lights on and off, and opening doors. When her name is called out in protest, she has been known to slam doors.

Someone (or something) more sinister likes to forcefully throw dishes through the air and apply pressure around the necks or on the chests of visitors. And the fireplace where the bodies were discovered occasionally emits heat as if it is burning wood, even though no fire is lit and no firewood is present. Could this be a final plea for justice from a trio cheated out of life?

Mississippi Petrified Forest

Flora, Mississippi

A petrified forest located in the middle of Mississippi? You betcha. Deposited by a powerful river that flowed more than 36 million years ago, logs turned to stone were uncovered in the 1850s when settlers searched out suitable land to farm.

Word would soon spread about this "petrified forest," said to be the only one of its type in the eastern United States. In a nod to its unique nature, the site would become a Registered National Landmark.

Today, visitors to the Mississippi Petrified Forest walk along nature trails that lead to its many points of interest. Some "stone logs" measure as long as ten feet and are thought to have come from trees ten times that length—far taller than trees that now populate the area. One stone tree is shaped just like a bench. Another appears uncannily like a frog. And you thought such petrified fun only existed out West!

Birthplace of Kermit the Frog Museum

Leland, Mississippi

This small museum, located at Leland's Chamber of Commerce, celebrates Jim Henson (1936–1990), the creator of Kermit the Frog, Miss Piggy, and other beloved Muppet characters.

Henson grew up in Leland and incorporated snippets from his childhood into his richly humorous characters. Kermit, for instance, actually evolved from Kermit Scott, a childhood playmate.

Information and photos cataloguing Henson's life are found here, alongside Muppet dolls and memorabilia. A wooden cutout of Kermit, all "frogged-up" in his finest threads, stands sentry rain or shine in front of the museum. Its obvious message? It ain't easy being green!

Christ of the Ozarks

Eureka Springs, Arkansas

In yet another giant testament to faith, this 67-foot rendition of Christ stands tall atop Magnetic Mountain. Somewhat cartoonlike in appearance, the giant statue has earned such unflattering nicknames as "Gumby Jesus" and "Our Milk Carton with Arms."

Christ of the Ozarks was originally intended to be the centerpiece of a religious theme park, but that venture never came to pass. Today, the statuesque savior welcomes visitors to an outdoor passion play held at a nearby 4,100-seat amphitheater.

Haunted Vino's Brewpub

Little Rock, Arkansas

Vino's is a brewery, a pizza parlor, and a great place to hear live music. After the establishment opened in 1990, it attracted a following among the living—but it has quite a group of nonliving fans too. The source of the haunting is unknown, but employees say that the building—which was constructed in 1909—has a creepy vibe. It features several spots that are permanently cold for no scientific reason, and other cold spots move around. When the building is relatively quiet, banging noises, thumps, and creaking are heard in seemingly empty parts of the building. After closing, staff members stack up the chairs to mop the floors and then leave them that way overnight; but when employees arrive the next day, they often find the chairs scattered around the restaurant.

Haunted Henderson State University

Arkadelphia, Arkansas

The ghost of Henderson State University is said to be the victim of a sad lover's tale. Around 1920, a young woman attended Ouachita Baptist University; her boyfriend was a student at Arkadelphia College (which is now Henderson State)—the Methodist college across the street. They were in love...or at least she thought so.

But the young man decided that the differences between their religions and schools were too much to overcome. When he invited another girl to the Homecoming Dance, the Ouachita student killed herself in despair. Now, each year during Homecoming Week, she is seen drifting through the women's dorms at Henderson, perhaps searching for the young lady who stole her man's heart.

Fouke Monster Mart

Fouke, Arkansas

Fouke, Arkansas, is famous for the Boggy Creek Monster—a half-man, half-ape creature along the lines of Bigfoot. For visitors who yearn to know more, Fouke (formerly Peavy's) Monster Mart is their number-one stop.

The monster was first sighted in these parts back in the 1940s. Eventually, he'd become so popular that a series of movies beginning with *The Legend of Boggy Creek* (1972) would commit him to hairy folk history.

At Fouke, a rather nondescript service station, the "Boggy Creek Monster" makes an appearance in the form of a hokey wooden cutout board.

Those wishing to learn more about the monster amble inside. There they will behold a plaster cast of Bigfoot, Fouke's featured exhibit since the Boggy Creek Monster's cast was supposedly lost to fire. After the excitement dies down, they continue on their journey all the richer for their efforts.

Crater of Diamonds State Park

Murfreesboro, Arkansas

Crater of Diamonds State Park is billed as the "world's only diamond site where you can search and keep what you find."

The 37-acre field, the eroded surface of an ancient, gem-bearing volcanic pipe, beckons get-rich-quick types with its implied promise. Several large diamonds found here have been cut into valuable "D" flawless stones. That said, the majority of stones uncovered by diamond prospectors are of the "rough" variety. Translation: They're worth a couple of bucks, tops, and are generally kept as souvenirs.

Still, the fun is in the hunt. And who knows? You may be the one to unearth the "biggie." The most recent "biggie" found at the park was discovered in 2006. The Roden Diamond, as it is called, was a whopping 6.35 carats. Happy hunting!

Abita Mystery House/UCM Museum

Abita Springs, Louisiana

Billed as Louisiana's Most Eccentric Attraction, this wonderful mishmash contains just about everything a traveler on a strange and unusual trip looks for. Take the sign that says, "If you have 3 or more it's a collection—A museum has over three collections."

The "museum" contains thousands of found objects and homemade inventions. Take a gander at the wind-driven whirligig standing beside a "Bassigator" (a 22-foot cross between a bass and an alligator). Next to these are a "Dogigator" (think alligator/dog crossbreed) and a Slipstream trailer that's been taken over by alien forces. How can we tell? A flying saucer has crashed into its side.

Owner John Preble used more than 50,000 recycled objects to create the bulk of his displays, and humor has been a steering force. At "Lil Dub's BBQ" diorama we're invited to "eat here and get gas." Another display puts an oil refinery smack up beside an antebellum plantation. This is Louisiana, after all.

A labor of love for artist John Preble, the UCM Museum (pronounced You-See-'Em Museum) is "Louisiana's most eccentric museum," and that is a serious understatement. The consummate roadside attraction features everything from the "House of Shards," bejeweled with chunks of shattered pottery, to "Aliens Trashed Our Airstream Trailer," a mobile home impaled by a flying saucer. Elsewhere, the museum houses Buford the Bassigator, collections of pocket combs and paint-by-number masterworks, a shrine to Elvis, and a miniature river town.

Home of the World's Tabasco Sauce Supply

Avery Island, Louisiana

Who would guess that all of the world's Tabasco sauce hails from this one island? It's true. Despite the fact that Tabasco sauce labels are printed in 21 languages and dialects, the sauce itself comes from here. Even more impressive, the McIlhenny Company, which started producing the sauce in 1868, still oversees the operation.

For those who've never experienced the "burn" of Tabasco sauce, a quick primer: The original Tabasco sauce measured 2,500 to 5,000 SHU on the Scoville Scale. Translation: It was one hot sauce. It is currently marketed in 160 different countries, and more than 700,000 bottles are produced each day at the Avery Island plant.

Tours of the facility are said to be one hot ticket. "See the original hottie" might make for a memorable slogan.

Too Hot to Handle

The Scoville Scale was named for its creator, Wilbur Scoville. In 1912, this American chemist devised a test to rate the heat of chili peppers. The scale ranges from 0 to 16,000,000 SHU. The hottest pepper in the world ranks a whopping 1,040,000 SHU.

Marie Laveau's House of Voodoo

New Orleans, Louisiana

Why visit knock-off voodoo shops when you can see the real thing? Marie Laveau's House of Voodoo is said to exist on the actual spot that legendary Voodoo queen Marie Laveau II called home. In fact, the queen is said to haunt her old haunts.

The store, rather smallish for so weighty an enterprise, features a Voodoo museum and sells Voodoo paraphernalia to neophytes (aka tourists) as well as seasoned practitioners. As one of New Orleans' most popular attractions, it's just the place to score that hard-to-find Voodoo doll or gris-gris bag.

Mardi Gras

New Orleans, Louisiana

French settlers in Alabama may have been the first to celebrate Mardi Gras in the New World, but these days nobody throws a bigger party than the good citizens of New Orleans. The tradition began when the French flag flew over New Orleans in the 1700s, but the Spanish government that followed put the kibosh on the event. It was resurrected after the U.S. government took over in the 1820s.

The annual celebration—held the two weeks before Catholic Lent, culminating in Fat Tuesday—is the nation's biggest blowout, a spectacle that's risque, chaotic, and over a million revelers strong. The parades are the true heart of Mardi Gras, organized by a number of "krewes" and featuring elaborate floats and the gaudiest assortment of costumes conceivable. For road-trippers who can't make it to the big party, there's a New Orleans museum—Mardi Gras World—that gives visitors a peek into the float-making process.

The Haunted LaLaurie Mansion

New Orleans, Louisiana

Marie Delphine LaLaurie was the crème de la crème of the high society of early 19th-century New Orleans. Rich, pretty, and intelligent, she entranced nearly everyone she met. But LaLaurie held a dark and diabolical secret: She delighted in torturing her slaves in heinous and despicable ways. Later, the spirits of those who died at LaLaurie's hand would come back to haunt the socialite's stately manor.

Social Butterflies

Marie was born in Louisiana around 1775. She was widowed twice and bore five children before marrying Dr. Leonard Louis LaLaurie in 1825. In the early 1830s, Marie and her husband moved into the stunning three-story mansion at 1140 Royal Street in New Orleans. It was regarded as one of the finest houses in the city and one that befit their social status, as the family was noted for its wealth and prominence in the community.

As visible parts of New Orleans society, the LaLauries frequently hosted grand parties that were attended by the city's most influential citizens. Like many wealthy people of the time, the LaLauries owned several slaves who cooked, cleaned, and maintained the property. Many guests remembered the finely dressed servants, who catered to their every need. But other LaLaurie slaves—sometimes glimpsed in passing—were surprisingly thin and hollow-chested. Rumors began to circulate that Madame LaLaurie was far from kind to her servants.

One neighbor claimed that he watched in horror as Madame LaLaurie chased a terrified female slave with a whip. The girl eventually made it to the roof of the mansion, where she chose to jump to her death rather than face her enraged owner's maniacal abuse. What happened to the girl's body remains a mystery: Some accounts say that it was buried on the property, while others report that it was dumped in an abandoned well.

A Fire Reveals All

The true extent of Marie LaLaurie's revolting cruelty was finally revealed in April 1834, when a fire broke out in the mansion. As the story goes, a cook who simply couldn't handle any more torture at the hands of Madame LaLaurie set the blaze. As the fire swept through the house and smoke filled the rooms, a crowd of onlookers gathered outside. Soon, the volunteer fire department arrived with buckets of water and bystanders offered their assistance. LaLaurie remained calm and directed the volunteers to save expensive paintings and smaller pieces of furniture. But when neighbors tried to enter the slave quarters to ensure that everyone got out safely, Madame LaLaurie refused to give them the key. Enraged, they broke down the door and were horrified to find several slaves tortured and mutilated. Many of the victims said that they'd been held captive for months.

The atrocities committed against the slaves in the LaLaurie home were depraved in the extreme. Some were found chained to the walls, and others were suspended by their necks with their limbs stretched and torn. One female slave was wearing a spiked iron collar that forced her head into an upright position. Some slaves were nearly starved to death, flayed with whips, and bound in painfully restrictive positions. Cruel experiments had been performed on some victims: Eyes were poked out, mouths were sewn shut, limbs were removed, and skulls were left open while they were still alive. The men who found the slaves were overwhelmed by the stench of death and decaying flesh, which permeated the confined chamber. A local newspaper reported that the bodies of tortured slaves were found buried around the grounds of the mansion.

When word of Marie LaLaurie's sadistic and grotesque crimes got out, an angry mob descended upon the mansion, breaking furniture, shattering windows, looting fine china and imported food, and destroying everything that it could find until only the walls remained. But by then, the LaLauries had already fled to France, never to be seen in New Orleans again.

Ghosts Take Up Residence

After the authorities restored order at the LaLaurie Mansion, the property was closed and sealed, and it sat completely empty for years...or so it seemed.

The spirits of the dead quickly claimed the house. Passersby often heard agonizing cries coming from the abandoned structure, and several people said that they saw apparitions of the murdered slaves walking on the home's balconies, peering out of windows, and roaming through the property's overgrown gardens. According to legend, vagrants who entered the building were never seen again.

The LaLaurie Mansion was purchased in 1837, but the buyer put it back on the market after only three months, claiming to have been driven out by weird noises and anguished cries in the night.

Hauntings Continue

In the years that followed, the LaLaurie Mansion was converted into a school for girls, abandoned again, and then converted into inexpensive apartments for immigrant laborers. Time and time again, the restless spirits of the tortured slaves made their presence known, much to the horror of the people who lived there. Once, a terrified tenant claimed that the spirit of a naked black man in chains attacked him and then vanished as quickly as it had appeared. Even cheap rent was not enough to convince tenants to stay for very long, and soon the house was vacant again.

The LaLaurie Mansion still stands today. Over the years, it has changed hands several times and has served as a saloon, a furniture store, a refuge for poor and homeless men, and an apartment building. In April 2007, actor Nicolas Cage purchased the property, but two and a half years later, it was back on the market. There have been no reports of ghostly activity there in recent years, but that doesn't mean the spirits of Marie LaLaurie's victims are resting in peace.

During a remodeling of the LaLaurie Mansion some years ago, workers discovered several unmarked graves under the floorboards of the house. This may explain why many of Madame LaLauries slaves simply disappeared, never to be seen again.

★ ★ ★ Midwest ★ ★ ★

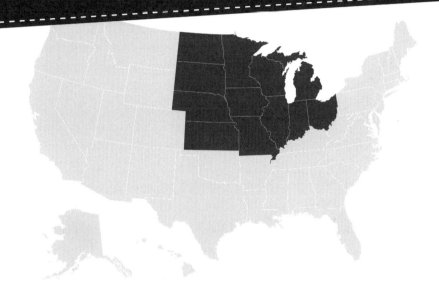

Vic Cook's Earthship

Pendleton, Indiana

In the late 1970s, Vic Cook was busy working as a high school music teacher and musician in Indiana. Unlike many of us, however, he was also busy dreaming of living a Walden-like existence in a low-cost, energy-efficient home in the woods.

While giving a guitar lesson one day, Cook told his student that he wanted to build a monument to nature but feared that the state's building codes would prevent it from happening. The student mentioned that his sister was trying to sell some wooded land in Pendleton, Indiana. Two weeks later, Cook purchased the land and had a site for his dream house. When he found an 1890s stove at a yard sale, he was on his way. Then he started digging.

Digging Deep

Cook eventually dug 22 feet down into the earth. He erected the walls of his house, each made from six inches of solid wood, which would also act as natural insulation for the house with the heat of the earth doing the rest. The result was that the house stayed around 68 degrees year-round, although a small kerosene heater is needed on rare occasions.

When it came to the roof and the structure that would be visible above ground, Cook wanted to make sure they were aesthetically pleasing and, more importantly, blended well with the natural environment. The roof, which included solar panels, was designed to be aerodynamic, making it able to withstand winds of 200 miles per hour. The panels used sunlight to power six solar batteries, which were capable of storing up to a month's supply of electricity for the entire house. A generator is kept on hand, though, just in case the sun decided not to make an appearance for several days.

All the Comforts of Home

Cook found his makeshift refrigerator one day when he came across a log in the woods. For the next six weeks, he worked on the refrigerator, hollowing it out, lining it with insulation, and adding a solar battery to it. The battery supposedly helped pull cool air out of the earth and into the log. Cook even added a freezer, which used nothing more than a microchip to cool down the earth's air.

The next comfort of home that Cook added to his house was running water. Obviously, he wasn't going to be able to get city water out in the woods and he wasn't keen on digging a well. Instead, he designed special tanks for the roof that could catch rainwater. Gravity was all it took to give Cook running water in the kitchen and bathroom. In keeping with the theme of the house being one with nature, Cook opted to go the composting route with his bathroom.

The most amazing thing of all is that Cook spent only about $30 each month on utilities, and because the house has no utility hookups, his property taxes were extremely low.

The Giant

Considering that the house had literally become one with the earth, Cook decided to name his labor of love the Earthship. Over the years, though, the house has acquired a nickname—the Giant—after Neil Armstrong's famous line about his "one giant leap for mankind." The line also reflected Cook's leap of faith into a one-man home-building project with a budget of less than $8,000. All in all, Cook spent more than a decade and 26,000 hours building his dream home. And before his death in 2010, he was always happy to show it off. For a time after his death, tours were still offered.

RV Hall of Fame
Elkhart, Indiana

The RV (Recreational Vehicle) Hall of Fame is a celebration of road trip adventure. Built in 1991, this 100,000-square-foot facility features Winnebagos, Airstreams, Holiday Ramblers, and scores of lesser-known vehicles. The hall-of-fame section includes the names of industry bigwigs and innovators. Dedicated RVers should be excused for not knowing any of them—after all, they were too darn busy RVing to pay the proper attention! They'd have it no other way.

Giant Ice Cream Man
Montpelier, Indiana

Looming tall over an ice cream stand, a man of uncommon size clutches a cone. Appearing to be a full 25 feet in height, this giant, replete with red blazer, wears a look of supreme satisfaction on his kisser. And why shouldn't he? With the Tin Lizzy Ice Cream Shop churning out endless refills below, he may well be in ice cream heaven. Yum!

The Mascot Hall of Fame

Whiting, Indiana

The Mascot Hall of Fame was originally founded by David Raymond who performed from 1978 to 1994 as the Phillie Phanatic. He was contacted by Whiting, Indiana, officials looking for something to complement its annual Pierogi Fest that brings 300,000 visitors to town. The three-story Mascot Hall of Fame opened there and brought its past inductees along.

Some of the mascot inductees include Mr. Met of the New York Mets, Big Red of Western Kentucky University, The Gorilla of the Phoenix Suns, and Brutus Buckeye of Ohio State University. In 2019, Benny the Bull of the Chicago Bulls, Tommy Hawk of the Chicago Blackhawks, Nittany Lion of Penn State University, and Sluggerrr of the Kansas City Royals were on hand for their induction ceremony.

Old Presque Isle Lighthouse

Presque Isle, Michigan

This lighthouse was decommissioned in 1870 and became a museum. In 1977, when George and Lorraine Parris were hired as caretakers, they ran the light regularly until the Coast Guard warned that running a decommissioned light was hazardous and illegal. To ensure it wouldn't happen again, the machinery that rotated the light was removed.

But since George's death in 1992, the lighthouse has frequently glowed at night—not so brightly as to cause harm but bright enough to be seen by passing ships and across the bay. Although the Coast Guard has classified it as an "unidentified" light, Lorraine believes that it is George, still happily working in his lighthouse.

American Museum of Magic

Marshall, Michigan

When modern-day magicians David Blaine and Criss Angel attempt a trick, they often expand on ideas originally dreamt up by the old masters. Harry Houdini, The Great Blackstone, and a score of others helped pave the way for today's breed; in their way, these newcomers give back by paying allegiance to their mystical predecessors. With such exchanges in mind, wouldn't it be great if there were a grand repository where magicians and fans alike could draw inspiration? There is. The American Museum of Magic lies a bit off the spotlight circuit in Marshall, Michigan, but it captivates nonetheless.

Bob Lund began collecting magicians' artifacts in the mid-1930s and didn't stop until his death in 1995. His cache is considered to be the world's largest privately-owned collection of magic bits, and that's saying something. Showcased in a three-story building, Lund's museum catalogues magic's numinous path from the days of Robert-Houdin (Houdini's idol and namesake) clear through to today's headliners.

Within its walls, magicphiles will find props, posters, costumes, films, photographs, virtually everything and anything pertaining to magic. Lund even aced the original Houdini "Milk Can" and Harry Blackstone's "Levitating Skull." It's unclear if Jean-Eugène Robert-Houdini makes ethereal appearances on Halloween, but if the great one were to return, we're certain he'd drop in for a visit.

Marvelous Marvin's Mechanical Museum

Farmington Hills, Michigan

Since 1990 when Marvin Tagoda turned his obsession for arcades and sideshows into a museum, we have all benefited. Who could live without old-time coin-operated machines or robotic fortune tellers? And that's just the normal stuff.

Tagoda's museum also features the Cardiff Giant, a knockoff of the real fake figure now located at Cooperstown, New York, and "The Drunkard's Dream," a 1935 coin-operated machine that illustrates what one sees when they've gone beyond their limit. The museum is so very offbeat it's listed in the *World Almanac's 100 Most Unusual Museums in the United States*.

Approximately 5,500 feet of floor space plays host to curiosities, animatronics dummies, pinball machines, posters, love and torture machines, and all manner of other techno-goodies. "Love and torture [machines] are the favorites," declares Tagoda. Somehow, we believe him.

The Paulding Ghost Lights

Paulding, Michigan

According to legend, an old railway brakeman was killed near the Choate Branch Railroad tracks that used to run near Paulding, Michigan, along the northern Wisconsin–Michigan border. People have observed strange lights near the tracks for decades, and it is said that they're from the railman's ghostly lantern swinging as he walks his old beat.

Others, armed with telescopes and binoculars, believe that the famed Paulding Light is actually caused by headlights shining from a highway a few miles away.

Still, many claim that the lights behave like anything but distant reflections. The lights are said to change from red to green, zoom up close as if peering into people's cars, chase people, flash through automobiles either cutting off all electric power or turning radios off and on, and zigzag through the nearby woods. Crowds flock to the Robins Wood Road site off Highway 45 to see the phenomenon for themselves, and a wooden sign has been erected complete with a drawing of a ghost swinging a lantern.

White River Light Station

Whitehall, Michigan

In the late 1850s, local mill owners and merchants became concerned about frequent shipwrecks occurring where the White River emptied into Lake Michigan near Whitehall, Michigan. The narrow river connected the lumber mills of White Lake (an area called "The Lumber Queen of the World") and the Great Lakes shipping channels. The state legislature responded by approving the construction of and funding for a lighthouse; however, the White River Light would not be built for another 12 years.

In 1872, a beacon light was set up at the area's South Pier, and shipping captain William Robinson was granted the position of light keeper. In 1875, the White River Light Station was built, and Robinson and his beloved wife, Sarah, moved into the keeper's residence, where they happily raised their 11 children. Robinson often said he was so happy there that he would stay until his dying day. That happiness was marred by Sarah's unexpected death in 1891. Robinson, who had expected to live with her at the lighthouse until his retirement, was inconsolable. Grief-stricken, he poured all of his attention into tending the lighthouse.

Like (Grand)father, Like (Grand)son

As Robinson grew older, the Lighthouse Board began to consider his replacement, finally awarding the post to his grandson (and assistant keeper), Captain William Bush, in 1915. Although the board expected Bush to immediately take over Robinson's duties, he kindly allowed his grandfather to continue as keeper and remain in the keeper's residence for several years.

In 1919, after 47 years of loyal service, the board demanded that Robinson vacate the premises, but he refused. The board allegedly met and agreed to take legal action against Robinson if he didn't leave, but they never got the chance. Two weeks later, on the day before the deadline, Robinson died in his sleep.

Bush moved into the residence, and the board was satisfied with their new man. But Captain Robinson stayed on, apparently still refusing to budge.

Thump, Thump, Tap

The lighthouse was decommissioned in 1960 and was turned into a museum in 1970. Today, museum staff and visitors believe that Robinson still occupies the building and continues his duties as lighthouse keeper. Curator Karen McDonnell lives in the lighthouse and reports hearing footsteps on the circular staircase in the middle of the night. She attributes this to Robinson, rather than natural causes, because of the unmistakable sound of his walking cane on the stairs.

McDonnell believes Robinson may have also gotten his wish—to stay in the lighthouse with his wife—because Sarah seems to have returned to the lighthouse as well. She helps with dusting and light housework, leaving display cases cleaner than they were before. Museum visitors often talk about feeling warm and safe inside the building and feeling a sense of love and peace. One tourist felt the presence of a smitten young couple, sitting in one of the window nooks.

We'll Leave the Light on for You

Visitors are welcome to explore the museum, which is open from June through October, and learn more about the shipping history of the Great Lakes. Perhaps you could even get a guided tour from the light's first and most loyal keeper—William Robinson, a man devoted to his wife and his job, who saw no reason why death should interfere with either.

Detroit Public Library–Skillman Branch

Detroit, Michigan

The Skillman Branch of the Detroit Public Library occupies the site of a former jailhouse where, in the early 1800s, prisoners were routinely executed. These tormented souls make their presence known by moaning and mumbling. They can be so disruptive that the stacks sometimes reverberate with the unsettling sounds.

The New Madrid Earthquake

New Madrid, Missouri

The New Madrid fault—near where Missouri, Kentucky, Arkansas, and Tennessee meet—witnessed an 8.0 or greater magnitude quake over 200 years ago. The shaking spread so far that church bells reportedly rang in Boston, more than 1,500 miles away! It had dramatic effects on the area's geography, lifting up land enough to make the Mississippi River appear to flow upstream. Fortunately, the sparsely populated area suffered only one death and minimal property damage.

In 1811 and 1812, Missouri and its surrounding states were rocked by devastating earthquakes. In late September 1811, Shawnee Chief Tecumseh did more than make an appeal for tribal unity against the whites–he vaunted himself a force of the highest order. "You do not believe the Great Spirit has sent me. You shall know," he reportedly said, "I...shall go straight to Detroit. When I arrive there, I will stamp on the ground with my foot and shake down every house in Tuckhabatchee."

On December 16, the day Tecumseh was thought to have arrived in Detroit, the first of a series of earthquakes—the most powerful ever to hit the United States—occurred in New Madrid, Missouri, and destroyed the small town of Tuckhabatchee.

In 1811, New Madrid was a popular destination for boatmen traveling the Mississippi River. New Madrid also sat directly on an active seismic fault zone three miles below the Earth's surface. By December, pressure that had been building up for centuries reached the breaking point.

December Jolt

The first quake happened on December 16 around 2:15 a.m. Suddenly, there was a sound like distant thunder. All at once the earth began to shake violently; people were thrown from their beds, furniture went flying across rooms, and trees snapped like twigs.

There was a "complete saturation of the atmosphere, with sulphurious vapor, causing total darkness," recalled an eyewitness. Lightning bathed the scene in eerie light. Ducks, geese, and other birds flew overhead, screeching loudly. Cattle stampeded. Panicked birds landed on human heads and shoulders. Chimneys crashed to the ground. "Confusion, terror and uproar presided," said one man.

New Madrid was not the only area hit hard. The town of Little Prairie, 30 miles downriver, was completely destroyed by the quake and its numerous aftershocks. One eyewitness saw the ground "rolling in waves of a few feet in height, with a visible depression between. By and by those swells burst, throwing up large volumes of water, sand and a species of charcoal."

On the water it was even worse. Boats were tossed around and swamped by the tremors. One boat was lifted 30 feet and propelled upriver for more than a mile—the Mississippi was running backward. "...All Nature was in a state of dissolution," one spectator later commented.

"The Devil Has Come Here"

For the next month, the earth continued its restless movement. On January 23, 1812, another quake struck. Eyewitness George Henrich Crist, who lived in north-central Kentucky, remembered:

"The earth quake or what ever it is come again today. It was as bad or worse than the one in December. We lost our Amandy Jane in this one—a log fell on her. A lot of people thinks that the devil has come here. Some thinks that this is the beginning of the world coming to a end."

Final Shot...?

Like a seasoned stage performer, Nature saved its biggest bang for the finale. The quake on February 7, which struck around 3:15 A.M., was as big or worse than the ones before it. It completely destroyed New Madrid. A boatman anchored off New Madrid wrote of "The agitated water all around us, full of trees and branches." He decided to keep his craft where it was as nearly two dozen other boaters frantically cut their mooring lines and headed for open water. They were never heard from again. A trapper hunting in Tennessee saw the ground "sink, sink, sink, carrying down a great park of trees."

"If we do not get away from here the ground is going to eat us alive," said Crist in Kentucky.

The New Madrid earthquakes were felt as far east as New York City (over 1,000 miles away) and as far south as Milledgeville, Georgia (575 miles). Only the area's scarce population prevented a greater loss of life.

Today the population of the area has grown enormously. And underneath them lies the New Madrid fault, like a ticking time bomb waiting to go off.

St. Joseph Public Library–Carnegie Branch

St. Joseph, Missouri

After hours, the ghostly footsteps of "Rose," who is thought to be a former librarian, are heard traipsing across the second floor. Although Rose is also blamed for phantom whispers and giggles, she takes her job very seriously and has been known to shush patrons. Rose also likes to put books back on the shelves, but she often puts them in the wrong place.

Branson's Wild World

Branson, Missouri

Far from the ocean, viewers can see deadly sharks along with more than 180 animal species at Branson's Wild World. This combination zoo and aquarium offers chances to interact directly with a number of animals. For those who want to drape a snake over their shoulder or dip their hand into a tank of fish, you know where to go.

Attractions as of this printing include "Deadly and Dangerous," featuring venomous snakes, spiders, and other threatening animals; the "Lemur Playground" that allows for interaction with adorable lemurs; and an outdoor wolf display called "Wolf Woods." The aquarium features sharks, eels, jellyfish, and piranha.

There's also a 3D blacklight miniature golf course where you can see fish along the way!

Leila's Hair Museum

Independence, Missouri

While Leila's Hair Museum sounds like it might feature luxurious tresses and locks, it actually displays items that were made from hair. Okay, so it's still plenty weird.

Cosmetologist Leila Cohoon was in a pickle in 1990. Her burgeoning hair-wreath collection was forcing her out of her digs. Confronted with the reality of losing her hairy companions forever, Cohoon wisely chose to allot them a display space at her new cosmetology studio.

Since then, the follicles have thrived. On display are some 2,000 pieces of hair jewelry, 150 hair wreaths, and a vast assortment of other hair-related items. "It could possibly be the only hair museum in the United States, maybe the world," boasts Leila. We shudder to think that this is true. There should be more. Hairs to us all!

Glore Psychiatric Museum

St. Joseph, Missouri

In a country raving-mad for its "mad" movie heroes (think R. P. McMurphy from *One Flew over the Cuckoo's Nest* or Michael Myers from *Halloween*), the Glore Psychiatric Museum was probably inevitable.

Chronicling the 130-year history of Missouri's "State Lunatic Asylum No. 2," the museum features replicas, artifacts, visual aids, and interactive displays that recall a time in psychiatric history when words for mental illness were more pointed and public perceptions more narrow.

Founder George Glore (an employee of Missouri's mental health system) spent 41 years assembling this collection into one so vast, it's recognized as "one of the 50 most unusual museums in the country."

Crazy exhibits abound but a few standouts are the "Bath of Surprise," a contraption that dumped a patient into icy water, and the "Giant Patient Treadmill," a gerbilesque megawheel where patients could walk their troubles away. One look at the treacherous "Tranquilizer Chair," and a patient could almost be scared out of insanity. Almost.

A. B. Safford Memorial Library

Cairo, Illinois

Resident spirit "Toby" likes to hang out on the second floor of the A. B. Safford Memorial Library. Staff members have heard his footsteps at night, and he's been blamed for the creaking noises that a rocking chair makes even when no one is in it and it's not moving. Toby has also been known to switch lights on and off. And library employees once witnessed a "ghostly light" emerge from behind a desk and travel down a hall before vanishing in the stacks.

Hippie Memorial

Arcola, Illinois

So said the Grateful Dead in their popular song, "Truckin." But the verse could just as easily apply to Bob Moomaw, creator of the self-proclaimed "world's only Hippie Memorial."

At some 62 feet long, Moomaw's personal journey (he lived for exactly 62 years) is catalogued in segments. The Great Depression, World War II, and 1950s hypocrisy crowds the first third. Next up is the Kennedy era and Moomaw's beloved Hippie invasion—a time span expressed by colorful peace symbols, freedom of expression scribbling, and a license plate reading, "WOODSTC." This era takes the memorial clear through to 1980, the year that Ronald Reagan was elected president. Moomaw celebrates this "downer" with 18 feet of plain rusted scrap.

Bob Moomaw disagreed with a great many things and an equal number of people during his lifetime, but he believed strongly in freedom of expression and the right to dissent. By all accounts, he'd fight to the death to preserve either. His Hippie Memorial stands as a fitting tribute to a man who was a thorn in the side of "established" America. Groovy.

Giant Uniroyal Woman Statue

Peoria, Illinois

When a person drives past Peoria Plaza Tire, they might be excused for thinking that they're witnessing the "Attack of the 50-foot Woman." In reality, this giant damsel is "only" 17.5 feet tall. Still, big is big no matter how you stack it.

In town since 1968, the ageless "Vanna Whitewall" (previously "Miss Uniroyal") isn't a jealous monster at all. She lives only to sell tires and hawk car repairs. At various times, the big gal has worn bikinis and skirts, and her hair color has seen some changes as well.

She currently sports a fetching blue skirt and red top. Her 108-72-108 measurements and 450-pound heft may not earn her a slot in a beauty contest, but she apparently plays well in Peoria.

Loveland Castle

Loveland, Ohio

Château Laroche ("stone castle"), or Loveland Castle, was the vision of Harry Andrews, an eccentric with a mission to propagate modern-day knighthood. Designed as a full-scale replica of a 10th-century French castle, the project was single-handedly built by Andrews from 1929 until his death in 1981. Even unfinished, the castle is a true fortification with 17 rooms, including an armory, banquet hall, chapel, master suite, great hall, and dungeon, as well as seven holes above the front door for pouring boiling oil upon invaders. Today, the castle is owned by a group of "knights"—medieval reenactors who uphold Andrews's vision. It is also reportedly home to a few resident ghosts.

Fairport Harbor Lighthouse

Fairport Harbor, Ohio

This lighthouse is rumored to have two rather playful ghosts. The first is of a keeper's young son who died. The second appears to be a charming gray kitten that routinely seeks out museum staff and visitors to play. Its spectral nature becomes apparent when visitors realize the kitten has no feet—it simply hovers above the ground. Although a former keeper's wife had a beloved kitten while she lived in the lighthouse, the "ghost cat" story was dismissed as silly until workers found the body of a cat in a crawl space there.

Futuro House

Carlisle, Ohio

The Futuro House of Carlisle, Ohio (one of a surprisingly large number of such structures located throughout the world), looks like it was lifted straight from a cartoon. Is the house a classic case of humanistic life forms copying art? Perhaps. Is it off-the-charts bizarre? Without a doubt.

The concept of the Futuro house was originally designed by Finnish architect Matti Suuronen in 1965. The Futuro in Carlisle, Ohio, features two oblong silver saucers connected by a tube/walkway. Nicknamed the "mating flying-saucer house" for this distinctive feature, the "risqué" structure really does come across as two spaceships "cozying up" for a visit.

"Y" Bridge

Zanesville, Ohio

One can only wonder how many unwitting souls have driven off of Zanesville, Ohio's, "Y" bridge. This sort of thing can easily occur on a bridge that's shaped like the letter "Y." What's the reason for such a funky configuration you might ask?

In its first incarnation as the Third Street Bridge (1813), designer Moses Dillon explained that the bridge would run, "from the point opposite Main Street in Zanesville to an Island at the mouth of the Licking River, thence north and south each way across the mouth of Licking Creek."

Since then, the unique span at the convergence of the Muskingum and Licking rivers has been rebuilt four times; its latest upgrade took place in 1984. As one of only two such bridges in the United States (the other is located in Galena, Missouri), the structure has become the pride of Zanesville. Citizens say that after crossing the span, you can still be on the side of the river from which you originated. A birds-eye view of the bridge shows that the boast is only partially true. No matter. It's still one crazy structure.

Today, the bridge stands gussied up with wider lanes and a modern stop light at its critical "Y" intersection. These, we presume, will keep unwary drivers from becoming sudden swimmers.

Wright-Patterson Air Force Base

Dayton, Ohio

An otherworldly legend makes its way from New Mexico to Ohio when the wreckage from Roswell ends up in the Midwest.

Even those who aren't UFO buffs have probably heard about the infamous Roswell Incident, where an alien spaceship supposedly crash-landed in the New Mexico desert, and the U.S. government covered the whole thing up. But what most people don't know is that according to legend, the mysterious aircraft was recovered (along with some alien bodies), secreted out of Roswell, and came to rest just outside of Dayton, Ohio.

Something Crashed in the Desert

While the exact date is unclear, sometime during the first week of July 1947, a local Roswell rancher by the name of Mac Brazel decided to go out and check his property for fallen trees and other damage after a night of heavy storms and lightning. Brazel allegedly came across an area of his property littered with strange debris unlike anything he had ever seen before. Some of the debris even had strange writing on it.

Brazel showed some of the debris to a few neighbors and then took it to the office of Roswell sheriff George Wilcox, who called authorities at Roswell Army Air Field. After speaking with Wilcox, intelligence officer Major Jesse Marcel drove out to the Brazel ranch and collected as much debris as he could. He then returned to the airfield and showed the debris to his commanding officer, Colonel William Blanchard, commander of the 509th Bomb Group that was stationed at the Roswell Air Field. Upon seeing the debris, Blanchard dispatched military vehicles and personnel back out to the Brazel ranch to see if they could recover anything else.

"Flying Saucer Captured!"

On July 8, 1947, Colonel Blanchard issued a press release stating that the wreckage of a "crashed disk" had been recovered. The bold headline of the July 8 edition of the *Roswell Daily Record* read: "RAAF Captures Flying Saucer on Ranch in Roswell Region." Newspapers around the world ran similar headlines. But then, within hours of the Blanchard release, General Roger M. Ramey, commander of the Eighth Air Force in Fort Worth, Texas, retracted Blanchard's release for him and issued another statement saying there was no UFO. Blanchard's men had simply recovered a fallen weather balloon.

Before long, the headlines that had earlier touted the capture of a UFO read: "It's a Weather Balloon" and "'Flying Disc' Turns Up as Just Hot Air." Later editions even ran a staged photograph of Major Jesse Marcel, who was first sent to investigate the incident, kneeling in front of weather balloon debris. Most of the general public seemed content with the explanation, but there were skeptics.

Whisked Away to Hangar 18?

Those who believe that aliens crash-landed near Roswell claim that, under cover of darkness, large portions of the alien spacecraft were brought out to the Roswell Air Field and loaded onto B-29 and C-54 aircrafts. Those planes were then supposedly flown to Wright-Patterson Air Force Base, just outside of Dayton. Once the planes landed, they were taxied over to Hangar 18 and unloaded. And according to legend, it's all still there.

There are some problems with the story, though. For one, none of the hangars on Wright-Patterson Air Force Base are officially known as "Hangar 18," and there are no buildings designated with the number 18. Rather, the hangars are labeled 1A, 1B, 1C, and so on. There's also the fact that none of the hangars seem large enough to house and conceal an alien spacecraft. But just because there's nothing listed as Hangar 18 on a Wright-Patterson map doesn't mean it's not there. Conspiracy theorists believe that hangars 4A, 4B, and 4C might be the infamous Hangar 18. As for the overall size of the hangars, it's believed that most of the wreckage has been stored in giant underground tunnels and chambers deep under the hangar, both to protect the debris and to keep it safe from prying eyes. It is said that Wright-Patterson is currently conducting experiments on the wreckage to see if scientists can reverse-engineer the technology.

So What's the Deal?

The story of Hangar 18 only got stranger as the years went on, starting with the government's Project Blue Book, a program designed to investigate reported UFO sightings across the United States. Between 1947 and 1969, Project Blue Book investigated more than 12,000 UFO sightings before being disbanded. And where was Project Blue Book headquartered? Wright-Patterson Air Force Base.

Then in the early 1960s, Arizona senator Barry Goldwater, himself a retired major general in the U.S. Army Air Corps (and a friend of Colonel Blanchard), became interested in what, if anything, had crashed in Roswell. When Goldwater discovered Hangar 18, he first wrote directly to Wright-Patterson and asked for permission to tour the facility but was quickly denied. He then approached another friend, General Curtis LeMay, and asked if he could see the "Green Room" where the UFO secret was being held. Goldwater claimed that LeMay gave him "holy hell" and screamed at Goldwater, "Not only can't you get into it, but don't you ever mention it to me again."

Most recently, in 1982, retired pilot Oliver "Pappy" Henderson attended a reunion and announced that he was one of the men who had flown alien bodies out of Roswell in a C-54 cargo plane. His destination? Hangar 18 at Wright-Patterson. Although no one is closer to a definitive answer, it seems that the legend of Hangar 18 will never die.

Abandoned Subway System

Cincinnati, Ohio

A plan to modernize the city that began at the turn of the century was abandoned and forgotten to history.

Attentive readers are probably scratching their heads, thinking, "Cincinnati doesn't have a subway."

They're partially right: The city does indeed have a subway, albeit an incomplete and abandoned one. It was designed to modernize the city but ended up as a symbol of how even the best-laid plans can go astray.

Cincinnati Needs a Facelift

With the dawning of the 20th century, Cincinnatians were looking for ways to modernize. When it came to transportation, the mode of choice was the Miami-Erie Canal, which made its way alongside the city. The waterway had been an efficient means of transporting people and goods, but that was back in Cincinnati's infancy. As the population grew, the canal became a literal cesspool filled with debris and disease-carrying insects. But rather than clean the canal, city officials decided to resurrect a plan that had been discussed since the 1870s instead: turn the canal into a subway line. It seemed like a massive undertaking, but as officials started talking about the logistics, the idea began making sense. The canal bed already existed, and once drained, it would provide a perfect foundation for a subway. Workers could simply follow the canal's path to lay the tracks down. Once they encased the whole thing in concrete and steel and added a couple of stations, voilà—instant subway! Because the canal was roughly 40 feet wide, workers could get right inside the bed to work, thereby keeping construction congestion to a minimum.

Planning the Subway

In 1905, the first official plans saw the light of day. The plans called for running four parallel tracks for two miles between Walnut and Race streets up to near the Western Hills Viaduct. From there, one set of tracks would connect with the existing Cincinnati and Westwood Interurban train line, while the second set connected with another train line to the north. But when it was discovered that all three tracks were different sizes and gauges, the idea was put on hold, and planners were sent back to the drawing board. In December 1914, developers presented a revised plan calling for a two-track, 16-mile loop around the city, referred to as the Rapid Transit Loop, as well as almost 20 stations. The report listed four different configurations, or "schemes," by which to lay out the tracks. A very excited Rapid Transit Commission immediately took steps to get a bond issue on an upcoming ballot and ensure the funds would be available to begin construction.

"Is This Thing Ever Gonna Get Built?"

A $6 million bond issue for the construction of the subway was approved in 1916. The commission eventually chose Scheme IV, which called for a four-mile stretch of track to be placed underground from Ludlow Avenue to 3rd Street in downtown. It seemed as though the wheels of progress were finally turning—that is, until April 1917, when the United States entered World War I. Because bonds were not allowed to be issued during times of war, Cincinnati was unable to get any of the expected $6 million, and breaking ground on the subway had to be postponed.

It wasn't until 1919 that workers began draining the canal and another year before actual construction began. But a $6 million bond from before the war did not hold the same value afterward. As a result, Scheme IV couldn't be completed as originally intended. After making a few adjustments and eliminating some stations along the route, however, it was full steam ahead on the construction. At least for a while.

The Bottom Drops Out

By 1925, a two-mile-long tunnel running from Walnut Street to just north of the Western Hills Viaduct had been constructed. Three underground stations had also been completed along the route—one at Brighton's Corner, another at Liberty, and one at Race Street—with a fourth station just beginning construction. Plans were also underway for an offshoot of the tracks on Walnut Street to go through downtown to a station at Fountain Square. Then it happened: The $6 million ran out.

With no money left and an estimated $10 million still needed to complete the subway, plans were once again put on hold. The project was still delayed in 1929 when the stock market crashed, paving the way for the Great Depression.

Years later, it was decided that the existing subway would be too costly to finish, and officials would instead modernize Cincinnati by creating a new motorway, Central Parkway, right over the existing subway. The Cincinnati Subway project was abandoned for good in 1948.

What Lies Beneath

Since the last digging tool was quieted within the subway more than 60 years ago, visitors can tour the abandoned tunnel, but city officials remain at a loss for what to do with it. It was furnished as a fallout shelter in 1962, but the need for it had ended by the 1980s.

Proposals to turn the subway into everything from an underground shopping mall to a massive wine cellar have been floated, but none have yet come to fruition. City officials are in a bind, because even filling in the tunnels is a costly proposition.

Too expensive to demolish and too archaic to resurrect, the Cincinnati subway sits quietly below ground, with only the dull rumble of cars on the Central Parkway overhead to keep it company.

The National Bobblehead Hall of Fame
Milwaukee, Wisconsin

The National Bobblehead Hall of Fame and Museum in Milwaukee, Wisconsin, displays 6,500 unique bobbleheads and boasts a collection that is 10,000 bobbleheads strong. The museum features dozens of exhibits, and a store with over 500 bobbleheads available for purchase. The collection is thought to be 75% sports-related with the rest being related to TV, movie, or pop culture.

The collection started when college buddies Brad Novak and Phil Sklar would attend sporting events on giveaway nights, that is, until the collection grew out of hand. The two are now co-owners of the museum and manufacture their own bobbleheads as well. At the museum patrons can design their own custom oversized plastic head or view a six-foot-tall life-sized bobblehead on display.

Fred Smith's Wisconsin Concrete Park
Phillips, Wisconsin

Born in 1886, Fred Smith operated as a north woods lumberjack until 1949. During his retirement—a time when many others relax and celebrate past victories—Smith got busy. Real busy.

The self-taught sculptor would build a veritable city of wood-framed concrete figures and distribute them around his Rock Garden Tavern, a business he acquired while lumberjacking. There would be miners, cowboys, Indians, and soldiers—all congregated in a splendid mishmash of Smith's folksy art. Just after the lumberjack/artist died in 1976, a storm leveled three-quarters of his figures. Luckily, the Kohler Foundation stepped in and restored all to their former glory.

Paul and Matilda Wegner Grotto
Sparta, Wisconsin

Borrowing a page from Fred Smith's playbook, Paul Wegner got antsy when confronted with retirement. After seeing Father Mathias's Dickeyville Grotto in 1929, Wegner's eureka moment arrived. With help from wife Matilda, he would build his own grotto from "found materials."

Actually, grotto is somewhat misleading in this case. The Wegner's series of concrete and glass sculptures are nondenominational and include such items as the Bremen, a 12-foot concrete model of the celebrated ocean liner; a glass church; an American flag; a peace model; and—to celebrate their 50th wedding anniversary—an ornate wedding cake.

After Paul's death in 1937, Matilda carried on until she too made her final exit in 1942. In 1986, the Kohler Foundation restored the grotto to its former glory and presented it as a gift to the county of Monroe. The Wegners' legacy lives on.

Statue of "Romeo," the Killer Elephant
Delavan, Wisconsin

In the 1800s, when 25 circuses wintered here, the town of Delavan was considered the "Circus Capital of the World." Needless to say, this place saw more than its share of pachyderms. Most of these behemoths did typical elephant tricks and acted in a typical elephant way. Then there was Romeo. Over a 15-year period, the "killer" elephant erased the lives of some five trainers via foot stomps, crushing accidents, and tusk impalements. Why wasn't the animal executed for his crimes? Here's where it gets good.

They say Romeo suffered a broken heart when his beloved Juliet passed on to that great elephant graveyard in the sky. So, in effect, his attacks were really a form of grief resolution. It's a great story but not at all true. In reality, Romeo was one ornery elephant. Period.

For reasons perhaps unfathomable, the good people of Delavan decided to honor Romeo with a full-size statue. Their fiberglass re-creation features the bloodthirsty fellow standing on his hind legs, eager to trounce. Below him, a clown blissfully unaware of his impending doom stands smiling. Folks, you just can't make this stuff up!

Rock in the House
Fountain City, Wisconsin

What would you do if a 55-ton boulder suddenly came crashing through your walls? If you were Maxine and Dwight Anderson, you would leave well enough alone and move out. The couple, who lived in a two-bedroom house along the Mighty Mississippi, experienced such terror on April 24, 1995, when a giant rock rolled some 400 feet down a cliff and came to rest in their bedroom. Thankfully, no one was injured.

The Andersons would ultimately sell their house to an enterprising gent named John Burt. In no time, the offbeat "Rock in the House" attraction would open. The premise was simple. Visitors would leave a buck (on the honor system) for strategic views of the rock. They'd also have an opportunity to purchase T-shirts at, we imagine, "rock-bottom prices." All's well that ends well, as they say. Rock on!

The Haunted Mounds Theater
St. Paul, Minnesota

In 1922, the Mounds Theatre opened on the east side of St. Paul, Minnesota, to showcase silent films. A few dramatic characters from that era are said to remain in the restored Art Deco building, but these entities are not confined to the silver screen.

The most frightening spook at the Mounds is the spectral male figure that lurks in the dusty, antiquated projection room. Building director Raeann Ruth and three paranormal investigators who spent a night in the room all reported hearing a male voice alternately cry and swear up a storm. They also witnessed an angry male ghost staring at them with dark, sunken eyes. It certainly didn't help to alleviate any fears when the group discovered an antique Ouija board lying amid the old projection equipment.

A more benign ghost is dressed as an usher and seems to be crying. According to legend, he was a theater worker who found his beloved cuddling with someone else. It is believed that after death, he stayed attached to the scene of his life's greatest tragedy.

Tragic may also be the best way to describe another Mounds Theatre ghost—a young girl who skips around the stage bouncing a ball. During a renovation (2001-2003), a small dress and a child's shoe were found hidden in the theater. Some believe that these items could be linked to a possible child assault, which could explain why the girl's spirit still roams the theater.

SPAM Museum

Austin, Minnesota

When World War II soldiers saw a tin of SPAM coming their way, some reportedly said, "Ham, SPAM ... Not that again!" Fortunately for Hormel Foods, maker of the famous luncheon meat, this was not the majority opinion.

In fact, SPAM (the lunch meat, not the unsolicited e-mail) is beloved. So much so that the company founded a mall-based museum in its honor in 1991. They chose Austin since it was here that George A. Hormel started his meat-making dynasty way back in 1891. Since that time, the processed meat marvel has "spammed" the decades. As has the museum, which now finds itself in a larger, tastier facility.

Inside, an electronic counter tallies all SPAM production; 3,390 SPAM cans rise tall in the lobby, and a display shows how SPAM helped the Allies win World War II, keeping the world safe for democracy and future SPAM consumption. Spamalicious!

Frank Lloyd Wright Gas Station

Cloquet, Minnesota

With modern-day gas stations taking us all "to the cleaners," a look at past offerings might be in order. In the case of Frank Lloyd Wright's contribution, that look is quite fetching indeed. Celebrated architect Wright built his prototype service station under a distinctive copper roof in 1956. He assumed it would wow the nation. It didn't. Most people passing through are oblivious to the great work standing over the requisite grease pit and gasoline drips, and that's a darned shame.

What folks might not realize is that this gas station is Wright's only realized design for "Broadacre City," his vision of a Utopian enclave. For this reason, a sign looms just below the giant Phillips 66 symbol. It reads: "World's only Frank Lloyd Wright service station." Despite an errant grease drop or three, it is that and so very much more.

Shrine of the Grotto of the Redemption

West Bend, Iowa

Had it not been for a bout of pneumonia, the Shrine of the Grotto of the Redemption would never have been built. At least that's how legend explains it. Father Paul Matthias Dobberstein (1872–1954), a German immigrant, was said to have developed pneumonia while studying at the Seminary of St. Francis outside of Milwaukee. At death's door, the seminarian prayed to the Blessed Virgin Mary and vowed to build her a shrine if he was spared. The grotto stands as his fulfillment of that promise.

Starting in 1912 and ending upon his death, Dobberstein created nine distinct grottos, each depicting a scene from the life of Jesus Christ. Featuring the Ten Commandments, The Trinity Grotto, Stations of the Cross, Grotto of the Resurrection, the Stable of Bethlehem and many more epic moments in Christianity, the grotto is so immense, it is touted as the world's largest. While we can't speak to that, we can say that the grotto is profoundly beautiful. It's truly a gift to behold.

Snake Alley

Burlington, Iowa

"There was a crooked man and he walked a crooked mile..." Should this nursery rhyme spring to life, the crooked man might just go in search of Snake Alley for a sliver of his convoluted jaunt. Billed as the "Crookedest Street in the World" by none other than Ripley's Believe It or Not, Snake Alley would certainly be up any crooked man's (or woman's) alley!

Built in 1894 as a way to tame a steep hillside, the experimental design would provide a direct link between Burlington's business district and a neighboring shopping area. Heralded as a "triumph in practical engineering" by local newspapers, the city proposed other such crooked streets, but the switchback design proved troublesome to horses, and plans were eventually scrapped.

The street remains intact to this day. Surprisingly, its brickwork is the very same batch originally laid down in 1894. How's that for far-sighted engineering?

Field of Dreams

Dyersville, Iowa

"If you build it, he will come." This simple sentence from the 1989 movie *Field of Dreams* has joined a prestigious list of Hollywood's most memorable lines. The wildly successful film, rooted in baseball and the culmination of dreams, touched a certain chord in people. Stories about second chances have an uncanny way of doing that.

The field, with its outermost reaches dissolving mysteriously into rows of corn, was in fact very real. It was built at the Lansing farm in the summer of 1988 solely for the movie.

When the film crew packed up, something rather startling happened. People, captivated by the story, flocked to see the field for themselves. They came from virtually everywhere and continue to come to this very day. While this surprises most of us, there's at least one man who has gotten used to it all by now. He answers to the nickname "Shoeless Joe." Some say he can be found out there amongst the cornrows.

Villisca Axe Murder House

Villisca, Iowa

This overnight lodge in Villisca, Iowa, offers something most others do not: Murder. Actually, they're selling a murder mystery here, but unlike a gaggle of other such faux operations, this one is completely legit. As a bonus, it's reportedly haunted. Should we put you down for a night?

The Villisca Axe Murder House was the site of one of the most grisly murders in Iowa history. On the morning of June 10, 1912, six members of the J. B. Moore family and two visiting children were chopped to bits as they lay sleeping in their beds.

Suspects were as numerous as motives, but nothing could be pinned down. At one point a preacher confessed to the murders, but he later recanted. Two trials and a grand jury investigation led absolutely nowhere. To this day, the grisly murders remain unsolved.

If you visit, owner Darwin Linn will scare the pants off you with tales of a creepy looking "love-lies-bleeding" plant that popped up unexpectedly during house renovations, or send chills down your spine by recounting an incident wherein a Des Moines disc jockey slept over and was awakened by the voices of nonexistent children. At $50 a night, the ax-murder house may just stop your heart. Says Linn ominously: "You're on your own until 8:00 a.m. the following morning." Once again, should we put you down for a night?

Ida Grove Castles

Smack dab in the middle of America's heartland, a profusion of castles sure do stand out. Are they a promotion of some sort, designed for their incongruity? Not at all. They are simply the end result of one man's burning passion. And this man had the means to turn his obsession into reality.

He went by the noble tag Byron LeRoy Godberson (1925–2003). As a wealthy inventor and industrialist, Godberson could pretty much do as he pleased. If it was castles that he liked, then it was castles that he'd build. And build he did.

The town of Ida Grove looks like something straight out of the Middle Ages with a castle tower welcoming visitors into town. Once inside, it becomes apparent that the castle theme is pervasive. The shopping center is shaped like a castle. So is the newspaper office. The local roller rink looks like something straight out of Disney World's Magic Kingdom. Even the town golf course features a medieval suspension bridge with imposing turrets on either end.

In addition to Ida Grove's castles, Godberson also created a half-scale replica of the sailing ship the HMS *Bounty.* The grand ship took 12 weeks to complete but when launched in Lake LaJune in 1970, it floated like a champ. In 1971, a group of Godberson's employees summoned sea recovery Captain Irving Johnson to Ida Grove. As a Christmas gift, the seaman presented Godberson with a bronze fitting from the original Bounty. The tall ship floats in the lake nearly four decades after its launch, a testament to its superb craftsmanship.

Lake LaJune was named for Godberson's wife, LaJune.

Hutchinson Public Library

Hutchinson, Kansas

After librarian Ida Day Holzapfel died in 1954, she began to hang around her former place of employment, the Hutchinson Public Library. One day in 1975, a librarian saw a strange woman hovering below the stairs, and after describing what she had seen to a coworker, her colleague identified the visitor as Holzapfel. Footsteps and disembodied voices have been heard in the basement, and some witnesses have glimpsed Holzapfel's apparition in the stacks.

Dalton Defenders and Coffeyville History Museum

Coffeyville, Kansas

By the late 1800s, citizens of the West were fast losing their patience with lawlessness and the perpetrators that forced it upon them. So on October 5, 1892, when the legendary Dalton Gang rode into Coffeyville hoping to separate the town's banks from their money, the citizens decided to take a stand. When the Daltons tried to launch their escape after the robbery, citizens armed to the teeth opened fire. The gun battle would leave four of the five gang members dead and would claim the lives of four Coffeyville defenders.

The Dalton Defenders and Coffeyville History Museum pays homage to its martyred liberators with a collection of photos and artifacts and has even seen fit to preserve the actual vault doorway of the banks. Perhaps their most prized possession is a wall-size photo of the four Dalton boys lying lifeless on a board. "'Twas the defenders that brought them down," the curator will quickly remind you. Indeed it was.

Monkey Island

Independence, Kansas

"Miss Able," a rhesus monkey hailing from Monkey Island's Ralph Mitchell Zoo, became one of the first living beings (alongside "Miss Baker," a squirrel monkey) to survive a trip into space aboard *Jupiter AM-18* on May 28, 1959.

The pint-size primate withstood speeds in excess of 10,000 mph during her heroic journey. Sadly, she was lost a day after her epic voyage during surgery to remove an electrode. Originally built in 1932, Miss Able's former home still operates, but it's a bit grown over these days. A prominent sign pays homage to the hairy dynamo that never had a chance to enjoy her fame.

Don Kracht's Castle Island

Junction City, Kansas

Who says math teachers lack imagination? As the builder of his very own medieval fortress, retired teacher Don Kracht dispelled this silly notion quicker than a charging knight thrusts his lance. And while we're slaying stereotypes, here's another one. Don Kracht never harbored visions of building a castle. "The castle just kinda came to me," said the unassuming man who went in search of projects for his retirement. "I just started doing it."

He most certainly did. Kracht's castle features bridges, sculptures, balconies, turrets, a courtyard fountain, gargoyles and angels, spiral staircases, and of course, the requisite lookout tower. Kracht continually added items to his castle; as a result, its features kept multiplying. Unfortunately, as of this printing, the castle can only be viewed from the road.

The Atomic Cannon

Junction City, Kansas

There are booms, and there are BOOMS. The destructive force produced by America's atomic cannons of the 1950s clearly fell into the latter category. Designed to lob nuclear shells at enemy forces while maintaining a safe distance, atomic cannons could hurl a 280mm shell up to 20 miles. This buffer zone was necessary since the bomb's yield was in the 15-kiloton range, or 15,000 tons of TNT, precisely the figure associated with the historic blast at Hiroshima.

A handful of these misery-makers exist, with the unit at Junction City purportedly the world's largest. Although deactivated in 1963, the launcher shows how very serious America's Cold War fears were. The fact that it's now displayed in a public park does little to soften the cannon's original intent.

Big Brutus

West Mineral, Kansas

Big Brutus, a genuine "monster" truck looms large at West Mineral's Mined Land Wildlife Area. Calling Big Brutus large is akin to calling Einstein smart. At 16 stories tall (160 feet) and 11 million pounds, this electric earth-moving shovel seems as if it could push the earth off its axis.

Designed to mine coal from southeastern Kansas coal beds, Brutus was active from 1963–1974. The behemoth's great hunger for electricity proved its ultimate downfall. Big Brutus wasn't the first to be done in by gluttony, and he certainly won't be the last. R.I.P. big boy.

Concrete Teepee

Lawrence, Kansas

When this giant teepee found its way onto the scene around 1930, the Wild West era had long passed. People now needed a place to sleep as they "rode" their gas-guzzling "horses" across the range, and the "Indian Village" complex was happy to oblige.

Comprised of a restaurant, filling station, and motor court featuring smaller teepees, travelers would step into this enormous weatherproof teepee to conduct their business. At 33 feet in diameter, more than a few "greenhorns" could be accommodated. Today, all that remains of the operation are a few abandoned outbuildings and the big teepee itself— slowly decaying mementos of a simpler, more playful time.

Carhenge

Alliance, Nebraska

Carhenge, the funky automotive version of England's mystical stone circle, emerged in 1987 from a plan that had as much to do with remembrance as it did with art. Built to memorialize the passing of artist Jim Reinders's father, a circle of 38 cars were planted and precariously balanced upon each other in a 96-foot footprint that precisely replicated Stonehenge.

The end result is part Druid, part Detroit, and undeniably wacky. In keeping with the original monoliths, all cars have been spray-painted a stonelike grey. This produces the proper look even as it staves off rust.

World's Largest Time Capsule

Seward, Nebraska

Buried beneath a pyramid (where else?), a grand cache billed as the world's largest time capsule spends, well, an inordinate amount of time. Scheduled for opening in 2025, this is a time capsule with a difference.

Harold Keith Davidson wanted to leave something to his grandkids. While granddads of the past have left tattered scrapbooks and sepia-toned photos to their descendants, Davidson decided to leave something a bit more substantive: his era.

Within the 5,000 items that Davidson deep-sixed, his grandchildren will find such 1970's mainstays as a leisure suit, bikini panties, a new Kawasaki motorcycle and Chevy Vega (it was the cheapest car Davidson could find), plus a plethora of assorted gear.

According to an attached plaque, the Pyramid, added for extra size in 1983, contains a "badly beaten up 1975 Toyota plus other memorabilia." If we were Davidson's grandkids, we'd hold out for the pristine Vega.

The Haunted Nebraska Wesleyan University

Lincoln, Nebraska

In 1912, Clarissa Mills was chosen to head up the music department and teach piano at Nebraska Wesleyan University. She was well liked by students and her peers, but in 1940, she died of unknown causes at her desk in the C. C. White building. For more than 20 years thereafter, all was normal, but in 1963, faculty member Coleen Buterbaugh stepped into Clarissa's old office and was never the same again. First she smelled the odor of gas, and then she felt an unknown presence in the room. In front of her stood the ghostly image of a tall, frail woman—Clarissa Mills. But that wasn't all: When she looked out the window, everything modern was gone. There were no paved streets, and a recently built sorority house was simply no longer there. Clarissa continued to haunt the building until it burned down in 1973. Some say Clara might still linger on the campus of Nebraska Wesleyan University.

Harold Warp's Pioneer Village

Minden, Nebraska

Judging by its name, you might expect to find Conestoga wagons and mock-ups of the Oregon Trail featured here, but pioneering covers far more than any one period. It's a fact not lost on Harold Warp. With Pioneer Village, the collector attempts to cover the period from 1830–1960, a super-productive span that ranks among the most fruitful in American history.

Making his fortune in plastics, Warp had the means to acquire some 50,000 artifacts but needed a place to showcase them. He accomplished this with 28 separate buildings and more than 100,000 square feet of display space.

Inside, visitors will find an eclectic hodgepodge of Americana including a frontier fort, general store, art collections, historic flying machines, antique tractors and automobiles, atomic power displays—pretty much everything and anything that helped bring America to its present point. Does this include a Conestoga wagon, the overland vehicle that opened up the West? You bet your pioneering spirit it does!

National Presidential Wax Museum

Keystone, South Dakota

Situated just below Mount Rushmore, the National Presidential Wax Museum features all 46 presidents and includes major scenes from history. Here's President Franklin

Delano Roosevelt at Yalta, there are the signers of the Declaration of Independence. You get the idea. A more recent exhibit pays homage to 9/11 with President George W. Bush hugging a fireman while standing on the debris pile at "Ground Zero."

Dinosaur Park
Rapid City, South Dakota

After Mount Rushmore was completed, the area around the monument experienced an economic boom. This was particularly true of Rapid City, a settlement of note sitting just to its east. Yet Dinosaur Park, a Rapid City attraction featuring full-scale replicas of our planet's prehistoric inhabitants, has never charged a dime for admission. What gives? The truth is Dinosaur Park represents the height of civility in a decidedly uncivilized world. Come again?

The idea for Dinosaur Park was concocted by the city and the WPA (Works Progress Administration) during the Great Depression. While it hoped to educate and entertain with its seven dinosaur displays, it would do so only as a by-product. Putting unemployed men back to work was its central mission. On May 22, 1936, huge dinosaurs joined equally huge presidents in the Black Hills region. They stand there today, looking a bit cartoonlike, but the big fellows have nevertheless accomplished their task. By instilling fear and wonder in tourist's hearts, they spared their hard working re-creators the incivility of a breadline. Thanks, T-Rex.

Wall Drug
Wall, South Dakota

Perhaps one of the more mainstream attractions within these covers, Wall Drug nevertheless deserves its ink. Apparently, its owners feel much the same since colorful Wall Drug billboards are plastered along a 500-mile stretch of I-90 from Minnesota to Billings, Montana. Each promises weary travelers an oasis of fun, food, and shopping just up ahead.

There's good reason for this. Wall Drug isn't so much a drugstore as a grand happening. Out here in the South Dakota hinterlands, where the people are sparse and the entertainment even more so, such diversions are as treasured as water in the desert.

And speaking of water, it was simple H2O that really got the ball rolling for this fun-time establishment. But that's getting a bit ahead of things. Here's the back story.

Wall Drug started on its path to commercial immortality back in 1931 when it was acquired by pharmacist Ted Hustead. Since it was located in an absurdly small town of just more than 300 residents, and an economic depression was underway, Ted's sales were less than stellar. Then, out of the blue, wife Dorothy seized upon an idea. Since thirst was a constant along the dusty roads of the region, Wall Drug would advertise free ice water to parched travelers. The gimmick worked. In no time, the Husteads saw a steady flow of customers. This translated to increased profits, which were then funneled into expansion, and Wall Drug—the happening—was created.

So, just what's at this place? Actually, what isn't here might be more fitting. Wall Drug includes a roaring T-Rex dinosaur; a miniature version of Mount Rushmore; an area to mine, pan, and dig for gold; a westward discovery show; a teepee; a stagecoach; a picnic area; a food shop; an art gallery; a jackalope display; an emporium; a chapel; a western boot and clothing store; a souvenir stand; and many, many more tourist lures. They even sell aspirin and prescriptions to anyone still interested in drug items. Crazy, huh?

These days, the enterprise still offers free ice water to thirsty travelers, and people keep right on coming. And why shouldn't they? As a much-welcomed respite from the long, boring road, the new, improved Wall Drug is simply without peer. A kazillion billboards can't be wrong!

Mitchell Corn Palace

There aren't many American travel guides that overlook the Mitchell Corn Palace. While this may sound like it qualifies the attraction for mainstream status, we assure you it does not. After all, how many buildings can you actually eat?

The original "Corn Belt Exposition" went up in 1892. It became an impromptu chamber of commerce where proud farmers would display their best crops on its exterior. Over the years the plantings continued. A grand tradition had begun.

These days, the third corn expo (now called the Mitchell Corn Palace) acts as a living canvas and features artful murals made from corn, grasses, straw, wheat, and other tasty bits extracted from good mother Earth.

An enormous festival is held at the Corn Palace each year. It brings national-level entertainment into Mitchell and kicks off a new design for the murals and panels. In 2007–2008, "Everyday Heroes" was chosen as a theme. It celebrated teachers, doctors, parents, crossing guards, social workers— basically everyone and anyone who has made a difference in our world.

Inside the Corn Palace, people do what they usually do in large spaces. From sporting events to stage shows, the ornate building proves it can entertain even as it continues to "grow."

Concrete USS *South Dakota*

As we learned with New Jersey's SS *Atlantus* and other floating "deadweights," concrete ships don't fare too well on the high seas. So it's a good thing the concrete USS *South*

Dakota is permanently dry-docked. Actually, that's somewhat misleading. The proud battleship was once a svelte, classy vessel made from steel. Her concrete overcoat came only after she was decommissioned and turned into a memorial.

But that too is misleading. Here's the scuttlebutt: In 1962, the USS *South Dakota* was scrapped. When her home state decided to memorialize her, instead of transporting the entire vessel to Sioux Falls, they kept a few guns, her propeller, anchor, and bell. Not enough to replicate an entire ship, you say? It is if you lay down a fake foot-high concrete outline and plant the genuine items in it.

The end result is a funky-looking "ship" that's part grassland, part armament, and totally strange. At 680 feet long, the unusual hybrid confounds, amuses, and memorializes. Only in America.

Salem Sue/World's Largest Holstein Cow
New Salem, North Dakota

With 50-foot-tall men and women running amok throughout America (not to mention this book), you may be wondering where they get their milk from. Well, wonder no more. Salem Sue, a fiberglass bovine of mind-boggling proportions, is "utterly" the best when it comes to milk production. She should be. Her belly is larger than a milk truck!

Sue is 38 feet tall by 50 feet long and visible for some five miles. Erected in 1974 by the New Salem Lions Club, the "big moo" was designed to promote Holstein herds. One can only imagine how well she does this since she's fully visible to busy I-94 traffic.

With Salem Sue's history now known, you may be wondering who milks the "grand dame of the barnyard." It's a tall order but we're guessing the Lions Club provides this service. In fact, it appears that they've been "milking" her since 1974. Moo!

Enchanted Highway

Regent, North Dakota

When it comes to "sizable" art, Gary Greff is without peer. The former schoolteacher, who is completely untrained in art and engineering, decided to undertake both to put his town on the map. What he ultimately built must be seen to be believed.

Greff's great works stand alongside a 32-mile road dubbed the Enchanted Highway. There, visitors will find what's billed as the world's largest steel sculptures. The claim may actually be true. Gary's *Geese in Flight* leads that vaunted category in the *Guinness Book of World Records*. Suffice to say, at 110 feet tall, 154 feet long, and loaded with geese, you wouldn't want to park your car beneath it.

Then there's *Grasshopper's Delight*. If you recall the 1950's flick *Them*, (where radiation-tainted ants grow huge and threaten the world) you sort of get the picture. Just replace the critters with a 40-foot-tall grasshopper and start running for shelter.

On a somewhat calmer note, observe *Theodore Roosevelt Rides Again*. In this sculpture, the famed "Rough Rider" barely controls a rearing horse. Nevertheless, "Teddy" manages to raise one hand in triumph, perhaps signaling that the West will soon be won. As with all of Greff's sculptures, this 51-foot-tall offering required the help of many volunteers.

In addition to this trio, four more whimsical sculptures loom large along the Enchanted Highway. All are made from discarded items, and all appear to have been created by a fine, seasoned artist. But then Gary Greff is a fine, seasoned artist. It's just that his seasoning is rather new.

Gary Greff's first sculptures were his *Tin Family*, constructed in 1991. The family consists of a Tin Lady, a Tin Man, and a Tin Boy. The Tin Man is the tallest (naturally) at 45 feet. Sixteen telephone poles help to hold him upright.

Fargo Walk of Fame

Fargo, North Dakota

A hand and foot up on the competition? That's what Fargo businessman Mike Stevens seemed to be thinking when he devised the Fargo Walk of Fame.

Patterned after the famous Grauman's (now Mann's) Chinese Theatre in Los Angeles, the walk contains more than 100 celebrity signatures, handprints, and footprints.

It's almost as if Fargo is throwing down the gauntlet and issuing Hollywood a challenge. With stars such as Garth Brooks, KISS, Neil Diamond, and Tiny Tim doing the Fargo plaster act, the west-coast star-factory had better beware. Bollywood (India's movie industry) is already nipping at Hollywood's toes. Can Fargo's Follywood be far behind?

World's Largest Buffalo

Jamestown, North Dakota

If World War III should erupt and food supplies become scarce, North Dakotan's could conceivably survive on steaks provided by the world's largest buffalo. Too bad the beast is made from stucco and cement.

Brought to "life" by Harold Newman and Elmer Peterson, the great one has been tempting carnivores since 1959. At 26 feet tall and 46 feet in length, this buffalo sitting just off I-94 is in fact the world's largest. It's also the first oversize animal sculpture to be displayed in the state.

Since Jamestown is nicknamed "The Buffalo City," you can easily see why his builders didn't produce a duck. Oddly, the huge Buffalo was never named or even nicknamed for that matter. Any ideas?

177

★★★ Mountain ★★★

Swetsville Zoo

Fort Collins, Colorado

A farmer by trade, Bill Swets began crafting his unique sculptures as a cure for insomnia. His zoo—a stone's throw from I-25—was populated with real and imagined beasts of all kinds, made from old car parts, farm equipment, and other industrial scraps. The menagerie ran the gamut from a swan made out of a motorcycle gas tank, to a scrap-metal version of Snoopy on his doghouse, to a three-piece "heavy metal" alligator band. In 2022, the site closed so that Bill could move south, and the sculptures were auctioned off.

Casa Bonita

Denver, Colorado

Said to be the largest restaurant in the western hemisphere (at 52,000 square feet!), Denver's Casa Bonita is one of the last vestiges of a regional chain of Mexican theme restaurants. The exterior, clad in pink stucco with a gilded dome tower that houses a statue of the Aztec Emperor Quahuatomec, masks an even more outrageous indoors: faux cliffs, faux caverns, and long lines for cafeteria-style Mexican dinners.

Coney Island

Bailey, Colorado

This hot dog–shape building is, not too surprisingly, a hot dog stand. While it actually began life on Colfax Avenue in Denver, it was relocated from its urban birthplace to the Rocky Mountain foothills in 1969 and has been a red-hot landmark en route to the great outdoors ever since.

The Great Stupa of Dharmakaya

Red Feather Lakes, Colorado

Tucked in the mountains northwest of Fort Collins, Colorado, this is the largest stupa—a monument to a great Buddhist teacher—in North America. Dedicated to the late Chogyam Trungpa, the 108-foot spire is a work of ornate and symbolic art, and it was built with a special formulation of concrete designed to last more than 1,000 years.

Buffalo Bill's Grave

Golden, Colorado

The final resting spot of Wild West performer William "Buffalo Bill" Cody is on Lookout Mountain—or maybe not. According to legend, a few of Cody's friends swapped his body with that of an anonymous cowboy and buried him just outside the town that he founded, Cody, Wyoming. Regardless, the official grave in Colorado was protected by National Guard troops for a spell before an impenetrable layer of concrete was poured over the site.

The Haunted Stanley Hotel

Estes Park, Colorado

The Stanley Hotel–a beautiful Georgian-style resort in Estes Park, Colorado–was the inspiration for the Overlook Hotel in Stephen King's famous novel *The Shining* and the movie adaptation, which starred Jack Nicholson. Fortunately, unlike at King's fictional inn, the ghosts of the Stanley Hotel are not malicious. But rest assured, there are definitely ghosts at this famous hotel.

How It All Began

In 1903, F. O. Stanley–inventor of the Stanley Steamer automobile–was suffering from tuberculosis and was told that he had just months to live. That year, Stanley and his wife, Flora, visited Estes Park hoping to find some relief in the thin mountain air. They fell in love with its majestic Rocky Mountain landscape and decided to move there permanently. Shortly thereafter, construction began on the Stanley Hotel, which was completed in 1909. (Stanley died in 1940 at the ripe old age of 91, so apparently the mountain air did the trick.)

Nestled in the mountains, the resort offers a spectacular view. Many notable guests have stayed at the Stanley Hotel, including John Philip Sousa, President Theodore Roosevelt, Japanese royalty, members of the Hollywood set–including Jim Carrey, Rebecca De Mornay, and Elliott Gould–and, of course, writer Stephen King.

Friendly Ghosts

King stayed in Room 237, which is the haunted room in *The Shining*. However, most of the paranormal activity at the Stanley seems to occur on the fourth floor, specifically in Room 418. There, guests have heard children laughing and playing, but when they complain that the children are too loud, no children are ever found.

In Room 407, a ghost likes to play with the lights. However, it's apparently a reasonable spook: When guests ask it to turn the lights back on, it does.

During his stay, Stephen King alerted the staff that a young boy on the second floor was calling for his nanny. Of course, the staff members at the Stanley were well aware of the ghostly boy, who had been spotted throughout the hotel many times over the years.

But the two most prominent spirits at the resort are those of F. O. Stanley and his wife. Flora makes her presence known by playing the piano in the ballroom. Even those who haven't seen her claim to hear piano music coming from the ballroom when it's empty, and some have seen the piano keys move up and down of their own accord.

F. O. Stanley's specter most often manifests in the lobby, the bar, and the billiard room, which were apparently his favorite spots in the building when he was alive.

A Ghostly Visitor

When Jason Hawes and Grant Wilson from the television show *Ghost Hunters* stayed at the Stanley Hotel in 2006, their investigation hit paranormal pay dirt. Hawes stayed in Room 401–purportedly one of the most haunted guest rooms–and set up a video camera to record anything that occurred while he was asleep. Although the picture is dark, the camera captured the distinct sounds of a door opening and glass breaking–all while Hawes was sound asleep. When he got up to investigate, he noticed that the closet door had been opened and a glass on the nightstand was broken. Later, the camera recorded the closet door closing–and latching–with no humans in sight.

Wilson had his own paranormal experience in Room 1302: He was sitting at a table with some other team members when the table lifted off the ground and crashed back down–all of its own accord. When the group tried to raise the table, they found it to be so heavy that it took several people to lift it even a few inches.

During a follow-up session at the Stanley Hotel, those in attendance were also treated to paranormal activity. K-2 meters were used to detect changes in the electromagnetic field (which indicate that a ghost is nearby), and they lit up time and again. Clear responses to questions directed at the resident spirits were also captured on audio recordings.

Meet the Spirits

The Stanley Hotel offers ghost tours to educate visitors about the paranormal activity within its walls. Or if you'd rather just stay in your room, you could always watch a movie–*The Shining* runs continuously on the guest-room televisions.

Herkimer, the Hercules Beetle

Colorado Springs, Colorado

This imposing Hercules beetle is the mascot of—and turnoff marker to—the John May Museum Center, best known for its permanent collection of about 100,000 insect specimens. Fittingly, Hercules beetles are also the world's largest real-life beetles, bugs so big (up to 6 $^3/_4$ inches long!) they've knocked down people unlucky enough to be in their flight path.

Mike the Headless Chicken

Fruita, Colorado

In 1945, Lloyd Olsen chopped a chicken's head off but missed its brain stem. Rather than getting fried, the bird, dubbed "Mike the Headless Chicken," lived for another 18 months, with Olsen feeding it with an eyedropper. Sculptor Lyle Nichols paid tribute to Mike's fortitude with this 300-pound interpretation, and the city of Fruita also plays host to an annual festival that invites visitors to "party their heads off."

Colorado Gators Reptile Park

Mosca, Colorado

Dubbed the world's only high-altitude alligator farm, Colorado Gators appears a bit out of the place in the Rockies, until you hear of its origins. The proprietors owned a fish farm and bought 100 baby alligators in 1987 to help dispose of waste from the fish. The reptiles thrived and multiplied, basking in the sun on snowbanks above a geothermal lagoon that stays 87 degrees Fahrenheit year-round. The farm has been known to throw an Alligator Rodeo and even offer gator wrestling classes.

Bishop Castle

Rye, Colorado

Jim Bishop is a man on a mission. Using rocks in the surrounding forest, he started building a one-room stone cottage in 1969 and just never stopped. He now has what he describes as "the largest one-man construction project in the country, quite possibly the world!" Highlights include a tower that ascends high into the sky and a fire-breathing steel dragon that crowns the main structure.

Arches National Park

Grand Couty, Utah

A fantasyland in rock, Arches National Park is filled with giant balanced rocks that look as though they are about to teeter and fall. There are pedestals and spires that resemble a child's drip castles expanded to enormous scale. Chiseled by the powerful forces of wind and water, this surprising natural rock garden contains one of the foremost collections of abstract sculpture in the world.

Giant Pink Dinosaur

Vernal, Utah

Originally designed to hold a sign hawking the Dine-A-Ville Motel, the 40-foot-tall Apatosaurus lost that gig when the motel fossilized. The lovable giant has now moved to the eastern end of town where he performs chamber of commerce duty. His new sign reads: "Vernal—Utah's Dinosaur Land." As if we couldn't tell.

Four Corners Monument

San Juan County, Utah

Name a well-traveled American who hasn't visited the Four Corners Monument and we'll show you a life hopelessly squandered. As the geographical meeting point of Arizona, Colorado, New Mexico and Utah, an impromptu straddling of all four states has become the savvy traveler's rite of passage.

What separates the four corners from other state meeting points is its unique corner intersection. It's also the only point in the United States that's shared by four states.

Bingham Canyon Mine–World's Biggest Pit

Bingham Canyon, Utah

This enormous copper pit mine is a fact-lover's dream. With a 17-million-ton yield thus far, it has produced more copper than any single mine in history.

Indeed, this is no ordinary mine. It is two-and-a-half miles wide and three-quarters of a mile deep.

Everything about the operation is humongous. Its electric shovels can scoop up to 98 tons in a single bite. Trucks that haul the mine's ore stand over 25 feet tall. Even the truck driver gets to feel larger than life as he rides in a cab suspended 18 feet above terra firma.

Perhaps the best gauge to the mine's size lies in this tidbit: If one attended a rock concert here, they could bring along nine million friends! Also, the mine is so deep that it could easily swallow two Willis Towers stacked upon each other.

Hollow Mountain Gas & Grocery

Hanksville, Utah

You have to admire American ingenuity and pragmatism. When developers blasted through a stubborn 40-foot rock to clear the way for a gas station, they abandoned the idea halfway through and hollowed out the inside instead. What they ended up with is something straight out of the *Flintstones*.

Like most service stations, Hollow Mountain Gas & Grocery sells the expected fuel and sundries, but how often does one get to pay for their purchases inside a hollowed-out "mountain"? While the owners likely refer to their staff as "attendants," we think "cave dwellers" carries a certain ring.

Hole in the Rock

Moab, Utah

Hole in the Rock in Moab is sort of like the Hollow Mountain Gas & Grocery on steroids. Well, apart from the fact that they don't sell gasoline. For a nominal fee, visitors are led on a tour of the intermountain digs and told about its builders, Albert and Gladys Christensen.

Albert started blasting his dream home out of this natural red cliff face in the 1940s. In 1952, he and wife Gladys finally moved in. When Albert passed on in 1957, Gladys continued improving their 14-room, 5000-square-foot cave house. She'd eventually open a gift shop and café—all the better to show the place off.

Today, a petting zoo adds to Hole in the Rock's interesting bits as does a not-too-faithful rendition of Franklin Delano Roosevelt carved into the rock beside the entrance. A descriptive blurb beneath declares, "Created and Sculptured by artist Albert L. Christensen."

Grafton Ghost Town

Grafton, Utah

Countless ghost towns exist within the Rocky Mountain region. Some are touristy affairs that smack of reproduction, others are more genuine. The one at Grafton is the real McCoy.

The town had its share of false starts. First settled in 1859, Grafton's first run lasted until 1862 when a flood swept it away. After being rebuilt a mile from its original location, Grafton existed until 1866 when a rash of Indian attacks sent its 28 families scurrying. In 1868, the town was repopulated. Grafton saw dwindling population numbers from this point forth. By the 1930s, most people had moved on.

Today, a handful of people live on the town's dusty periphery, and many of its old buildings still remain. Among these are a church that was built in 1886 and a two-story private residence that is now boarded up. Nearby, the town's cemetery bears testament to its existence. Occasional tumbleweeds blowing down Grafton Road complete the desolate picture.

Sri Sri Radha Krishna Temple

Spanish Fork, Utah

What could seem more out of place than a temple built in the middle of nowhere? A Hare Krishna Temple built in this no man's land, which happens to be an acknowledged Mormon stronghold. But build it, the Krishnas certainly did. In fact, the group received a great deal of help from their Mormon brethren.

The 50-foot-tall temple juts up from its elevated plain like a proud citadel should. Exquisitely beautiful, the domed sanctuary is modeled after Kusum Sarovar, a famous palace in India.

More than 40,000 visitors tour the temple annually. Hot vegetarian meals are fed to those who hunger physically as well as spiritually, and gifts, books, and apparel are sold as souvenirs. Such is the peaceful coexistence of faiths.

Penguin Statue

Cut Bank, Montana

Before you start in with the Tennessee Tuxedo cracks, understand that this abnormally "big bird" has likely heard them all by now. Besides, at 27 feet tall and some 10,000 pounds, you wouldn't want to push ol' Tennessee's buttons.

Strike that. Actually you do want to push this sea bird's buttons, at least the rather prominent one that starts him talking. So, what does he say? The tuxedoed one merely echoes the slogan painted at his base: "Welcome to Cut Bank," he enthusiastically warbles, "the coldest spot in the nation!"

Considering his heritage and overall size, we have to take his word for it.

FREE LONG DIST
0 $ BREAKFAST

Old Montana Prison

Deer Lodge, Montana

In 1871, the Old Montana Prison opened its gates in Deer Lodge after citizens of the territory realized that laws needed to be enforced and the wilder elements of the region needed to be punished. Like many other prisons of the day, this facility soon became overcrowded, which led to sickness, poor living conditions, prisoner unrest, and the taut emotions that lead to restless spirits and residual hauntings.

No Escape

The year 1890 marked the beginning of the Conley era–a time when prison warden Frank Conley ruled with an iron fist and put his prisoners to work. But Conley also made significant improvements to both the prison itself and the lives of the inmates. He even established camps that sent the prisoners outside to work in the community.

However, this outside work was a privilege, and in 1908, two prisoners who were not allowed this freedom decided to take matters into their own hands. Their attempted escape resulted in the murder of the deputy prison warden and 103 stitches in the back and neck of Warden Conley. The two would-be escapees were hanged in the prison yard for their crime.

After that, the prison underwent many changes, including the end of prisoners working outside the facility, the addition of a women's prison, and the creation of a license plate manufacturing plant.

In 1959, the Old Montana Prison experienced a riot that lasted for three days and nights. Several inmates attempted to escape by holding the warden hostage and killing the deputy warden on the spot. After the National Guard was called in to end the melee, the two ringleaders died in a murder/suicide.

The Main Attraction

The Old Montana Prison closed for good in 1979, and a year later, the building opened its doors to the public as a museum. In addition to offering historical tours, the museum also offers tours for those who are interested in things that go bump in the night. In fact, so much paranormal activity has been experienced at the Old Montana Prison that several ghost-hunting television shows have traveled there to investigate and film episodes.

In 2010, a *Ghost Lab* episode titled "No Escape" depicted Brad and Barry Klinge's (founders of *Everyday Paranormal*) visit to the prison. A wealth of high-tech ghost-hunting equipment helped the investigators uncover supernatural phenomena ranging from mysterious whispers and the sound of footsteps in empty rooms and hallways to objects flying through the air. The investigators also experienced a general feeling of dread and the unshakeable sensation that they were being watched.

See for Yourself

While touring the old prison, one can almost imagine the place as it was in the old days. Many people report hearing the shuffling of cards in the cellblocks, as well as mumbled voices and footsteps. Arguments have even been known to break out between people who aren't visible.

Shadows and ghostly figures are common sights at the museum, and some visitors have reported seeing objects flying through the air in violent, threatening ways. People have also experienced a myriad of emotions and sensations: Some have reported feeling deep sadness or dread overtake them. And even more frightening, others have perceived that someone or something is choking or attacking them.

Living With the Ghosts

Museum Director Julia Brewer is rather matter-of-fact about the hauntings in the old prison. After all, she has smelled burning flesh in her office for the better part of a decade, so you could say that she's a believer.

Brewer leads many of the groups that tour the facility, so she knows most of the prison lore. She also knows how to treat the spirits, and cautions visitors to treat the dead with respect...or else face the consequences.

A place known as the Death Tower produces a high level of otherworldly energy–it's where inmates Jerry Myles and Lee Smart died in a murder/suicide during the 1959 riot. A place called the Steam Hole carries some heavy energy of its own. Prisoners who were deemed unruly were often sent there; at least one prisoner died in the Steam Hole under suspicious circumstances, and another inmate took his own life there by hanging himself from a pipe.

Several ghosts are known to haunt the prison grounds, and many visitors–especially psychics and ghost hunters who are sensitive to the spirit world–have experienced odd and sinister sensations. Some have even reported feeling physically ill.

Playful Spirits

A couple of ghosts are even known to hang around the museum's gift shop. One is the spirit of an inmate named Calvin, who was beaten to death in a corner of the room when it was an industrial area of the prison. Now the site houses a shelf of dolls, perhaps to neutralize the violence. A spirit that the staff refers to as "Stinker" also frequents the gift shop. The jokester of the pair, he likes to play pranks, such as moving merchandise around.

You'd think that ghosts would stick to their old haunts within the prison, but another place on the grounds that definitely seems haunted is the Montana Auto Museum, which is located just outside the gift shop. Staffers and visitors have seen ghostly figures there, and people have heard car doors slam when no one else is around.

And then there's the spirit of a young girl that has been observed by visitors at the auto museum. When a group reached the building on one ghost tour, the leader invited any spirits to show themselves by turning on a flashlight; the playful ghost did. The group also asked her to move a chain that was cordoning off the cars; she did that too.

In a place that's harbored more than its share of violence and despair, the ghost of a little girl seems pretty benign. But as tour guides warn groups about the spirits of the Old Montana Prison: Be careful...they might just follow you home.

World's Largest Steer

Baker, Montana

Born in 1923, the world's largest steer measured 5 feet, 11 inches in height, 10 feet, 4 inches in length, and 9 feet, 2 inches in girth. He tipped the scales at a portly 3,980 pounds.

Named "Steer Montana" by his owner Jack Guth, the outsize bovine (technically a Roan Polled Shorthorn) would appear in more than 60 state fairs during his lifetime. Upon his death in 1938, Steer Montana's skeletal remains continued to thrill crowds.

These days, Steer Montana can be found at Baker's O'Fallon Historical Museum. The world-class bovine stands beside a two-headed calf and a female mannequin done up in bizarre hair curlers. Is nothing sacred?

Radon Health Mines

Basin, Montana

In a nod to holistic treatments of the atomic age, we present the radon "health" mines of Basin, Montana. While companies exist solely to rid basements of dangerous radioactive radon gas, visitors to the health mines voluntarily expose themselves to it. Why?

It is believed by some that exposure to the gas can prove fruitful, particularly in the treatment of such ailments as arthritis and asthma. Each year, hundreds of people come to innocuously named places such as the Earth Angel and Sunshine Health Mines to take the cure by simply hanging around for a week or two. Others actually ingest radioactive water tainted by radon in hopes of improving their health.

Radon levels in the mines reach 175 times the federal safety standard for houses, yet the people keep on coming. Perhaps they've read a report submitted by the *British Journal of Rheumatology* that concludes, "This component of rehabilitative intervention can induce beneficial long-term effects." Who knew?

Our Lady of the Rockies

Butte, Montana

Our Lady of the Rockies stands 90 feet tall and is precariously perched more than 8,500 feet up on the Continental Divide, offering an unobstructed view of some 100 miles.

Completed in 1985, the statue pays homage to all women and features a memorial wall consisting of the names of 13,000 that have come before. According to David Adickes, noted sculptor of the enormous Sam Houston statue in Texas, the steel-framed lady was created to boost the town's spirits when its copper mines were shut down.

Visitors can enter the statue and peer down upon Butte, far below. For many, this is a religious experience all by itself.

The Haunted Sweetwater County Library

Green River, Wyoming

It's not surprising that the Sweetwater County Library is haunted; after all, it's built on the site of a graveyard. Since the mid-1980s, lights have mysteriously turned on and off by themselves, and orbs of light have been known to move along the walls inside the art gallery, even when it's empty. Strange flapping sounds are heard throughout the building at night, and two old electric typewriters once began operating on their own. The paranormal activity at the library is so common that in 1993, staff members started a "Ghost Log" to document their experiences.

The Haunted Wyoming Frontier Prison

Rawlins, Wyoming

"It's a gas!" is the saying most likely heard after a visit to the Wyoming Frontier Prison Museum. Such wisecracks are part and parcel of a museum that features a genuine gas chamber (used for five executions; visitors are actually encouraged to sit in its death seat), shoes made from the skin of an executed killer (his name was Big Nose George–it's unclear whether this was just a nickname or described an actual physical trait), and a pipe holder fashioned from the doomed man's skull.

The old prison dates back to 1902 but hasn't seen an inmate since 1981. Tours take visitors past the prison's infirmary, exercise yard, cellblocks, and visiting rooms. "There's a place behind bars for you," reads the prison museum's macabre welcoming sign.

The Old Pen was known for the use of severe torture and the mistreatment of its inmates. Fourteen prisoners were executed on the premises, and several more were killed during a botched escape attempt when death-row inmates hit a gas line while trying to tunnel their way to freedom; someone lit a match to identify the obstruction and the men died instantly. They may have been the lucky ones, however: Nine other death-row prisoners were victims of a poorly constructed gallows. The contraption didn't drop the men far enough to break their necks, and they ended up dying slow, agonizing deaths by strangulation.

The Old Pen is now the site of several residual hauntings that feed off the negative energy of the place. Residual hauntings often create an atmosphere of unpleasantness, as if the agony that occurred there still lingers. People have reported unusual odors, screams, wailing, and a sense of intense fear. Because these are mostly residual hauntings, the spirits at the Old Pen don't seem to acknowledge the living at all, which is probably a good thing.

Jackalope Capital of the World

Douglas, Wyoming

Western towns have made some grandiose claims over the years; declaring oneself the "Jackalope Capital of the World" is not to be taken lightly. First off, no one seems 100 percent sure whether jackalopes (deer and/or antelope crossbred with a jackrabbit) really exist. Scientists say such a species is as probable as $1 gasoline, but others aren't quite as sure.

Nevertheless, the town of Douglas sure appears to be a worthy contender in jackalope supremacy. Why? Because they say so, that's why. And they've been saying so since the 1940s!

If that's still not enough to convince people that Douglas is the jackalope capital of the world, the town offers proof. It comes in the convincing form of an eight-foot-tall concrete statue in Douglas's downtown district; through images of the ever-elusive animal on park benches; via pictures of the shy ones on buildings. There's even a jackalope on the side of Douglas's fire trucks.

If still in doubt, here's the absolute clincher. Every June, Douglas plays host to "Jackalope Day." This event features such crowd-pleasers as a mud volleyball tournament, motorcycle show and rally, and a greased pig run. Could the town hold such an affair if they weren't number one?

Then too, there's the matter of hunting licenses. Douglas issues thousands of jackalope hunting licenses a year. These are rather specific since hunters can only hunt between midnight and 2:00 a.m. each June 31 and must possess an I.Q. under 72. So there you go.

Long live the jackalope!

World's Largest Elkhorn Arch

Afton, Wyoming

Elk are a pretty big deal in Wyoming, which explains Afton's arch to end all arches. Comprised of some 3,000 elk antlers, the arch stretches some 75 feet across four lanes of Highway 89. It weighs a whopping 15 tons.

"To duplicate this arch at today's prices, the cost would be over $300,000 for the antlers alone," proclaims an informative sign. So, who's even trying?

World's Largest Mineral Hot Spring

Thermopolis, Wyoming

When you enter the town of Thermopolis (Greek for "Hot City"), you're in for some thermal fun. Here, you'll derive soothing pleasure from the world's largest mineral hot spring.

The teal-colored spring issues 3.6 million gallons of water per day, making it the world's largest mineral hot spring. Its 127-degree temperature makes it perfect for baths, and numerous concessions make such soaks available to tourists.

It's believed that the spring possesses curative properties due to its abundance of minerals. We can't speak to that, but we will say that Thermopolis is the hot spot to end all hot spots.

Mormon Handcart Visitors' Center

Alcova, Wyoming

America likes its victories, but it loves its tragedies. Case in point? The Mormon Handcart story.

In July 1856, Mormon pioneers some 600 strong departed Iowa for a 1,200-mile trek to Salt Lake City. Leaving late in the season, most pulled their belongings behind them in carts. Almost immediately, trouble hit when the carts started to break. In order to lessen their load, heavy objects including blankets and winter clothes were discarded. It proved to be a deadly move. In late October, a blizzard killed 150 of the emigrants who made up the Martin party, with most perishing due to exposure.

In 1997, the Mormon Handcart Visitor's Center began to tell their story. More than 1,000 visitors arrive each day in summer to see where the tragedy occurred. Far fewer come in fall, which is not too surprising considering....

Hell's Half Acre

Powder River, Wyoming

In a region brimming with geologic features, Hell's Half Acre causes even locals to take notice. Such excitement can occur when a flat plain 320 acres wide suddenly drops away to a 150-foot-deep depression for no apparent reason.

Throw in tortured rock spires painted an unnatural shade, add the requisite forbidding feel, and you have yourself an ethereal wonder.

Scientific types will spoil the fun by pointing to water and wind as the culprits responsible for this desolate hole. We prefer to think that alien bugs really did walk here once. From the look of things, they may still be out there.

The scouting team for the 1997 sci-fi movie *Starship Troopers* recognized the eerie quality of this site and quickly set up shop beside the rocks. Since they were looking to simulate an alien bug planet, the fit was ideal. All they had to do was supply the creepy crawlers and yell "Action."

Golf Ball House

Yucca, Arizona

Part of a futuristic community that never quite sprouted, this spheroid was originally envisioned as a supper club and nightclub. However, after plans for the rest of the forward-thinking development were scrapped, the structure deteriorated for a spell before being fixed up as a private residence.

Titan Missile Silo

Sahuarita, Arizona

Just a little south of Tucson, Arizona, lies the Sonoran Desert, a barren, desolate area where nothing seems to be happening. That's exactly why, during the Cold War, the U.S. government hid an underground Titan Missile silo there.

Inside the missile silo, one of dozens that once littered the area, a Titan 2 Missile could be armed and launched in just under 90 seconds. Until it was finally abandoned in the 1990s, the government manned the silo 24 hours a day, with every member being trained to "turn the key" and launch the missile at a moment's notice. Today, the silo is open to the public as the Titan Missile Museum. Visitors can take a look at one of the few remaining Titan 2 missiles in existence, still sitting on the launch pad (relax, it's been disarmed). Folks with extra dough can also spend the night inside the silo and play the role of one of the crew members assigned to prepare to launch the missile at a moment's notice.

Hotel Vendome

Prescott, Arizona

As a quaint and welcoming community in the Arizona mountains, Prescott holds a lot of history. Former manager Abby Byr and her cat, Noble, are said to haunt this hotel, which was built in 1917. At around that same time, Abby, who suffered from tuberculosis, moved to Arizona for health reasons. There, she met and married her husband, and the couple bought the Hotel Vendome. They soon lost the place due to unpaid taxes, but the next owners hired them to run it. One night in 1921, Abby sent her husband out for medicine; he never returned. She died a short time later, and employees, guests, and ghost hunters have all felt her presence lingering at the hotel.

Some have even seen her apparition in Room 16, where she and her husband lived. Is it Abby who makes noise by moving hangers around in the closet? Guests have also reported having their possessions inexplicably moved around the room, and some report getting sudden whiffs of strong perfume.

Jerome Grand Hotel
Jerome, Arizona

Jerome, Arizona, got its start as a mining town in the late 1800s. In the late 1920s, the United Verde Copper Company built a hospital there to treat sick and injured miners. In addition to the many deaths that are typically associated with a hospital, several violent ends occurred in the building as well. In 1935, an orderly was found crushed beneath the elevator, and another fell from a fifth-floor balcony; both deaths are thought to have been murders. A suicide also took place at the hospital when a patient rolled his wheelchair over a balcony and onto the street below.

The hospital closed its doors in 1950 and the building sat vacant for nearly half a century until two brothers opened the Jerome Grand Hotel there in 1997. The third floor has seen the most paranormal activity, but disembodied voices and coughing, a dusty smell, and apparitions have been reported throughout the building; they're most likely the antics of spirits left over from the days when the sick and injured lived and died there.

The Haunted Phoenix Theater
Phoenix, Arizona

Audiences that saw *A Chorus Line* at the Phoenix Theatre in 2005 got a little more than they bargained for when an unpaid and uncredited dancer twirled her way between the chorus-line performers. Those who saw her may have thought it was odd that a ballerina was prancing around in a show about Broadway dancers. Of course, they may have found it even stranger if they realized that she was just one of the many ghosts that inhabit the theater, which opened in 1951.

Members of Arizona's Phoenix Theatre Company have been entertaining locals and visitors with a variety of productions since 1920. As the oldest arts institution in Arizona, it makes sense that a few of its ghosts want to make one last curtain call.

The aforementioned ghost—which the staff affectionately calls "Tiny Dancer"–is not the only spirit at the Phoenix Theatre with artistic inclinations. "Mr. Electrics" is the spirit of an old man who is sometimes seen sitting on the pipes that hold the lighting instruments. He also appears late at night to help the technicians by manipulating buttons. Another ghost that deals with lighting is referred to as "Light Board Lenny;" he hangs around the lighting booth and has been known to playfully lock out light-board operators and spotlight technicians if they leave their positions in the booth. The spirit known as the "Prop Master" takes a cue from Lenny and sometimes locks people out of the prop room so that it can dig through the props.

Unfortunately, not all the spirits at the Phoenix Theatre are so lighthearted. One of the theater's ghosts is believed to be the angry spirit of Freddy, an actor who was fired from a production and then was killed while riding his bicycle home. Freddy generally likes to make a racket by slamming doors and stomping around in the theater's upstairs rooms.

With all the extra help, it's no wonder that the Phoenix Theatre Company is one of the nation's oldest continuously operating artistic troupes. Hopefully, they will be successful for years to come because ghosts hate auditioning.

Yuma Territorial Prison State Historic Park

Yuma, Arizona

What could be worse than being locked in a prison cell for life? How about being locked in a prison that you were forced to help build? That's what happened to the first seven inmates at the Yuma Territorial Prison back in 1876. Is it any wonder that the place is considered one of the most haunted locations in Arizona

There were no minimum- or maximum-security prisons in the 1800s, so inmates at the Yuma Prison ranged from petty thieves to murderers. By the time the prison closed in 1909, more than 3,000 convicts had been held within its walls. Compared to today's standards, prison life back then was hard. Each cell measured only nine feet by nine feet, and it was not uncommon for the indoor temperature to reach 110 degrees in the summer. A punishment known as the "Dark Cell" was similar to what we now call solitary confinement. And a ball and chain were used to punish prisoners who tried to escape. It must have worked because plenty of souls never left this place.

The Good, the Bad, and the Ghostly

Despite the brutal conditions, a library and educational programs were available to inmates, and a prison clinic even gave them access to medical care. But the jail soon became overcrowded, and in such close quarters, tuberculosis ran rampant. During its 33-year history, 111 prisoners died there, many from TB; eight were gunned down in unsuccessful escape attempts.

From 1910 to 1914, the former prison building housed Yuma High School. Considering the restless souls that were left over from the structure's days as a prison, it probably did not make for the best educational experience. During the Great Depression, homeless families sought shelter within its walls. And later, local residents who wanted to have a little piece of Arizona history "borrowed" stones from the building's walls for their personal construction projects.

Solitary Spirits

Today, all that remains of the former Yuma Territorial Prison are some cells, the main gate, a guard tower, the prison cemetery—and the ghosts. A museum is located on the site, and visitors and employees report that spirits have settled there as well. Lights turn on and off randomly; objects are moved from one place to another; and once, the coins from the gift shop's cash register leaped into the air and then fell back into place.

The Dark Cell is also a focal point for ghostly activity: The restless spirits of prisoners who were sent there for disobeying rules are thought to linger. At least two inmates were transferred directly from that cell to an insane asylum, but whether anyone actually died there is unknown. It makes for a few unsettled spirits, though, doesn't it?

Linda Offeney, an employee at the prison site, once reported feeling an unseen presence in the Dark Cell. And a tourist who visited the prison in the 1930s had her photo taken near the Dark Cell; the picture looked perfectly normal—except for the ghostly figure of a man standing behind her within the cell.

Offeney also tells the story of a writer for *Arizona Highways* magazine who witnessed the hauntings: The journalist wanted to spend two days and two nights in the cell just as prisoners would have—in the dark, with only bread and water. She only made it a few hours before she called for assistance, explaining that she couldn't shake the feeling that something was in the cell with her.

In June 2005, Arizona Desert Ghost Hunters spent the night at the Yuma Territorial Prison and gathered enough evidence to convince them that the place is indeed haunted. Photos taken of the guard tower and in Cell 14 both show suspicious activity: An orb can be seen near the tower and a misty figure is clearly visible in Cell 14, where inmate John Ryan hung himself in 1903. The investigators also captured EVPs (electronic voice phenomena) in Cell 14, where a voice said, "Get away," and in the Dark Cell, where a male spirit told the group to "Get out of here."

Although the Yuma Territorial Prison only operated for 33 years, it certainly spawned its fair share of paranormal activity. This begs the questions: Was the prison built so soundly that for many, there was no escape, even in death? Or did the inmates just give up and choose to stay there forever?

London Bridge
Lake Havasu City, Arizona

After local authorities determined the old London Bridge was sinking into the Thames River, the crumbling granite went up for auction as plans were drawn for a replacement. The winning bidder—Lake Havasu City founder Robert McCulloch—paid about $2.5 million for the old one, then shipped it to Long Beach, trucked it to Arizona, and rebuilt it over a manufactured lagoon as a tourist attraction.

Longhorn Grill

Amado, Arizona

It's difficult to imagine a restaurant more Western than one shaped like a giant longhorn skull. That's the case at the Longhorn Grill, a desert outpost of an eatery located in the saguaro-studded sands between Tucson, Arizona, and Nogales, Mexico. Besides functioning as a restaurant, the building has been used as a location for several movies, including *Alice Doesn't Live Here Anymore*.

Hotel Brunswick

Kingman, Arizona

For the most part, the ghosts at the Hotel Brunswick seem to be friendly, and some are downright playful. A spectral young girl has been seen in the dining room, and elsewhere in the hotel, several guests have seen a small ghost-child, who seems to be seeking a playmate. Others have reported that something tugged on their legs or feet while they were sleeping. One family woke up in the morning to discover that their necks had yellow marks on them. (Fortunately, the marks washed off easily with soap and water.) Old coins were found in stacks lined up in hallways and near the bar, which a former owner interpreted as the spirits letting him know that prosperous times were ahead.

Another owner saw a ghostly man walking up the stairs when he opened the cellar door; he got chills as the figure passed right through him. Guests have experienced similar shadow phenomena in the second-floor hallway. It is not known who most of these ghosts were in life, but some believe that one of the spirits is W. D. McKnight, a wealthy gentleman who died in his room at the Hotel Brunswick in 1915. Although it can be a bit unsettling to bunk with a ghost, no one has reported any harmful encounters with the hotel's resident spirits.

Mystery Castle

Phoenix, Arizona

This curious dwelling was build by Boyce Gulley out of desert rocks and salvaged materials of all kind, including auto parts and recycled appliances. Over sixteen years, the castle bloomed into a unique 18-room abode with quirks around every corner.

International UFO Museum and Research Center

Roswell, New Mexico

The International UFO Museum is ground zero for the controversy surrounding the events of July 1947, when a UFO allegedly crashed in the countryside near Roswell. It's the centerpiece of the city's downtown and the natural starting point for an alien-related vacation of any kind.

Los Alamos National Laboratory

Los Alamos County, New Mexico

Until recently, the U.S. government refused to acknowledge the Los Alamos National Laboratory's existence. But in the early 1940s, the lab was created near Los Alamos, New Mexico, to develop the first nuclear weapons in what would become known as the Manhattan Project. Back then, the facility was so top secret it didn't even have a name. It was simply referred to as Site Y. No matter what it was called, the lab produced two nuclear bombs, nicknamed Little Boy and Fat Man—bombs that would be dropped on Hiroshima and Nagasaki, effectively ending World War II. Today, tours of portions of the facility can be arranged through the Lab's Public Affairs Department.

New Mexico State Penitentiary

Santa Fe, New Mexico

A riot at the New Mexico State Penitentiary in 1980 resulted in more than enough trauma to create unsettled spirits. In a rebellion that was driven by rage rather than well-thought-out plans, 33 inmates lost their lives. Twelve guards were taken hostage, and more than 100 people were injured.

If heightened energy and emotions are the ingredients for paranormal activity, then the New Mexico State Pen should be one of the most haunted prisons in the world. And perhaps it is. Doors have been observed opening and closing on their own, lights turn on and off by themselves, unusual noises are heard, and visitors report a general feeling of unease when entering Cellblocks 3 and 4, where the worst fighting of the riots occurred. New Mexico's governor closed the prison in 1998 because of its "uncontrollable disturbances"; it has since been used in the production of films such as The Longest Yard (2005).

Tinkertown

Sandia Park, New Mexico

A lifetime of carving and collecting by the late Ross Ward is the bedrock for a sprawling and charmingly eclectic tourist attraction northeast of Albuquerque on Old Route 66. The museum is surrounded by barricades fashioned from bottles and includes a miniature town—Tinkertown—that Ward began carving in the early 1960s.

The Haunted KiMo Theatre

Albuquerque, New Mexico

In 1951, Bobby Darnall was just six years old when the boiler at the KiMo Theatre exploded and killed him. The boiler was located in the lobby behind the concession stand in the 1927 Pueblo Deco-style building; Bobby had been watching a film with his friends but decided to get a snack. Just as he approached the concession stand, the boiler blew; the force of the explosion demolished part of the lobby. These days, employees appease Bobby's hungry spirit by leaving doughnuts on a pipe that runs along the back wall of the theater, behind the stage. If any doughnuts remain the next morning, they sometimes contain child-sized bite marks. Bobby has also been seen playing by the stairs wearing jeans and a striped T-shirt, but he is not the only ghost in the theater: A woman in a bonnet has also been seen roaming the building, but she generally keeps to herself. The KiMo Theatre closed in 1968, but it was restored and reopened in 2000, just in time for Route 66's 75th anniversary celebration.

The Haunted Carrie Tingley Children's Hospital

Albuquerque, New Mexico

Originally established in the city of Truth or Consequences, New Mexico, Carrie Tingley Children's Hospital was founded in 1937 to help kids suffering from polio. It was later moved to Albuquerque, where it became affiliated with the University of New Mexico Medical Center. Some unused areas of the hospital are said to have invisible force fields that sometimes prevent people from moving through certain hallways or doors. Employees know to listen for a telltale hissing sound that is heard just before a barrier is encountered. Glowing rooms, disembodied voices, and phantom heartbeats and sobbing are all elements of the haunting there.

The Lodge

Cloudcroft, New Mexico

Opened in the early 1900s, The Lodge has attracted famous visitors such as Pancho Villa, Judy Garland, and Clark Gable. And since 1901, every New Mexico governor has stayed in the spacious Governor's Suite.

The Lodge is reportedly haunted by the ghost of a beautiful young chambermaid named Rebecca, who was murdered by her lumberjack boyfriend when he caught her cheating on him. Her apparition has frequently been spotted in the hallways, and her playful, mischievous spirit has bedeviled guests in the rooms. She is now accepted as part of the hotel's history, and there is even a stained-glass window with her likeness prominently displayed at The Lodge.

The hotel's Red Dog Saloon is reputedly one of Rebecca's favorite spots. There she makes her presence known by turning lights on and off, causing alcohol to disappear, moving objects around, and playing music long after the tavern has closed. Several bartenders claim to have seen the reflection of a pretty, red-haired woman in the bar's mirror, but when they turn around to talk to her, she disappears.

Specters on the Strip
Las Vegas, Nevada

According to the popular slogan, "What happens in Vegas stays in Vegas." As it turns out, some celebrities never leave Las Vegas–even after they're dead.

Benjamin "Bugsy" Siegel (1906-1947)

When gangster Benjamin "Bugsy" Siegel first arrived in Las Vegas in the 1930s, the town was still a sleepy backwater in the Nevada desert. But soon, Siegel had Vegas on its way to becoming the world's premier gambling mecca. However, on June 20, 1947, Siegel's associates rewarded him for his hard work by blasting him into oblivion at his girlfriend's Beverly Hills home. Since then, his ghost has been seen there running and ducking as if trying to avoid being struck by a hail of bullets. Siegel's specter is also often spotted at his Flamingo Hotel, where he's seen dressed in a smoking jacket and sporting a wide grin. He usually hangs out in the hotel's Presidential Suite, which is where he spent much of his mortal time. And later in the evening, when the pool area isn't particularly crowded, Siegel often shows up there.

Elvis Presley (1935-1977)

Clad in the famous white-sequined jumpsuit that he often wore in his later years, the spirit of Elvis is reportedly seen at the same Hilton hotel in Las Vegas where he used to perform. The spectral "King" has been glimpsed wandering around backstage and sometimes even taking a final bow.

Redd Foxx (1922-1991)

Redd Foxx's ghost supposedly still resides at his former home in Las Vegas, playing pranks on the house's current occupants. He likes to make himself known by opening and closing doors and randomly turning computers on and off. But considering that Foxx was a comedian and a prankster in life, this doesn't seem all that unusual for the former star of *Sanford and Son*.

Liberace Museum Collection

Las Vegas, Nevada

The late "Mr. Showmanship," Liberace was a Las Vegas legend known for both twinkling the ivories and his over-the-top style. The Liberace Museum Collection that bears his name reflects his love for all things extravagant with collections of his cars, costumes, and pianos. Highlights include a Rolls-Royce sheathed entirely in mirrored tiles and etched with the image of horses, a gold ring in the shape of a piano decorated with 260 diamonds, and hundreds of costumes, ranging from a mink cape lined with rhinestones to a 200-pound aquatic-themed costume.

Claims Stake Prospector Statue

Washoe Valley, Nevada

This 18-foot-tall prospector brandishes an oversize chunk of faux gold in order to attract chocoholics to the Chocolate Nugget Candy Factory, located between Reno and Carson City on U.S. 395. Before his stint hocking candy, he was the mascot of the Prospector, a casino/hotel in nearby Sparks.

Area 51

Alien autopsies. Covert military operations. Tests on bizarre aircraft. These are all things rumored to be going on inside Area 51—a top secret location inside the Nevada Test and Training Range (NTTR) about an hour northwest of Las Vegas. Though shrouded in secrecy, some of the history of Area 51 is known. For instance, this desert area was used as a bombing test site during World War II, but no facility existed on the site until 1955. At that time, the area was chosen as the perfect location to develop and test the U-2 spy plane. Originally known as Watertown, it came to be called Area 51 in 1958 when 38,000 acres were designated for military use. The entire area was simply marked "Area 51" on military maps. Today, the facility is rumored to contain approximately 575 square miles. But you won't find it on a map because, officially, it doesn't exist.

An Impenetrable Fortress

Getting a clear idea of the size of Area 51, or even a glimpse of the place, is next to impossible. Years ago, curiosity seekers could get a good view of the facility by hiking to the top of two nearby mountain peaks known as White Sides and Freedom Ridge. But government officials soon grew weary of people climbing up there and snapping pictures, so in 1995, they seized control of both. Currently, the only way to legally catch a glimpse of the base is to scale 7,913-foot-tall Tikaboo Peak. Even if you make it that far, you're still not guaranteed to see anything because the facility is more than 25 miles away and is only visible on clear days with no haze.

The main entrance to Area 51 is along Groom Lake Road. Those brave (or foolhardy) souls who have ventured down the road to investigate quickly realize they are being watched. Video cameras and motion sensors are hidden along the road, and signs alert the curious that if they continue any further, they will be entering a military installation, which is illegal "without the written permission of the installation commander." If that's not enough to get unwanted guests to turn around, one sign clearly states: "Use of deadly force authorized." Simply put, take one step over that imaginary line in the dirt, and they will get you.

Camo Dudes

And just exactly who are "they"? They are the "Camo Dudes," mysterious figures watching trespassers from nearby hillsides and jeeps. If they spot something suspicious, they might call for backup—Blackhawk helicopters that will come in for a closer look. All things considered, it would probably be best to just turn around and go back home. And lest you think about hiring someone to fly you over Area 51, the entire area is considered restricted air space, meaning that unauthorized aircraft are not permitted to fly over, or even near, the facility.

Who Works There?

Most employees are general contractors who work for companies in the area. But rather than allow these workers to commute individually, the facility has them ushered in secretly and en masse in one of two ways. The first is a mysterious white bus with tinted windows that picks up employees at several unmarked stops before whisking them through the front gates of the facility. Every evening, the bus leaves the facility and drops the employees off.

The second mode of commuter transport, an even more secretive way, is JANET, the code name given to the secret planes that carry workers back and forth from Area 51 and Las Vegas McCarran Airport. JANET has its own terminal, which is located at the far end of the airport behind fences with special security gates. It even has its own private parking lot. Several times a day, planes from the JANET fleet take off and land at the airport.

Bob Lazar

The most famous Area 51 employee is someone who may or may not have actually worked there. In the late 1980s, Bob Lazar claimed that he'd worked at the secret facility he referred to as S-4. In addition, Lazar said that he was assigned the task of reverse engineering a recovered spaceship in order to determine how it worked. Lazar had only been at the facility for a short time, but he and his team had progressed to the point where they were test flying the alien spaceship. That's when Lazar made a big mistake. He decided to bring some friends out to Groom Lake Road when he knew the alien craft was being flown. He was caught and subsequently fired.

During his initial interviews with a local TV station, Lazar seemed credible and quite knowledgeable as to the inner workings of Area 51. But when people started trying to verify the information Lazar was giving, not only was it next to impossible to confirm most of his story, his education and employment history could not be verified either. Skeptics immediately proclaimed that Lazar was a fraud. To this day, Lazar contends that everything he said was factual and that the government deleted all his records in order to set him up and make him look like a fake. Whether or not he's telling the truth, Lazar will be remembered as the man who first brought up the idea that alien spaceships were being experimented on at Area 51.

What's Really Going On?

So what really goes on inside Area 51? One thing we do know is that they work on and test aircraft. Whether they are alien spacecraft or not is still open to debate. Some of the planes worked on and tested at Area 51 include the SR-71 Blackbird and the F-117 Nighthawk stealth fighter. Currently, there are rumors that a craft known only by the codename Aurora is being worked on at the facility.

If you want to try and catch a glimpse of some of these strange craft being tested, you'll need to hang out at the "Black Mailbox" along Highway 375, also known as the Extraterrestrial Highway. It's really nothing more than a

mailbox along the side of the road. But as with most things associated with Area 51, nothing is as it sounds, so it should come as no surprise that the "Black Mailbox" is actually white. It belongs to a rancher, who owns the property nearby. Still, this is the spot where people have been known to camp out all night just for a chance to see something strange floating in the night sky.

The Lawsuit

In 1994, a landmark lawsuit was filed against the U.S. Air Force by five unnamed contractors and the widows of two others. The suit claimed that the contractors had been present at Area 51 when large quantities of "unknown chemicals" were burned in trenches and pits. As a result of coming into contact with the fumes of the chemicals, the suit alleged that two of the contractors died, and the five survivors suffered respiratory problems and skin sores. Reporters worldwide jumped on the story, not only because it proved that Area 51 existed but also because the suit was asking for many classified documents to be entered as evidence. Would some of those documents refer to alien beings or spacecraft? The world would never know because in September 1995, while petitions for the case were still going on, President Bill Clinton signed Presidential Determination No. 95–45, which basically stated that Area 51 was exempt from federal, state, local, and interstate hazardous and solid waste laws. Shortly thereafter, the lawsuit was dismissed due to a lack of evidence, and all attempts at appeals were rejected. In 2002, President George W. Bush renewed Area 51's exemptions, ensuring once and for all that what goes on inside Area 51 stays inside Area 51.

So at the end of the day, we're still left scratching our heads about Area 51. We know it exists and we have some idea of what goes on there, but there is still so much more we don't know. More than likely, we never will know everything, but then again, what fun is a mystery if you know all the answers?

Idaho Potato Museum

Blackfoot, Idaho

Located in a state famous for its spuds, the Idaho Potato Museum features the world's largest (artificial) baked potato as well as the world's largest potato chip (it's edible but well-guarded).

From there, the display launches into all things potato, educating as it entertains. For instance, did you know that potatoes are comprised of 80 percent water and 20 percent solids? Or that French fries were introduced to America by Thomas Jefferson?

Neither did we, but the Potato Museum changed all that.

Dog Bark Park Inn

Cottonwood, Idaho

Inside what may be the world's largest beagle, dog-tired guests spend luxurious hours dogging it. Confused? No need. The beagle in question is actually the Dog Bark Park Inn, a.k.a "Sweet Willy"—a two-story rental unit fashioned after the popular breed. Guests are generally dog-crazy types caught up by the wonder of it all.

The inn is run by a husband and wife team who double as chainsaw carvers. In addition to hosting duties, the artists create doggie carvings for most popular breeds. Since the team is constantly beleaguered with questions about Sweet Willy, they've thoughtfully produced a souvenir book that tells his story from snout to tail. It's just the thing should one wish to "put on the dog" when they return home.

Ruff! Ruff!

World's Largest Captive Geyser

Soda Springs, Idaho

Who would have thought that a geyser more reliable than Old Faithful existed? This one spews every hour on the hour, but there is a catch. It's regulated by man. Still, as the world's largest captive geyser, it's worth a visit.

The gushing, 150-foot-high waterspout was discovered in 1937 when a driller accidentally penetrated an underground chamber. Once the geyser sprang forth, it simply wouldn't stop erupting. Soon, enterprising types interested in tourism found a way to cap it.

Today, the water feature goes off without a hitch unless high winds preclude its release. A visitor's center explains the science behind the big gusher. Ready set, BLOW!

Craters of the Moon

Arco, Idaho

In Idaho there's a landmass so unusual, Apollo 14 astronauts used it to prepare for their moon mission. In reality, the craters found at Craters of the Moon National Monument and Preserve are of the volcanic variety, not the result of errant meteor strikes like those found on the moon. Still, their resemblance to lunar pockmarks is almost uncanny.

Comprised of cinder cones, lava tubes, and several types of lava flows, the 60-mile-wide plain is the result of 15,000 years of volcanic activity. A seven-mile loop road takes visitors past the park's most notable volcanic features, and foot trails lead to the rest.

Shoshone Ice Caves

Shoshone, Idaho

This natural wonder is indeed stange and unusual. You'll find ice here in the middle of summer! A wooden bridge leads through the cave to a natural dead-end wall where the ice is extra thick. This is the big payoff —a sizable conglomeration of out-of-season ice.

The Miner's Hat

Kellogg, Idaho

The onetime mining hotbed of the Silver Valley is a natural home for this structure, shaped like a miner's hat with a carbide lamp, at the foot of mountains once scoured for silver and gold. Originally a drive-in restaurant, the building has housed the offices of Miner's Hat Realty since the 1960s.

Idaho State Penitentiary

Boise, Idaho

The early inmates at the Idaho State Penitentiary (which opened around 1870) were model prisoners, but by the 1930s, the convicts admitted there were much more violent and cunning. The prison closed in the 1970s due to riots brought on by the prison's pitiful living conditions. Where there is violence, there's also a good chance that spirits will linger behind. It's no surprise that a tremendous feeling of sadness is experienced in the execution chamber, but visitors' reactions to it are unusually strong: Some have become agitated and overcome with a feeling of dread, while others have dissolved into tears and reported feeling physically ill. And then there are the noises—crying, moaning, and the sounds of guards walking the halls emanate from this facility's walls. The prison, which is now an official historic site, is used as a museum and is open for public tours.

★ ★ ★ Pacific ★ ★ ★

The Vietnamese Catholic Martyrs Church

Sacramento, California

Tales of "crying" statues have become almost commonplace. Sometimes they're revealed as hoaxes, but other times they can truly confound the senses. The Mother Mary statue that cries "tears of blood" at the Vietnamese Catholic Martyrs Church in Sacramento apparently began crying in November 2005 when parishioners discovered a dark reddish substance flowing from her left eye. A priest wiped it away only to see it miraculously reappear a moment later. News of the incident spread like...well, like news of a crying Mother Mary statue. Soon, hordes of the faithful made a pilgrimage to witness the miracle.

Skeptics say that black paint used as eyeliner on the statue is the true culprit and that her "tears" are closer to this color than red. The faithful think the nonbelievers are blinded by anything but the light because the tears continually reappear even after the excess substance is wiped away.

Linda Vista Community Hospital
Los Angeles, California

A hospital with too many unexplained deaths sounds like the perfect place to find a ghost or two. Linda Vista, which was built in 1904, is now closed and is said to be haunted by both patients and staff. Elevators start and stop by themselves; a green light glows faintly throughout the night and other lights flicker on and off; moans and screams have been heard; the image of a doctor has been observed in an upper window; and on the third floor, unexplained foul odors can often be smelled. Visitors also report seeing a spectral girl playing outside and hearing her laugh.

Apparently Hollywood types don't scare too easily: The building has been used in movies, music videos, and commercials, as well as the pilot episode of NBC's long-running hospital drama *ER* (1994).

The Haunted Hollywood Roosevelt Hotel
Los Angeles, California

Hollywood boasts a number of haunted hotels, but the Hollywood Roosevelt, which opened in 1927, is the most famous. Since 1984, when the hotel underwent renovations, the ghosts have been putting in frequent appearances.

One of the hotel's famous ghosts is Marilyn Monroe. Her image is sometimes seen in a mirror that hangs near the elevators.

The specter of Montgomery Clift, who stayed at the hotel in 1952 while filming *From Here to Eternity* has been seen pacing restlessly in the corridor outside of Room 928, where he appears to be rehearsing his lines and learning to play the bugle, which was required for his role in the movie.

Staff members and guests have frequently reported other unexplained phenomena, such as loud voices in empty rooms and hallways; lights being turned on in empty, locked rooms; a typewriter that began typing on its own in a dark, locked office; phantom guests that disappeared when approached; and beds that make and unmake themselves. Those Hollywood ghosts can be so demanding!

Colorado Street Bridge

Pasadena, California

When the Colorado Street Bridge opened in Pasadena, California, in 1913, it was one of the many impressive bridges that Route 66 crossed before it terminated in Santa Monica. But these days, it is commonly referred to as "Suicide Bridge" because it is believed that 100 to 200 people have ended their lives by jumping off this high span; many of these deaths took place during the Great Depression.

But the high suicide rate can't be blamed entirely on economic circumstances because the first one occurred there only six years after construction was finished. It is also believed that a construction worker died there six months before the bridge was complete, when he fell off the structure into a concrete pit supporting a pillar; his body was never recovered, but legend has it that his ghost lures people to follow him.

Many people have witnessed a spectral woman in a flowing robe throwing herself off the bridge. She may be the ghost of a mother who flung her baby and then herself from the span in 1937. (The baby actually landed on some treetops and survived.) People have also heard strange cries coming from the canyon 150 feet below the bridge.

The Brides of March

San Francisco, California

This annual March event aligns with the famous quip, "Take my wife, PLEASE!" as it has some fun with America's most sacred institution.

Designed to lampoon America's commercial wedding culture, the event was born in 1999 through the genius of a member of San Francisco's Cacophony Society.

The premise is quite simple. Procure a used wedding dress, put it on, and join event-goers in a bar-to-bar slosh through San Francisco. Photo opportunities, visits to jewelry stores, and mock weddings round out the special day.

Salvation Mountain

Calipatria, California

Leonard Knight loves God, and he loves all of humankind. To underscore his feelings, the artist created a 50-foot-tall masterpiece on a barren hillside.

Festooned upon a layer of adobe clay, Knight's "canvas" includes paintings of biblical scripture, waterfalls, bluebirds, trees, flowers, and other colorful objects. A large heart situated in the middle of the piece drives the main message home.

Knight adores visitors but eschews cash contributions. He's far more interested in donations of labor and acrylic paint. Although Knight's magnum opus has been created on state land, a 2002 ruling entered it into the congressional record as a national treasure.

Until he died in 2014, Knight lived in a "house" built on the back of his two-ton 1939 Chevrolet truck, which was elaborately decorated to match the mountain he created. He had no modern amenities and chose to rise and rest with the sun.

Giant Sequoia Trees

Tulare County, California

Ancient giant sequoia trees are nature's ever-growing wonders. Giant sequoias grow naturally on the western slopes of California's Sierra Nevada Mountains at elevations from 5,000 to 7,000 feet. Some are as tall as a 26-story building, with their trunks spanning up to 100 feet and the bark on the older specimens reaching two to four feet thick.

California's Sequoia National Park is home to several noteworthy giants, including the General Sherman, which is the world's largest tree by volume, measuring 274.9 feet high, almost 103 feet around, and comprising 52,508 cubic feet of wood. Giant sequoia trees are estimated to be between 1,800 and 2,700 years old. Depending on the tree and where it is situated, giant sequoias can grow up to two feet in height every year, producing almost 40 cubic feet of additional wood each year.

Kinetic Grand Championship
Ventura, California

"Where Art and Engineering Collide," reads the tagline. If this sounds perplexing, understand that this fun-filled, three-day endurance race consists of funky sculptures powered solely by humans. Further challenge lies in the fact that the race traverses pavement, mud, sand, and water.

The offshoot of a 1969 tricycle race, the Kinetic Sculpture Race features homemade contraptions that use Rube Goldberg-like engineering to transform human energy into motive force.

Alternately known as the "Triathlon of the Art World," contestants are openly encouraged to cheat (yeah!) as they strive to attain the number one spot. Gentlemen, start your legs!

The race started when local sculptor Hobart Brown "improved" the look of his son's tricycle by adding extra wheels and ornamentation. Jack Mays then challenged him to a race down the street, and the two competitors, along with about a dozen other machines, raced for the first time. Neither H. Brown nor Mays won, however.

The first winner of the Kinetic Sculpture Race was Bob Brown, whose sculpture was a smoke-emitting turtle that laid eggs.

Grandma Prisbrey's Bottle Village

Simi Valley, California

Apparently, Grandma Tressa Prisbrey (1896–1988) hit the bottle pretty hard. At the age of 62, the intrepid woman began building bottle houses. By the time she finished in the 1980s, 33 full bottle-based structures had been completed.

Her first bottle house acted as an enclosure for her pencil collection (she had more than 10,000 pencils); her second housed a doll collection. From there, things got out of hand, but in a good way.

More than one million bottles were used to construct the village, and the mindset behind it is quite refreshing. "Anyone can do anything with a million dollars," said Prisbrey, "but it takes more than money to make something out of nothing." Indeed.

Tressa Prisbrey's life was not easy. She married her first husband when she was 15; he was 52. She had seven children by him, six of whom died. During her lifetime, death also struck two of her husbands, a fiancé, and all but one of her siblings. To Prisbrey, the Bottle Village was her physical means of creating something delightful out of discard and sorrow. This is reflected in the many references to maternity and sympathetic magic, such as dolls, child-size buildings, wishing wells, and religious structures.

Great Statues of Auburn

Auburn, California

While lesser street artists build their statues from delicate materials, dentist Ken Fox, the artist responsible for the Great Statues of Auburn, constructs his from solid concrete. And he likes to build BIG—a fact evidenced by the 35- to 40-foot height of his figures.

Fox began building his statues in the 1960s, a time when political statements were almost a given. Built in 1972, another of Fox's giant statues depicts an Asian laborer pushing a wheelbarrow. It's more than a little controversial. On the other end of the spectrum, *Fox's Coal Miner* appeals directly to the mainstream in this gold-rush territory; so much so, it was originally commissioned by the town.

The artist's statues are distributed throughout Auburn, but his most risqué works stand beside his dental office. *Freedom of Prayer* features a naked young woman with her arms projected skyward. For certain patients about to undergo root canal, this could prove more effective than Novocain.

When Fox first began raising his statues he had quite a bit of opposition from the town. They even rerouted school buses to keep the children from seeing the contentious sculptures. But the town eventually warmed up to his creations.

Gilroy Gardens

Gilroy, California

If not for one very specific area, Gilroy Gardens would be interchangeable with most any themed amusement park. However, the gardens in Gilroy Gardens set it far, far apart.

The most outstanding items found among the enterprise's six gardens are its Circus Trees. These topiary (trees shaped by grafting, bending, and pruning) differ from conventional trees much the way a Salvador Dalí painting differs from a static photograph.

Two of its more famous offerings are the "Basket Tree," a tree shaped like–you guessed it–a basket, and the "Four-Legged Giant," an otherworldly tree with four separate trunks that merge into one.

Seventeen additional Circus Trees will further confound visitors' senses. Luckily, a wealth of standard garden features offset the grouping. These help viewers to maintain a foothold in reality. And then, last but not least, there are the thrill rides. Whoopee!

Official Center of the World

Felicity, California

Who would believe that a fictional children's book was responsible for designating the official center of the world? It's completely true. *COE the Good Dragon at the Center of the World*, a book written by native frenchman Jacques-Andre Istel, places the point inside a pyramid at Felicity, California, a town that he himself founded.

Somehow, some way, Istel managed to convince Imperial County, California, that Felicity was indeed the world's center. They backed his assertion by declaring Felicity the official Center of the World.

And why shouldn't they? After all, the center of the world is completely dependent upon perspective. Theoretically, every point and any point on planet Earth can represent the center of the world, so Felicity is as good a place as any.

As self-appointed mayor of Felicity (the town is named after Istel's wife Felicia Lee), Istel believes the eye-catching pyramid, lofty designation, and official center of the world metal disc help place his rural town on the map. We wonder if all the hoopla was really necessary. After all, Felicity is centrally located.

Desert Christ Park

Yucca Valley, California

Is Desert Christ Park a theme park for the faithful? Yes and no. While the park surely draws its share of believers, the 35 alabaster figures glistening in the hot, desert sun also snare the eyes of the uncommitted.

Sculptor Antone Martin created his figures and scenes in the 1950s. Constructed in concrete and painted a striking white color, the creations contrast starkly with the muted desert tones in which they're set.

A depiction of the Last Supper stands beside apostles in contemplation. The Tomb of Christ and the Garden of Gethsemane also make an appearance, alongside the Sermon on the Mount.

A few of the statues suffered "beheadings" at the hands of a 1992 earthquake, but by and large Desert Christ Park stands intact, ready to welcome those of faith and curiosity alike.

Don't just capture a picture of the Last Supper; join it! The bas-relief has a convenient window (next to Jesus, of course) that allows you to enter the photo op.

Forestiere Underground Gardens

Fresno, California

Baldasare Forestiere can best be described as a modern-day mole man. To escape the unrelenting heat of the San Joaquin Valley, Forestiere started boring underground in the early 1900s. Some 40 years later, he had created a subterranean complex of caverns, grottoes, and garden courts that were as pretty as they were surreal. Since Forestiere's death in 1946, the 90 rooms that constitute the underground gardens have been operated as a museum.

Today's visitor walks through a land of Roman arches, columns, and domes that provide a striking backdrop for a vast assortment of plants and trees. These include black fig, tangerine, persimmon, avocado, grapefruit, orange, mulberry, and more. Some trees are planted as deep as 22 feet below ground level. They stand as a living testament to the "mole man's" tenacity and fortitude.

Forestiere created his subterranean gardens by hand and with no blueprints. Rather he based them after the "visions stored in [his] mind." He continued to extend and shape the complex throughout his life.

World's Ugliest Dog Competition
Petaluma, California

When does the crack "get a load of that ugly mug!" symbolize something positive? When you own a mongrel that's been entered in the World's Ugliest Dog Competition. The contest, part of the annual Sonoma-Marin Fair, is open to any breed of dog that possesses uncommon repulsiveness. Aside from the prestige of being named the "World's Ugliest Dog," the animal's owner stands to pull down a cool $1,000 cash prize if they win.

In the last decade, there have been a variety of dogs who have won this unfortunate title. There are several Chinese Crested Chihuahuas who have won, and this breed in particular seems well suited for the title. Some of the other winners are chihuahua mixes, olders mutts, and dogs like boxers and mastiffs whose faces are overcome by jowls filled with saliva. In 2006, scandal erupted when an unidentified person gained unauthorized electronic access to the contest's internet voting page. There the offender deleted tens of thousands of votes from the top two leading dogs. The internet voting had to be started from scratch before the panel of judges could select an official winner.

Hollywood Sign

Hollywood, California

Before it became an icon of impending celebrity to newcomers with stars in their eyes, the Hollywood sign was a real estate promotion that actually read "Hollywoodland." The last four letters didn't survive, but the first nine did–albiet barely: By 1973, the sign was falling apart–one 'O' had toppled down the hill, and an arsonist had set fire to an 'L'–prompting a $250,000 reconstruction.

Bubblegum Alley

San Luis Obispo, California

Colorful, unusual, and a bit repulsive, the tradition of leaving one's chewing gum behind in Bubblegum Alley dates back to the 1960s. The alley is interactive and user-friendly: Several nearby downtown merchants conveniently have gumball machines in front of their stores.

Fisherman's Wharf

San Francisco, California

What is now San Francisco's most popular tourist destination has been the heart of its fishing and crabbing industry for more than a century. Often accessed by the world-famous San Francisco cable cars, Fisherman's Wharf is home to a plethora of tourist attractions, including a wax museum, an aquarium, a frolicking population of sea lions, and Oracle Park, the home of baseball's San Francisco Giants.

Museum of Neon Art

Glendale, California

Once nicknamed "liquid fire," neon has evolved into the ink of the American road. It's fitting that Los Angeles County is home to the only museum dedicated to neon art—a Packard dealership here became home to the first neon signs in the United States in 1923.

Founded in 1981, the Museum of Neon Art is located in downtown Glendale's loft district. It plays host to several temporary exhibits each year and also offers classes in neon art and sign-seeing "cruises" of the neon-laden city.

The Haunted *Queen Mary*

Long Beach, California

Once one of the world's most luxurious cruise liners, the *Queen Mary* played host to rich and famous guests such as Clark Gable, Charlie Chaplin, and Elizabeth Taylor. But since 1967, the stately ship has been permanently docked at the Port of Long Beach in California. In the early 1970s, she was transformed into a luxury hotel that includes several restaurants, bars, and lounges. She remains a very popular tourist attraction today.

What many patrons may not know, however, is that this former grande dame of the sea has a history of paranormal activity, which has been witnessed by passengers and crew members alike. In the early 1980s, Tom Hennessy, a columnist for the *Long Beach Press-Telegram*, decided to check out the ship's alleged hauntings for himself. An avowed skeptic, Hennessy didn't expect to find much, but after just one rather frightening night aboard the ship, he left a believer.

Bizarre Activity

Hennessy interviewed several people who had worked aboard the *Queen Mary*, and many of them talked candidly about their experiences with the ship's ghosts. A security guard told Hennessy that it wasn't uncommon for lights to mysteriously switch on and off and for doors to slam shut on G Deck, which is where some believe the ship's morgue was located. The guard also described bizarre activity in the ship's artifacts section, such as motion sensors being tripped even though the room was empty and locked up tight.

Other individuals who had worked on the ship told Hennessy that they'd heard odd clanging noises in the engine room, as if someone was hard at work. But the noises almost always occurred after hours, when the room was unoccupied.

Face to Face With Ghosts

Another security officer revealed to Hennessy that once, while she was standing on the stairs leading to the swimming pool, she saw a woman in an old-fashioned swimsuit preparing to dive into the empty pool. When the guard hollered to stop her, the woman vanished.

Another time, the same guard was riding the escalator from the engine room exhibit when she had the eerie feeling that she was being watched. When she turned around, she saw a man dressed in gray overalls standing on the escalator directly behind her. Assuming that the man was a maintenance worker, she stepped aside to let him pass, but instead, he mysteriously disappeared.

Other witnesses have also encountered this spectral man in overalls. He has dark hair and a long beard and is believed to have been a mechanic or maintenance worker in the 1930s.

The *Queen Mary* also has its own resident "Lady in White." Who this woman was in life is unknown, but she haunts the Queen's Salon. She wears a long white evening gown, and witnesses say that she dances alone near the grand piano as if listening to music that only she can hear.

Tour guides aboard the *Queen Mary* have also reported frightening phenomena, including hearing odd noises and seeing weird lights. One guide said that he heard an unseen man clear his throat, and then he watched as the chain across the entryway to the engine room began to shake violently.

Phantom voices, disembodied footsteps, cold spots, and inexplicable breezes that blow through closed-off areas are some of the other eerie occurrences that take place aboard the *Queen Mary*. While touring the ship, one guest felt someone tugging at her purse, pulling her sweater, and stroking her hair. Cold chills crept down her spine when she realized that no one was near her at the time.

Made a Believer

Hennessy's personal experience aboard the *Queen Mary* was equally odd. During the half hour he spent alone in the portion of the ship that houses the propeller shafts, the journalist heard weird clanging noises that ceased when he ran toward them and then started again when he walked away. He also reported finding an oil drum blocking an entryway where no oil drum had been before. Later, upon returning to the same passageway, he found two drums blocking the way. Hennessy also experienced rushing air in a supposedly airtight room, mysterious vibrations on a metal catwalk, and the sounds of a nearby conversation–even though the closest crew members were two decks away.

It is natural to assume that the spooks that haunt the *Queen Mary* are former guests and crew members, but their exact identities are unknown. Some speculate that the sounds of rolling metal that are occasionally heard in a particular hatchway may be related to a crewman who was crushed to death during World War II when the *Queen Mary* was used as a troopship. And odd activity in one kitchen, including disappearing utensils, is believed to be the antics of an unpopular Navy cook who was killed during a riot aboard the ship. During the melee, the cook was allegedly shoved into a hot oven, where he burned to death.

The ghosts of the *Queen Mary* are apparently more into mischief than mayhem. No one has been hurt or threatened by the spirits, and press reports of the ship's paranormal activity have only served to attract more tourists. The *Queen Mary* may no longer be seafaring, but thanks in part to the spirits that remain on board, she's as popular as ever.

The *Queen Mary* was fast–at the outbreak of World War II, she was the world's fastest transatlantic liner. With a cruising speed of 28.5 knots, she often sailed unescorted, as German subs could not catch or keep up with her. The *Queen Mary* is also huge: In July 1943, she set the still-standing record for the most people on a single voyage with 16,683 soldiers and crew members on board.

Galco's Soda Pop Stop

Los Angeles, California

John Nese has a thing for carbonation. After a prolonged period of underwhelming business at his Italian deli, Nese decided to carry soda, soda, and more soda still. Exclusively.

Since this occurred in 1990 and the businessman's doors still remain open, it appears that Nese's gamble paid off. And why not? Everyone seems to enjoy a refreshing soda now and then, and Nese carries varieties of the bubbly liquid that defy the imagination.

If you're looking for real cola (made with real sugar as opposed to high-fructose corn syrup), he's got it. Turns out the sweet concoction is bottled in Mexico by independent types with an obvious "sweet tooth."

If you fancy a sip of rose-flavored soda (and who doesn't?), Nese has that base covered as well. Marketed as Nuky Rose Soda, the Florida-made beverage is actually prepared from crushed rose petals. Slurp!

From Red Ribbon Cherry Supreme, a soda colored neon-pink, to Special Espresso Coffee Soda, a drink that uncannily resembles mud, Galco's Soda Pop Stop carries more than 500 different varieties of pop that run the gamut from sweet to oh-so-sweet. Could one of these smile-makers have your name on it?

Queen Califia's *Magical Circle*
Escondido, California

This colorful sculpture garden created by noted French artist Niki de Saint Phalle (1930–2002), consists of nine large-scale sculptures painted in a vibrant mosaic of shades.

Named for the legendary Amazon Queen, the *Magical Circle* includes an 11-foot-tall version of Queen Califia holding court beside a 13-foot-tall eagle. These in turn flank other sculptures, a maze entryway, native shrubs, and contemplative integrated benches.

Encircling the garden is a 400-foot undulating wall that features playful serpents that seem ready to strike.

Billed as "the last major international project created by Niki de Saint Phalle," Queen Califia's Magical Circle is as captivating as it is confusing. Art done right is like that sometimes.

Living Memorial Sculpture Garden
Mt. Shasta, California

The Living Memorial Sculpture Garden is the antithesis of most feel-good folk-art displays. Designed to enlighten people to the plight of war and the warriors affected by such confrontations, the memorial tells a stark tale of futility as it honors those that have passed before.

Created by artist Dennis Smith, each sculpture tells a specific story. *The Refugees* looks at those souls uprooted, transplanted, and jostled about by the ever-fickle demands of war. "This type of thing happens a lot," explains Smith. "It is one of the side effects of war."

The POW-MIA Cage depicts a prisoner-of-war cell that speaks to the horrors of such confinement. "This statue is for all those who have been wrongfully locked up. Imagine confinement, mosquitoes, leeches, rats, rotten rice, rotten fish, abusive guards, and little chance of survival. Hope is reaching for the will to hang on!"

Those Left Behind features a survivor, arms outstretched in defeat, symbolically questioning what comes next. "Who can repay those who have lost loved ones in combat?" asks the artist. "What on this earth can compensate for the loss of life?"

Winchester Mystery House

San Jose, California

By the time she was 22, Sarah Pardee was seriously popular—she spoke four languages, played the piano, and was exceedingly pretty. Nicknamed the "Belle of New Haven," she had her pick of suitors.

She chose a young man named William W. Winchester, the only son of Oliver Winchester, a stockholder with the successful New Haven Arms Company. When Sarah and William married in 1862, William had plans to expand the business by buying out some of his competition and introducing the repeating rifle, so named because its lever action allowed a gunman to fire many shots in succession. The gun became known as "The Gun that Won the West," and the now fabulously wealthy Winchester name was woven into the fabric of American history.

Can't Buy Me Love

In the summer of 1866, Sarah gave birth to a daughter, but the joy of a new baby was brief. The child was born sickly, diagnosed with marasmus, a protein deficiency that typically afflicts infants in third-world countries. The baby was unable to gain weight and succumbed to the disease in just a few weeks.

Sarah and William were both bereft, but Sarah took it the hardest. She sank into a serious depression from which she would never totally recover.

Fifteen years later, when Oliver Winchester passed away, William stepped into his dad's shoes at the family business. However, he had only held the job for a few months when he lost a battle with tuberculosis and died in 1881.

Sarah was now 41 years old and without the family she had built her life around. She was also extremely wealthy. In the late 1880s, the average family income hovered around $500 per year. Sarah was pulling in about $1,000 per day! Because her husband left her everything, she had more than 700 shares of stock in addition to income from current sales. Sarah was up to her eyeballs in money. When William's mother died in 1898, Sarah inherited 2,000 more shares, which meant that she owned about 50 percent of the business. Sarah Winchester was all dressed up and had absolutely nowhere to go—even if she did have someplace, there was no one with whom she could share it.

"I See Dead People"

Today, most people regard psychics with more than a little suspicion and skepticism, but in the late 19th century, psychics had grabbed much of the public's attention and trust. The period after the Civil War and the onslaught of new industry had left so much destruction and created so much change for people that many were looking for answers in a confusing world. With claims that they could commune with the "Great Beyond," psychics were consulted by thousands hoping for some insight.

Sarah was not doing well after the death of her husband. Losing her child had been a debilitating blow, but after her husband's passing, she was barely able to function. Fearing for her life, one of Sarah's close friends suggested she visit a psychic to see if she could contact her husband or daughter or both.

Sarah agreed to visit a Boston medium named Adam Coons, who wasted no time in telling her that William was trying to communicate with her, and the message wasn't good.

Apparently, William was desperate to tell Sarah that the family was cursed as a result of the invention of the repeating rifle. Native Americans, settlers, and soldiers all over the world were dead, largely due to the Winchester family. The spirits of these people were out for Sarah next, said William through the medium. The only way for her to prolong her life was to "head toward the setting sun," which meant, "move to California." The medium told her that once she got there, she would have to build a house where all those spirits could live happily together—but the house had to be built big and built often. Sarah was told that construction on the house could never cease, or the spirits would claim her and she would die. So Sarah packed up and left New Haven for California in 1884.

Now That's a House!

Sarah bought an eight-room farmhouse on the outskirts of the burgeoning town of San Jose, on the southern end of San Francisco Bay. Legend has it that she hired more than 20 workmen and a foreman and kept them working 24 hours a day, 365 days a year. To ensure that they would keep quiet about what they were doing—and not leave because the house was more than a little weird—she paid them a whopping $3 per day—more than twice the going rate of the time.

The workmen took the money and built as their client wished, though it made no sense whatsoever. Sarah was not an architect, but she gave the orders for the house's design. Sarah's odd requests, the constant construction, and an endless stream of money resulted in a rather unusual abode—

stairs lead to ceilings, windows open into brick walls, and some rooms have no doors. There are also Tiffany windows all over the place, many containing the number 13, with which Sarah was obsessed. There are spiderweb-paned windows, which, although lovely, didn't do much to dispel rumors that Sarah was preoccupied with death and the occult.

The house kept on growing, all because the spirits were supposedly "advising" Sarah. Chimneys were built and never used. There were so many rooms that counting them was pointless. Reportedly, one stairway in the house went up seven steps and down eleven, and one of the linen closets is bigger than most three-bedroom apartments.

Very few people ever saw the lady of the house. When she shopped in town, merchants came to her car, as she rarely stepped out. Rumors were rampant in San Jose: Who was this crazy lady? Was the house haunted by spirits or just the energy of the aggrieved widow who lived there? Would the hammers ever stop banging? The workers knew how weird the house was, but no one knew for sure what went on inside Sarah's head.

Still, Sarah was generous in the community. She donated to the poor, occasionally socialized, and, in the early days, even threw a party every once in a while. She had a maid she was quite fond of and was exceedingly kind to any children she encountered. But as the house grew and the years passed, the rumors became more prevalent and the increasingly private Winchester retreated further into her bizarre hermitage.

The End

In 1922, Sarah Winchester died in her sleep, and the construction finally ceased after 38 years. In her will, Sarah left huge chunks of her estate to nieces, nephews, and loyal employees. The will was divided into exactly 13 parts and was signed 13 times. Her belongings, everything from ornate furniture to chandeliers to silver dinner services, were auctioned off. It took six weeks to remove everything.

And as for the house itself, it wasn't going to find a buyer any time soon: The structure at the time of Sarah's passing covered several acres and had more than 10,000 window panes, 160 rooms, 467 doorways, 47 fireplaces, 40 stairways, and 6 kitchens. A group of investors bought the house in hopes of turning it into a tourist attraction, which they did. What they didn't do was employ guides or security, however, so for a small fee, thousands of curious people came from all over the country to traipse through the house, scribbling graffiti on the walls and stealing bits of wallpaper. It wasn't until the house was purchased in the 1970s and renamed the Winchester Mystery House that it was restored to its original state. Millions of people have visited the house, which continues to be one of the top tourist attractions in California.

The Footnote

With so many people going in and out of the house over the years, it's not surprising that there are tales of "strange happenings" in the Winchester mansion. People have claimed that they've heard and seen banging doors, mysterious voices, cold spots, moving lights, doorknobs that turn by themselves, and more than a few say that Sarah herself still roams the many rooms. Psychics who have visited the house solemnly swear that it is indeed haunted.

This can't be proven, of course, but it doesn't stop the claims, and it didn't stop the lady of the house from undertaking one of the world's most incredible construction projects.

La Brea Tarpits

Los Angeles, California

The animals are much smaller than they used to be—no saber-toothed cats or woolly mammoths—but the famous pits continue to trap critters like lizards and birds.

Tar pits are created when crude oil seeps through a fissure in the earth's crust. When oil hits the surface, the less dense elements of the oil evaporate, leaving behind a gooey, sticky substance known as asphalt, or tar. La Brea is a Spanish name that translates literally to "the tar." These famed pits are located in Hancock Park in Los Angeles; they constitute the only active archeological excavation site to be situated in a major metropolitan area. The pits are tended by staff members of the George C. Page Museum, which is nearby. It is at the museum that the fossils currently being excavated from the pits are cleaned and examined.

Not only do the staff members get to parse through the well-preserved remnants of prehistory, but they also sometimes witness the natural process by which these remnants are preserved. An average of ten animals every 30 years get trapped in the pits.

The tar pits, which are about 40,000 years old, work like a large-scale glue trap. If an animal lets just one paw hit the surface of the asphalt, it sticks (especially on warm days, when the asphalt is at its stickiest). In its frenzy to free itself, the animal gets more stuck. Eventually, its nose and mouth will be covered, and then it's all over—just one more carcass for scientists to excavate.

Watts Towers

Los Angeles, California

In the annals of American folk art, few endeavors have drawn as much attention as the Watts Towers. The tall sculptural pieces, located in the economically depressed community of Watts, continue to elicit responses both positive and negative. At one point, detractors threatened to topple the tall towers, taking one man's personal creativity and art of self-expression down for the count.

In 1921, Italian immigrant Sabato "Simon" Rodia (1879–1965) had a date with artistic destiny. At his home in the Watts section of Los Angeles, the laborer dreamt of "doing something big." To accomplish the task, he gathered whatever materials he could find and started to build. Along the way, Rodia himself admitted he had little idea what would eventually materialize. Thirty years later, the folk artist would know for sure.

Using steel pipes and rods, mortar and wire mesh, Rodia built a virtual city on his tiny, one-third acre lot. Performing the task completely alone, Rodia's artistic offering featured tall towers (two approach 100 feet in height), plazas, fountains, walkways, and a gazebo. To offset their starkness, many of his works featured eye-catching shards of glass, bits of shiny porcelain, and tile. In 1955, Rodia declared his work Nuestro Pueblo (Spanish for "our town") and stepped aside. His masterpiece was complete.

Rodia moved from Watts in 1954, and a downward spiral of vandalism and disrepair turned many against his creation. Eventually, the city of Los Angeles declared the towers "an unauthorized public hazard" and scheduled a test of their structural integrity. If the towers could withstand a 10,000-pound stress test, the equivalent of a 76 mile-per-hour windstorm, they would be spared. If not, Simon Rodia's life work would be reduced to a pile of rubble. On October 10, 1959, the test commenced. A crowd of 1,000 supporters drew sighs of relief when the towers held firm. Later that year, the towers were opened to the public for a fifty-cent charge. Things were looking up. Literally.

Today, the Watts Towers stand as symbol of self-expression and survival. They have garnered enough popularity to earn a spot on the National Register of Historic Places, a feat not often awarded to folk art. If "doing something big" was Rodia's principal goal, it's a safe bet to say he succeeded. Defiant, hulking towers stand as proof.

The Haunted White Eagle Saloon

Portland, Oregon

The building housing the White Eagle Saloon in Portland, Oregon, has been many things since it was constructed in the early 1900s: a hotel, a brothel, a rooming house, and, most recently, a tavern that features live music. For much of its history, it has also been haunted.

Over the years, a great deal of paranormal activity has been reported at the White Eagle Saloon. Most of it has been harmless—but not all of it. For example, many years ago, a waitress was walking to the basement after closing to tabulate the day's receipts when something unseen shoved her down the stairs. The woman's hysterical screams got the attention of the bartender and doorman, who had a bucket hurled at them by an invisible force. Not surprisingly, the waitress quit the next day.

To date, this is the most violent outburst from the spirits at the White Eagle Saloon; however, many other, more innocuous events that simply defy explanation have occurred there.

Weirdness in the Bathroom

One of the White Eagle's ghosts seems to enjoy flushing the toilet in the men's room. Many people have observed this unusual activity, usually after closing. A faulty toilet? No way, says owner Chuck Hughes—the flushing has occurred with two different commodes, and it is sometimes accompanied by the sound of footsteps in the hallway outside the restroom.

Hughes has experienced quite a bit of unexplained phenomena over the years. For example, one day he was removing a lock from a door on the second floor when he heard what sounded like a woman crying at the other end of the hallway. But as he walked toward the source of the noise, the crying ceased. Hughes checked all of the rooms on the second floor but found nothing. When he returned to his work on the door, the crying began again. Hughes again tried to find the source of the sound, and this time, he felt an overwhelming chill.

Frightened, Hughes rushed downstairs and exited the tavern. Looking back at the building, he saw what he later described as a ghostly shape in one of the second-floor windows. After moving to the back of the building, Hughes saw the same specter at another window. Shaken, he refused to go upstairs again for nearly a year.

A Ghost Named Sam

It is believed that one of the ghosts haunting the White Eagle Saloon is a former employee named Sam, who some say was adopted at a young age by one of the building's early owners. A burly guy, Sam lived and worked at the White Eagle until his death in the 1930s.

After Sam died in his room at the White Eagle, his boss had his body removed and then locked the room and left it pretty much the way it was for a long time. Is Sam still hanging around the tavern? Many believe so. Hughes recalled that after he bought the White Eagle, the door to Sam's room would not stay open. Time after time, the door was left open, only to be found shut—and locked—a couple of days later. Apparently, Sam likes his privacy.

Hughes says that he's experienced enough unexplained phenomena at the White Eagle to fill a book. For example, he used to keep a bed in the basement to use when he worked late; one night, he awoke to find himself being nudged by invisible hands. Understandably disconcerted, he got dressed and went home.

While working in the basement after hours, Hughes often heard voices and footsteps above him; sometimes the voices even called his name. But every time he went to investigate, no one was there.

Suspected Spooks

The White Eagle Saloon has hosted its share of wild times and even wilder characters over the years, so it's no surprise that it's haunted. Sam is believed to be the spook that flushes the men's room toilet, and the crying woman may be the spirit of one of the many prostitutes who worked there when the building housed a brothel.

But who pushed the waitress down the cellar stairs? Some suspect that it was the ghost of a Chinese bouncer known for harshly treating the African American prostitutes who worked in the basement. One day, the guy simply disappeared. Was he murdered? If so, it might explain why his angry spirit is still attached to the White Eagle.

The Haunted Heathman Hotel
Portland, Oregon

Choose your room at the Heathman Hotel carefully because there's a certain column of rooms that reportedly sees quite a bit of paranormal action: You should pick rooms ending in 03 (between 303 and 1003) only if you don't mind spending the night with a ghostly companion. George Heathman built the hotel in 1927 for lumber and railroad tycoons who sought luxurious lodging in the West.

No one knows what actually caused the hauntings, but ghost hunters speculate that someone fell or jumped out of a window and now haunts the rooms that he or she passed on the way down. Today, guests in those rooms experience odd occurrences, such as towels being used and glasses and chairs being moved when no one else has been in the room. Visitors have also felt a strange presence in some rooms; one guest even awoke to find himself wrapped up tightly in his sheets.

Out 'N' About Treehouse Treesort
Takilma, Oregon

Though it's a bit off the beaten path, this "treesort" promises an unforgettable experience—each unit is a different tree house. Each tree house has a different theme: You can choose to stay in the saloon-inspired "Treeloon," the "TreePee," the "Cavaltree Fort," or you can really go out on a limb and stay in the highest tree house, the 37-foot-high "Treezebo."

If a whole night in a tree house is more than you want, take one of the daily tours of unoccupied units and the "Mountain View Treeway," a high-rise walkway that includes a 90-foot suspension bridge.

Petersen Rock Garden

Redmond, Oregon

Folk artist Rasmus Petersen created this four-acre rock garden to pay homage to life in America. He started collecting rocks he found on his property, such as agate, obsidian, and malachite, in 1906 and began to build monuments, bridges, and buildings in 1935.

The garden features replicas of the Statue of Liberty and Independence Hall, and the adjoining museum offers a florescent rock display.

The Bomber

Milwaukie, Oregon

Before this long-standing drive-in restaurant closed, a World War II–era B-17G bomber graced its premises. The Bomber served up thick milk shakes and Bomber Burgers since 1948, a year after Art Lacey bought the "flying fortress" and flew it to Oregon to use as an advertising gimmick for his gas station. Though the gas station closed in 1991, the restaurant was still run by Art Lacey's family for a couple more decades.

Voodoo Doughnut

Portland, Oregon

More than a mere doughnut shop, Voodoo Doughnut is a night owl's dream–open from 10p.m. to 10 a.m.–and a licensed wedding chapel. Their giant doughnuts come in a wide selection, from the namesake "Voodoo Doughnut" to the "Memphis Mafia" (with a peanut butter-banana-chocolate glaze). Doughnuts and coffee for ten are part of the wedding ceremony package.

Mitchell Recreation Area & Memorial

Lake County, Oregon

When the Japanese attacked Pearl Harbor on December 7, 1941, 2,390 lives were lost and the United States was dragged into World War II. But it is a mistake to believe that no one was killed on the U.S. mainland as a result of the war.

On May 5, 1945, a Japanese balloon bomb killed six Americans picnicking near the town of Bly, Oregon. The Japanese launched some 9,000 balloon bombs against the United States during World War II. They attached incendiary and anti-personnel bombs to large hydrogen-filled balloons and released them into the jet-stream winds to float 5,000 miles across the Pacific Ocean and explode in the forested regions of Western states. This, they hoped, would cause widespread forest fires and divert U.S. manpower and resources away from the war in the Pacific.

Officially, only 285 of the balloon bombs reached North America, though experts estimate that approximately 1,000 made it across the Pacific Ocean. The U.S. military successfully orchestrated a media blackout of the bombings to deny the Japanese any publicity of success. The first balloon landed near San Pedro, California, on November 4, 1944. The bombs traveled as far north as Canada, as far south as the Arizona border with Mexico, and as far east as Farmington, Michigan, just ten miles from Detroit. The U.S. military shot some down, while others landed without exploding. None, however, succeeded in creating the major forest fires Japan desired.

When a 13-year-old girl on a church picnic in the woods near Bly, Oregon, discovered one of the balloon bombs, she attempted to pull it from a tree. It exploded, killing the girl, the church minister's wife, and four other children. These six were the only war casualties on the U.S. mainland during World War II. Had the Japanese perfected the balloon bombs and used germ or biological weapons, that statistic, and the outcome of the war, might have been very different.

Today, a memorial stands to honor the victims of Japan's balloon bomb attack during World War II. Inside the Fremont-Winema National Forest near Bly you can find the Mitchell Memorial in the Mitchell Recreation Area.

Coastal Ghost Forests

Tillamook County, Oregon

The gnarled, twisted shapes rising up from Oregon's coastline are macabre memorials to the magnificent forests that stood here ages ago. Like a ghost town eerily preserved in time, these "ghost forests" are shrouded in mystery: What caused the mighty trees to fall? Why are they still here? And where are they going?

An Eerie Appearance

These groves of ancient tree stumps—called "ghost forests" because of their age (approximately 1,000 to 4,000 years old) and bleak appearance—emerge along the 46-mile stretch between Lincoln City and Tillamook. For years, tourists and scientists alike have been perplexed by the forests' strange beauty. Some trees extend out of the sand like angular sculptures; others are just visible as tiny tips poking through the water.

All are remnants of the giant Sitka spruce forests, which towered 200 feet above Oregon's coastline for years. That is, until something knocked them down.

A Cataclysmic Collapse

No one knows for sure just what that "something" was, but experts agree that for such forests to be preserved, the trees must have been very suddenly submerged in sand, clay, or mud. This submersion would not only kill the trees but also keep them frozen in time by shutting off their oxygen.

The original (and still widely held) belief is that a giant earthquake, which suddenly dropped the ground 25 feet below sea level and immersed the trees in sand and water, toppled the forests. Another theory is that it wasn't an earthquake but a tsunami that struck, drowning the trees under a massive tidal wave. A third theory suggests that it was a combination of the two—an earthquake buried the trees and then caused a tsunami that lopped off the tree tops, leaving only stumps behind.

A newer theory is that the trees died as a result of sudden landscape changes, with sand levels rising over the course of a few decades (that's "sudden" when you're speaking in geologic terms) to eventually overwhelm the forest.

Seasonal Specters

For decades, ghost forests were seen only occasionally during the harsh winter months, when violent waves strip away layers of sand, exposing the tree stumps just briefly before the calmer waves of spring and summer carry sand back to the shores and bury them once again.

But lately, the ghost forests have become less of a rarity. Since 1998, more and more spooky spruces have been popping up—the result of a decade of rough winters, washing away as much as 17 feet of sand in some areas, combined with less sand recovery in the spring and summer.

In 2007, Arch Cape saw stumps for the first time in 40 years, along with the mud-cliff remains of a forest floor, and in the winter of 2008, an unprecedented ten-foot drop in sand level revealed a new forest at Cape Kiwanda.

Just a few miles away at Hug Point, the waves uncovered stumps that could date back 80,000 years to the Pleistocene era, when woolly mammoths and saber-toothed tigers roamed the earth. And the remains of roots marred by saws at Moolack Beach show that early European settlers harvested the trees for fire and shelter. Oregon's most impressive and most famous ghost forest is found at Neskowin, where 100 twisted shapes can be seen poking through the water year-round.

Erosional Riptide

But the erosion that has newly exposed these phantom forests may also be destroying them. The stumps at Neskowin and Cape Lookout are reportedly showing so much that waves are ripping them out by the roots.

Some experts believe this increased erosion means the coastline is gradually disappearing—and taking the ghost forests with it. Perhaps soon, the ghost forests of Oregon will haunt only our memories.

Caveman

Grants Pass, Oregon

In 1874, a hunter uncovered a cave system near Grants Pass. The men in the community eventually used it as the launching pad for an Elks-like club named the Cavemen. After a secret subterranean ceremony in 1922, the group dressed in skins and marched in local parades. The club isn't as visible today, but members left a lasting mark on the town in the form of an 18-foot fiberglass Neanderthal who welcomes visitors.

Yaquina Bay Lighthouse

Newport, Oregon

In 1899, Lischen M. Miller wrote a story for *Pacific Monthly* about a girl who disappeared at the Yaquina Bay Lighthouse. The girl, a captain's daughter, was left with a caretaker while her father was at sea. One day she and her friends went to explore the abandoned lighthouse.

When she got separated from her friends, they heard her shriek. They searched for her but only found some blood and her handkerchief. A door that had been open only moments before was locked. Although many maintain that this story is pure fiction, the spectral figure of a girl has been seen around the tower.

The Haunted Heceta Head Lighthouse

Florence, Oregon

Home of Rue (aka "the Gray Lady"), this former lighthouse is now a bed-and-breakfast. It is believed that Rue was the mother of a baby who was found buried on the grounds. Perhaps she feels the need to stay and protect her child, but if that's the case, she finds plenty of other ways to stay busy: Objects are moved, cupboard doors open and close by themselves, and a fire alarm was once mysteriously set off.

Although Rue doesn't seem to mean any harm, she once frightened a workman so terribly that he accidentally broke a window and fled, leaving broken glass all over the floor. That night, workers heard a scraping noise coming from upstairs; in the morning, they found that the broken glass had been swept into a nice, neat pile.

Prehistoric Gardens

Gold Beach, Oregon

Prehistoric Gardens, the life work of Earnie Nelson, features 23 life-size prehistoric animal sculptures going about their daily lives within a soupy, natural rain forest.

Each steel and mortar replica was designed to be as scientifically correct as possible, but we could still detect a twinkle in the eye of even the most fearful specimens.

While this is no Jurassic Park (thank goodness!), the rain forest setting provides the correct backdrop to approximate the prehistoric age. Explanatory boards label each specimen and offer up tidbits about their imposing existence. If you ever wish to feel small, this is the place.

Gerhke's Windmill Garden

Grand Coulee, Washington

If you're going to build yourself a windmill garden, it seems right and proper that it be erected in Electric City. After all, a windmill produces electricity–and Electric City, with its close proximity to the Grand Coulee Dam, seems to be the kingpin of current flow.

Despite their powerful implications, the windmills were actually built for decoration. Emile Gehrke (1884–1979) originally constructed the "wind spinners" in his backyard, but after his death much of his whimsical works were moved to a fenced-in display along a main road in nearby Grand Coulee.

Here, visitors will find windmills designed like kettles, plates, funnels, bicycle wheels, spoons, pots and pans, and hard hats. Gehrke's presence looms large over his creations, which is none too surprising since their relationship was written on the wind.

Cedar Creek Treehouse

Ashford, Washington

Adventure seekers looking for unique digs will be hard-pressed to outdo the Cedar Creek Treehouse, located at the base of majestic Mount Rainier. From a 50-foot perch on a fragrant cedar tree, these accommodations offer a bird's-eye view of the mountain. Built in 1982 and placed within the "arms" of a Western Red Cedar tree, the 16- by 16-foot cabin generally operates as a bed-and-breakfast, although the owners are currently on break. An 80-foot suspension bridge followed by a five-story stairwell takes one up, up, up to the unique lodge. Guests who've stayed at the treehouse speak of deliciously fresh air, spiritual renewal, and a newfound sense of peace. Funny, we thought a blister or sprain might work its way into their tales. Amenities include a one-hour guided tour of the area, which takes place approximately 100 feet in the sky! Guests are free to video and photograph the incredible sights.

The Haunted Northern State Mental Hospital

Sedro-Woolley, Washington

Built in 1912, the Northern State Mental Hospital was intended to treat nonviolent but mentally unstable patients. Because it was a humane facility with beautiful grounds and educational and vocational opportunities for the patients, it quickly became known as the place to send the mentally ill. But all that changed in 1950, when Dr. Charles Jones took over the hospital. He began performing a new, innovative, and highly experimental procedure known as the trans-orbital lobotomy, which involved slicing into the brain to disable certain functions.

The exact number of deaths that occurred at this hospital is unknown, but it is estimated to be around a thousand.

One ghost, which is known simply as "Fred," enjoys tossing pans and other objects through the air. Witnesses have also spotted the apparitions of a young girl playing with a red ball and her father chasing after her.

Hobo Inn

Elbe, Washington

Near the foot of majestic Mount Rainier, the Hobo Inn is the place to bed down for the night for an experience that melds creature comforts with the hobo lifestyle. The proprietors have converted about a half-dozen vintage cabooses into motel rooms (scarf on a stick not included).

Seafair Milk Carton Derby

Seattle, Washington

Got milk? If so, you may wish to save your milk carton and at least 49 others. Only then can you enter Seattle's Milk Carton Derby.

Kicking off Seattle's Seafair celebration for better than three decades, the derby pits ordinary citizens against corporate and military teams. The object? Make it across 1,200 feet of water in a human-powered craft built from a minimum of 50 half-gallon milk cartons.

Awards are presented in a number of categories, but the number one objective appears to be basic survival. Since a milk carton only supports four pounds of weight, there are more than a few Titanic incidents. Bottoms up!

Fremont Troll

Seattle, Washington

Do you remember the childhood fairy tale that spoke of a troll that lived beneath a bridge? If you do, and if you're haunted by such a frightening prospect (as we most certainly aren't) don't go anywhere near Seattle's Aurora Bridge. A hideous beast dwells beneath it. The troll "sculpture" stands 18 feet tall, with a head at least half that high, and can scare a small child (and certain writers) out of a year's growth.

While it's officially said to have been sculpted by four area artists in 1990, we're not so sure. The evil gnome clutches a Volkswagen Beetle in his grimy paws. Our guess is he snatched it from the roadway above! Some foolhardy types take their chances and clamber on top of the beast. That's a bit too risky for us.

Once upon a time the troll's Beetle contained Elvis memorabilia. This time capsule was removed after the car was vandalized, including having its California license plate stolen.

Fremont Rocket

Seattle, Washington

Erected in 1994, this genuine 1950s rocket once graced a surplus shop in Belltown. Now it stands poised for moon shots. Well, sort of.

Bedecked in snazzy metalwork, neon lights, and shiny paint, the Fremont Rocket stands before a colorful mural of clouds and distant galaxies. At regular intervals, plumes of vapor issue through its nozzles suggesting an imminent launch.

Since it's moored to the corner of the Ah Nuts Junk Shop, an escape from Earth is about as likely as an escape from income taxes, but the dreamers among us shall not be deterred.

5, 4, 3, 2, 1...blast off!

Lenin Statue

Seattle, Washington

What can an ultra-progressive, artistic community such as Fremont add to their enclave that might have a hope of "pushing buttons"? The world's largest Lenin statue, of course.

If your history is up to snuff, you'll recall that former Soviet Union leader Vladimir Lenin (1870–1924) was the poster boy for communism, a regime that apple-pie-loving Americans have had more than a few problems with throughout the years. Why then should good Washingtonians display a statue of him? Simple. Because as members of a free nation, they still can.

The 16-foot-tall bronze statue originally hails from Poprad, Slovakia (the former Czechoslovakia), where it was erected in 1988. When the Soviet regime went down for the count in 1989, the statue was unceremoniously tossed into a Poprad dumpsite. Rescued by American Lewis Carpenter, it was shipped to its new home in Seattle.

The statue depicts Lenin marching with a determined gait, on his way to impending revolution. The contrast of the immense communist figure standing beside thriving capitalist stores is pronounced. It suggests that, for now at least, capitalism is alive and well.

Lewis Carpenter managed to finance the salvage and move of the statue in large by mortgaging his home. When he died in a car accident in 1994, the statue (and its debt) was left in the hands of his estate.

His family loaned the statue to the Fremont district until a buyer could be found; the asking price was $150,000. They are still seeking a buyer. As of 2015, the price had been raised to $250,000.

Fremont Fair Solstice Parade

Seattle, Washington

When budding counter-culturists and unabashed freedom lovers seek a place to "get their groove on" they head straight for Fremont's annual Solstice Parade. Since the event features just about anything that can be conjured up artistically, plus oodles of self-expression displayed in its many, varied forms, the procession ranks as one of the most eclectic in the world.

Detractors speak of the parade's crazy pop-art, antiestablishment statements, and general lunacy. Backers point to its freedom of expression, transcendence of boundaries, and philanthropic roots. But all, and we repeat ALL, will tell you of its frequent nudity and the throng of naked bicycle riders that "crash" the event each year. It's a real show-stopper and a renewable lure that continually draws in crowds.

When the first parade was held in 1989, it drew about 300 people. Thirty years later, Seattleites in the tens of thousands wait with bated breath to see what will go down next. Main moral: People love to mix.

RichArt's Ruins

Centralia, Washington

Factually speaking, RichArt's Ruins was a conglomeration of trash that artist Richard Tracy assembled before his 2022 death. Comprised of discarded metal pieces, chunks of Styrofoam, light bulbs, plastic balls, and countless other items, all seem placed in a happenstance way along multiple "walls" throughout the complex.

From certain angles, RichArt's Ruins looked precisely like a mass of junk stuck together. From others, artistic possibilities and even small triumphs materialized. The latter was enough to keep visitors walking along to see what they would uncover next. Perhaps this was RichArt's intent all along?

Bob's Java Jive

Tacoma, Washington

A stellar example of programmatic architecture, Bob's Java House is a throwback to a fun era that featured many such wondrous establishments. The fact that it still stands makes it one rare pot indeed.

Originally dubbed the Coffee Pot Restaurant when it opened in 1927, the 25-foot tall, 30-foot diameter coffee pot served, among other things, piping hot coffee. It operated in this capacity for a few years then morphed into a drive–through restaurant. At one point during its illustrious history, it even became a speakeasy.

In 1955, the establishment was purchased by Bob and Lylabell Radonich and rechristened Bob's Java Jive, a nighttime "hot" spot. After remorphing into a karaoke bar and then a go-go club, the coffee pot poured its way into the new millennium, only slightly worse for all its wear.

Today, the pot has become a beloved icon and an instantly recognizable feature on the Tacoma landscape. It is still owned by the Radonich family (Bob Radonich passed into that great percolator in the sky in 2002 at the seasoned age of 83) and currently features area rock 'n' roll bands over strong cups of Joe.

But the main thing is that Bob's Java Jive, a chuck of artistic pop culture from a far-off time, is still standing. Somehow, almost inexplicably, this little-pot-that-could has weathered repeated storms of change and warmed the hearts (and bellies) of us all as it has spanned the ages. For that, we should all raise our cups.

The famous coffee pot has served as a unique backdrop for movies *Say Anything* (1989) and *I Love You To Death* (1990). The films boast big names such as John Cusack, Kevin Kline, and Keanu Reeves.

Programmatic Architecture

Programmatic, or "Mimic," architecture is a form of construction that characterizes what an operation builds or sells. While this sounds buttoned-up and businesslike, the end result is anything but. From coffee shops shaped like mugs to hot dog stands shaped like wieners, this waning form of construction enchants as it entices.

Prime examples of this technique are found at the Longaberger Company headquarters (an office building shaped like a picnic basket) in Newark, Ohio, Randy's Donuts (with a giant donut on its roof) in Los Angeles, California, and the catsup bottle water tower (hawking Brooks Catsup) in Collinsville, Illinois. Fun, fun, fun!

World's Largest Frying Pan: Almost

Long Beach, Washington

What was once billed as the world's largest frying pan has sadly slipped from the top shelf—and there's not a can of PAM in sight to blame it on. The fact is, this giant nine-foot, six-inch pan was simply outpanned by other towns.

Record holders only rent the marks that they hold, and all must eventually release the reins. Still, Long Beach's pan makes for great photo ops and will always be a unique conversation piece.

From time to time, the big pan travels throughout the northwest to promote the Long Beach area.

Land of Metal People

Raymond, Washington

In and around the town of Raymond, mysterious metal figures dot the landscape. These silhouette sculptures depict Native Americans, loggers, bears, horses, oxen, foxes, birds, and other things. What are they and why are they here?

The artistic effort in steel is known as the "Raymond Wildlife Heritage Sculptures Corridor." Its purpose is to reflect the area's rich heritage.

Numbering some 200 pieces in all, the sculptures spice up Highway 101, State Route 6, and parts of the town.

Heavily rusted and gritty after years spent in a wet climate, the statues suggest equal grit in the people and animals they personify. But there seems to be one out-of-place offering. Does a girl feeding an ice-cream cone to a dog conjure up particularly hard times? If so, sign us up!

Think the statues are so neat that you'd like one for yourself? Replicas are available for purchase through the Raymond Chamber of Commerce.

Waterfront Exercise Bikes

Vashon Island, Puget Sound, Washington

Here's one that's so silly it had to be included. Six fully functional exercise bicycles sit overlooking Puget Sound on a land bridge connecting Vashon Island with Maury Island. How and why they are here is anyone's guess.

Could the bicycle donor be an exercise junky looking for an on-the-fly endorphin release? Might he/she be a person who has declared war on calories? Is the bicycle enthusiast a few spokes shy of a full wheel?

These earth-shattering questions may never find an answer, but that's not important. There's much peddling to do, ladies and gentlemen, so have at it!

See a Moose in Anchorage

Anchorage, Alaska

Moose regularly wander into Anchorage. True. Moose can show up nearly anywhere in Alaska (including most towns) at any time of year. They aren't playthings; they are wild animals that can be very grumpy and dangerous, so don't toy with them.

By definition, the worst location in Alaska is between a sow grizzly and her cubs. The second worst is between a cow moose and her calf, and moose are far more numerous than bears.

Christmas in Alaska

North Pole, Alaska

A luxury Christmas cruise to Alaska has become one of the most popular cruises for Americans to take, and it's not hard to figure out why. It is a myth that there is no sunlight in southern Alaska during the winter months (though the days are quite short), and nothing could possibly convey the spirit of the season better than the rugged, subarctic beauty of the 49th state. Alaska offers American travelers the adventure and exoticism they crave while still maintaining the safety and comfort of home, and this combo makes it a wonderful place to enjoy the winter holidays.

Apart, Yet a Part of Us

Alaska may be as American as apple pie, but you won't find apple pie at most Alaskans' Christmas celebrations. Maple-frosted doughnuts are the traditional sweet served on Christmas Eve, but they come after the main course, which includes such Native Alaskan delights as *maktak* (raw whale), walrus, caribou, and owl. Too far out of your comfort zone? Try the *nigiglik* (duck), *piruk* (fish pie), or smoked salmon.

Though Alaska is the least religious state in the Union, with only 22 percent of its citizens identifying themselves as church-goers, the Christian faith was well-established by Catholic, Protestant, and Eastern Orthodox missionaries. Many Native Alaskans as well as other residents consider themselves to be Christian, and the Aleut phrase *Gristuusaaq suu'uq,* or "Christ is born" is seen and heard often during the Christmas season.

Christmas in North Pole

Of course, nowhere in Alaska is Christmas more popular than in the North Pole, where the "Christmas in Ice" festival features beautiful ice sculptures by artists who come from as far as China to share their talent. Music, food, and special events for the kids make this a truly memorable Christmas event.

The First Alaska Highway
Fairbanks, Alaska

The 1,500-mile Alaska Highway, which runs from Dawson Creek in Canada's Yukon to Fairbanks, Alaska, was not the first Alaskan highway. Sure, it got the name and fame, but it was a highway-come-lately compared to the 1,150-mile Iditarod Trail between Seward and Nome. The Iditarod opened in 1915; the Alaska Highway in 1942. Granted, the Alaska Highway is open year-round and is paved, while the decidedly more rustic Iditarod Trail is just, well, a trail, navigable only in winter and only by dogsled.

Still, the Iditarod has an international claim to fame. Each winter since 1973, dog mushers from every snowy corner of the world gather to race over the trail in the "Last Great Race on Earth," an annual tribute the history and contributions of the dog sleds, from the gold prospectors who opened Alaska's interior (the dogs would haul the gold), to the dogs that ran serum vaccines to isolated Nome to prevent a diphtheria epidemic in 1925.

So, what exactly is an "Iditarod"? It's a ghost town that was once the midpoint on the trail.

World Ice Art Championship

Fairbanks, Alaska

Originating in the 1930s as the Fairbanks Winter Carnival and Dog Derby, the World Ice Art Championships evolved into an annual tradition in the late 1980s. Teams from all over the world carve blocks of ice into ornate sculptures of all kinds. Over the years, sculptures have included stingrays, dragons, 100-foot towers, and truly inspired abstract works. The blocks used are harvested from a frozen pond; past events have used 1,500 tons of ice.

Aurora Ice Museum

Fairbanks, Alaska

If you're going to build an ice museum, Fairbanks, Alaska, appears to be a good spot. In 2004, the Chena Hot Springs Resort got busy and built the "Aurora Ice Hotel." It contained carved ice crystals, ice sculptures, a functional chess set, jousting knights, and galleries of assorted ice themes. Unfortunately, due to a run of 90-degree days (can this really be Alaska?), it melted.

In 2005, with the help of World Champion ice carver Steve Brice (and a high-tech patented "absorption chiller") another attempt was made. This time, the frosted figures froze frigidly, and the operation was rechristened the "Aurora Ice Museum." Visitors could now see a frozen "polar bear" bedroom, an igloo, chandeliers shaped like the Aurora Borealis, even a frosty outhouse.

Today, the ice sculptures remain at a constant 20-degree level and await the arrival of warm-blooded mammalians. The good folks at Chena Hot Springs Resort offer you a parka for your visit.

Need to "chill out" after taking a tour? The museum boasts an ice bar where you can order a variety of drinks, including an "apple-tini," which is served in an ice-carved martini glass. But don't worry about getting too cold; there's an ice fireplace nearby to warm your hands.

Anchorage Light Speed Planet Walk

Anchorage, Alaska

The Anchorage Light Speed Planet Walk has people traveling faster than they ever thought humanly possible.

So what is it? Basically it's a scale-model built to human dimensions and spread throughout the city. An eight-minute walk starting at the sun will deliver one to Earth—the time it takes a light beam to cover the distance across the cosmos.

For math aficionados, this means each step equals the distance that light travels in one second, or 186,000 miles. And you thought drag-racers were fast.

Service High School graduate Eli Menaker devised the model as a way for people to wrap their minds around the enormous size of our solar system. Each planet is represented at different locations around the city and a special indoor solar system exhibit lies on the path to Mercury. It's a small universe, after all.

Menaker worked with artist Julie Matthews to guarantee the accuracy of the sunspots on the star's replica.

Watching the Aurora Borealis

Yukon-Koyukuk County, Alaska

The aurora borealis (also called the northern lights) consists of awe-inspiring twirls of light in the sky, caused by "solar wind"—electrically charged particles interacting with Earth's magnetic field. The aurora borealis can be up to 2,000 miles wide, but it fluctuates in size, shape, and color, with green being the most common color close to the horizon while purples and reds appear higher.

Named after Aurora, Roman goddess of dawn, and Boreas, Greek god of the north wind, these ribbons of color are best viewed in northern climates like Alaska, but have been seen as far south as Arizona.

Santa Claus House

North Pole, Alaska

In the early 1950s, Con and Nellie Miller relocated to Alaska. Mr. Miller wore an old red Santa suit and soon became "Santa" in the eyes of local children. The name caught on, and the couple built this gift shop and trading post to celebrate the spirit of Christmas all year.

A giant Santa marks the entrance to the shop, and reindeer can be found on the grounds. You can even order a personalized letter from Santa proclaiming the recipient to be on the "Good List."

Igloo City Resort

Cantwell, Alaska

The icelike exterior of this four-story igloo located between Fairbanks and Anchorage sheaths an unfinished interior: The developers ran out of money before the planned grand opening of the ill-fated resort. Regardless, the place is a hard-to-miss monument to what could have been, with a gas station and gift shop in lieu of rooms for rent.

Iolani Palace

Honolulu, Hawaii

Built in 1882, Iolani Palace is the only royal palace in the
United States and was the official residence of the Hawaiian
Kingdom's last two monarchs. King Kalakaua, who had the
palace built, was succeeded by his sister, Queen Lili'uokalani.
Queen Lili'oukalani was overthrown in 1893 and imprisoned
in a palace bedroom for five years. This ornate and opulent
palace is now open for tours.

Kalaupapa National Historic Park

Moloka'i, Hawaii

One of modern time's most notorious leper colonies was
on the Hawaiian island of Molokai, which was established
in 1866. Hawaiian kings and American officials banished
sufferers to this remote peninsula ringed by jagged lava rock
and towering sea cliffs. Molokai became one of the world's
largest leper colonies—its population peaked in 1890 at
1,174—and more than 8,000 people were forcibly confined
there before the practice was finally ended in 1969.

The early days of Molokai were horrible. The banished were
abandoned in a lawless place where they received minimal
care and had to fight with others for food, water, blankets,
and shelter. Public condemnation led to improved conditions
on Molokai, but residents later became freaks on display
as Hollywood celebrities flocked to the colony on macabre
sightseeing tours.

Today the area is managed by the Kalaupapa National
Historic Park, and a permit is still recquired to enter.

Punalu'u Black Sand Beach

Hawaii County, Hawaii

Some places have beautiful beaches with sand that's white, or various shades of tan, or maybe even dark gray. Rarely, however, does one see sand that's as black as charcoal. The peculiar sand of Punalu'u is made of lava that exploded when it hit the water and has since been ground very fine. If that isn't strange enough, there are freshwater springs beneath the saltwater surf.

The Upside Down Waterfall

Oahu, Hawaii

The lush Nu'uanu Valley on the eastern coast of Oahu stretches from Honolulu to the Ko'olau Range and ends quite suddenly in steep cliffs, called the Pali.

Here, on only the rainiest and windiest of days, visitors can see the famous Upside-Down Waterfall, so called because water cascading from the 3,150-foot summit of Mount Konahuanui falls only a few feet before strong trade winds blow it back up in the air. The water dissipates into mist, creating the illusion of water slowly falling upward.

Natives call the waterfall Waipuhia, or "blown water." According to one legend, Waipuhia was named for a young girl who lived in the hills of the Nu'uanu Valley and whose bright eyes pleased the gods. One tragic day, the girl's true love was lost in a storm, and when she wept for him, her tears were caught halfway down the cliff by the god of wind and tossed into the spray by the god of mist.

Lookout Lore

Weather permitting, the best view of the waterfall is from the 1,186-foot Nu'uanu Pali Lookout, itself an infamous spot in Hawaiian lore. As the legend goes, in 1795, King Kamehameha I drove the Oahu warriors up the Nu'uanu Valley to the Pali, where thousands of them were driven over the cliffs to their deaths.

While scholars pooh-pooh the story, natives say that at night the cries of long-dead warriors can be heard echoing through the valley. Others tell of seeing a ghostly white figure—perhaps the king—on the Pali Highway leading up to the Lookout, as well as ghost warriors falling from cliffs. What eventually became the Pali Highway was built in 1898 by Honolulu native (and future mayor) John Wilson. Apparently, Wilson's workers encountered several bones during the project—and simply laid the road right over them.